Three and A Half Minutes of F

C000094849

by

Alex Boucher

ISBN: 9781916864207 (paperback)

Interior Layout by Welly Artcore - artcorefanzine@gmail.com

10 9 8 7 6 5 4 3 2 1

Published by Earth Island Books
Pickforde Lodge
Pickforde Lane
Ticehurst
TN5 7BN
www.earthislandbooks.com

Printed in the U.K.

THREE AND A HALF MINUTES OF FAME

ALEX BOUCHER

THE SETLIST

Prologue - 23rd July 1992

PART ONE

PART TWO

PART THREE

PART FOUR

FOR SAM

The events that happen in this book are based on my own experiences
and interpretations. Some names have been changed.

INTRODUCTION

The lives of successful artists do not always make for the best stories. I am always drawn to the underdog and find myself rooting for them as they battle every adversity life can throw at them. Anyone who has the guts to seek a career as a professional musician has my respect, the odds are always stacked against you and it often requires Herculean feats of self-belief to get yourself up on stage in front of your friends, let alone a disinterested unruly mob, waiting to see the band you are opening up for. In an all too cynical world, the story of a group of teenagers, banding together to make a living playing their songs, seems almost impossibly romantic, but it is one I am drawn to time and again.

I met Alex in the spring of 1992 when I was working as an A&R Man for EMI Music Publishing, searching out promising new bands and doing my best to help them realise their dreams. I had a side hustle, running an independent record label with two friends, and Alex was playing drums with first band we wanted to sign. He had an irrepressible energy and played with great flair, looking the part behind grunge length hair. He was not the most talkative member of the band, but I really appreciated his willingness to push the band as hard as he could, and his enthusiasm was infectious. He was a great listener, and this book more than shows his ability to take in everything that was going on around him and serve it up with great honesty and humour.

Few musicians are fortunate enough to turn their talent into a career, but it is a testament to Alex's determination and robust nature that regardless of the knocks, he continues pushing forward in the music industry. The number one rule is to keep turning up and to his credit he always does. This story though is so much more than the tale of a drummer trying to survive, it captures the spirit of the music scene in the nineties as it was for so many hard-working bands that perhaps didn't get to enjoy the attention of the charts and the paparazzi.

There is no attempt to make this existence more glamourous than it is, but the love of music, of performance and of the whole absurd merry-go-round of the music business is what drives the tale forwards. It is a superb document of a world that no longer exists, a music scene before the digital age, before streaming and social media followers decided your fate. A time when people like me would make decisions based on simply how much we loved a band, rather than whether the analytics told us it was a sure thing.

Mike Smith, Music Industry Legend

AUTHOR'S NOTE

Dear reader,

This is a love letter to the 90's. It's a time capsule too. A chance for me to document everything I saw, felt, and experienced during that special time. I turned sixteen in 1990. Over the next ten years I would see Nirvana break through, Richie Manic cut up his forearm, Oasis sell out Knebworth, and Tony Blair bring in the first Labour government since 1979.

From an early age, I was passionate about music. I witnessed how it could bring people together, provide a sense of elation, divide opinions, and define a generation. I started a diary when I was fourteen. I kept going, becoming an archivist for my life on a regular basis. I would list the songs I liked, the band's albums I wanted to buy, and the lyrics I liked the best. I would compile mixtapes before I made them, write about the girls I fancied and why I had no chance with them. Someone once said its best not to wallow in the past but to give it a respectful nod. I'll confess, I'm a wallower. Give me a time machine and I'll be back in the '90's in a heartbeat. I'll even tell you what specific event I'd go back to - it's jumping around my bedroom like a crazy person as I listen to the song High as a Kite by Kingmaker.

Music from that era puts fire in my belly, adds a swagger in my step, makes me cry and gives me goosebumps. I miss the '90s. That sense of freedom and wild abandon, not influenced by a pithy tweet or an email I've read in the wrong tone of voice. In those days, you could either speak on the phone or send a letter. Those were the only 2 options. These days, that seems incomprehensible.

Travelling is my second love. I never grew tired of visiting a new town, even though the local venue was all I would see. I had no problem spending hours in a van, listening to music, watching the world go by. As a kid on holiday, I would always explore the hotel, wander the corridors, and open random doors to reveal a cavernous ballroom or function room. I would always gravitate to the lobby. It's the first room you see when you enter, bringing a nervous buzz if you've never been there before, that strange air of uncertainty as if you're about to enter Narnia.

Music venues were the same - walking into an empty room, placing our cases down by our feet and looking around. Knowing in a few short hours it would be alive, full (hopefully) of an expectant crowd.

Being on the road, in the '90's with the best music in my ears is a special recipe I can never repeat. But because of my diary I'm able to serve up something close to the real thing. So here it is. I hope you enjoy it.

Alex

PROLOGUE
23RD JULY
1992

Ollie opens the dressing room door. "You've got ten minutes until you're on stage". My stomach somersaults and I half shudder and nod at the same time as he runs off to find Matt and Steve. Laurence is sitting cross-legged in the corner of our tiny room, noodling on his bass guitar. He never gets nervous, bastard. Suede took so long doing their soundcheck we had to rush through ours. We were still onstage getting the levels right as people entered the Town and Country Club, a big venue close to Kentish Town tube. The early birds are already running down to the front, ensuring they have a prime spot to see us and then Suede, Mega City Four and headliners Blur.

I glance at the setlist. Stages can sometimes be super dark, so I want to memorize it before laying it down near the drum kit alongside the obligatory can of beer.

I look around and then turn to Laurence:

"Shit, where's the beer?" Lol, are we out of beer?"

His reply comes from behind long hair:

"Yep. Well. No. We've stashed it in the van for the ride home."

"Where's Toby? I need to get in the van."

"Dunno"

Great. Always the last to know. Less than five minutes until we're on, and no beverage to keep me lubricated between songs. Having a beer beside me has become a sort of ritual, I'm superstitious that I'll play badly if there isn't one next to me. Stupid I know, but it keeps the nerves at bay. I start to panic. Maybe I can ask Brett for one? Or Damon? Don't be ridiculous, I think, asking them would make me more nervous. Water won't do; that's a sacking offence. Nothing for it. I need to get one from the bar. I navigate the musty backstage corridors and find a side door leading to the venue, guarded by a security man. I flash my red all-access sticker emblazoned on my denim jacket, and he stands aside. The venue is starting to fill up. Everywhere I look, there are oversized band T-shirts worn by rosy-cheeked indie kids eager to find their mates. Their curtain-style haircuts can't conceal the boozy apple odour, so the air reeks of cider. It seems everyone is half-tanked on Merrydown. It's the '90s, so smoking isn't banned indoors yet, and a hazy cloud fills the cavernous room.

The bar nearest the stage is busy. Will I complete this mini errand in time? Thankfully, I spot Mike at the end of the bar, a welcoming face that slowly morphs into a confused one.

"Alex, what the hell are you doing down here?? Aren't you on soon? Like, now?"

"I need a beer."

"Don't you have a rider?"

"Yeah, normally, but it's been, er, transferred somewhere else."

I clearly didn't need to be this technical. He can tell I'm fraught. I'm standing on tiptoes, waving my arms, failing to catch the attention of the picky bar staff. Mike notices my attempt at semaphore is getting me nowhere.

"What are you having?"

"One pint. Stella. Cheers Mike"

As Mike is tall and looks somewhat important, he nods at the bar staff and gets served straight away.

I say a quick cheers, then walk/run back to the side door, sipping from the glass, and trying not to spill lager everywhere.

When I return to the dressing room, there's a collective sigh of relief when they see me. I suddenly realized how dependent they are on the drummer being present.

"Look everyone, Alex got himself a beer but didn't bother to get anyone else one. Time to go" Ollie says, pushing past me. We make our way to the stage.

A burly sound tech wanders over and tells us we're on after we hear the next song, "Dragging Me Down" by Inspiral Carpets. I'm glad it isn't the current number one single, "Ain't no Doubt" by Jimmy Nail. I look out across the stage and into the venue, one of the biggest we've played. Going on before an act dubbed "The Best New Band in Britain" is not going to be easy, nor is the challenge to steal their thunder. I have another shaky look at the setlist as the song finishes, and the lights go down. This is our cue.

We wander on in the dark. There are a few whoops and yeahs, and I make sure to step over the cables and gaffer tape littering the stage. I place my pint down and sit at the kit, picking up my sticks. The smoke machine lets out an intrusive hiss, and I hold my breath as it creeps over the drums. I check the kit, tighten the stands, pull the hi-hat stand closer and give the bass drum a solid "DUN DUN", to alert the crowd we're about to play.

I look up at Matt, Laurence, and Steve, who all give me the nod. The blisters on my fingers and palms have hardened from gripping my sticks over the years. Oh well, I'll be making fresh ones in the next thirty minutes.

I tentatively raise my sticks and count us in.

ONE, TWO, THREE, FOUR...

CHAPTER 1

1,2,3,4

But first, let's rewind to the early 1980s. A live show called Top of the Pops on BBC1 on a Thursday evening. For me, it's an essential slot in the week. It's hosted by a smiley-faced mullet-clad presenter, holding a bulbous microphone, ready to take you through half an hour of chart hits, broadcasting live on telly.

With a glass of Ribena in hand, I sit cross-legged in my pyjamas on the carpet, eager to see who has entered the charts, who is climbing up and who's down five places. TOTP is diverse, having to feature bands that make the Top 20, meaning you have Cliff Richard, All About Eve and Bobby Brown on the same show. As I watch, entranced, I notice how much fun everyone is having: the performers, the audience; it's one big party. It made me want to have music on all the time, a constant soundtrack to my life: in the car, on the family stereo, in my room. It became a weekly quest to find new music, seeing what CD's my parents had bought or click-clacking through the plastic cases at the local library and taking a chance on obscure bands and ones that I'd seen performing on the show. As my collection grew, I'd record them on to cassette and build my musical archive. I would set up a cassette player in the bathroom and listen to whole albums whilst having a soak until someone knocked on the door needing the loo. What stood out to me with all these records was the drumming and percussion. One listen to the drums on "Seeds of Love" by Tears for Fears (Badman's Song especially) or "Paradise" on the album "Love" by Aztec Camera, just got me enthralled. "Wages Day" by Deacon Blue would have me air-drumming ferociously as I played their CD at full volume in my bedroom.

Living in Stansted Mountfitchet, Essex, it is a middle-classy, village, set-up. Family holidays in Majorca or The Lake District. My Dad worked for NatWest; Mum was a part-time receptionist. My twin sister was a bookworm who begrudgingly played the clarinet until I broke it one day while trying to do a handstand on her bed.

We had a string of family dogs with cute names and a procession of cats that would sun themselves in the conservatory. It was a typical family with Sunday roasts, card games at Christmas and regular visits to the grandparents, who would regale us with stories from World War II and try to understand the current crop of pop stars on the telly.

Having played football all his young life, and then having a go at every sport invented, my dad would have been glad for me to have the same interests. It took a failed visit to the local artificial ski slope and a short attempt at Rugby club to prove that these genes hadn't been passed on. But their unwavering support lingered on as I sprinted down the side of the pitch, rugby ball under my arm, weaving in and out, avoiding muddy arms as chasers reached for my feet, yelling "Come on, Alex."

Even though I was spurred on to excel, it was soon clear that I was happier listening to music in the car than what the destination had in store.

My obsession with music grew with the creative process of making mix tapes. As Antiques Roadshow groaned on in the background, I would be writing my next killer compilation, figuring out the best order for each song, and orchestrating the dynamic ebb and flow of side A and side B. Would "Imagination" by Belouis Some segue well into "Need You Tonight" by INXS? Maybe I need to add "Like a Prayer" by Madonna to keep the energy going. I'd decorate the tapes with stickers, give it a punchy name, like "Stuff! By the Dude, part XIII" and eagerly push it into the stereo the next time we went to the garden centre.

Inspired, I asked to learn the drums.

Drum lessons start around my 8th birthday. Every Saturday, I invest an hour with my tall teacher Alan whilst the folks look in on my grandparents. The classroom is a spare room in his house, with a self-made practice kit made of foam and plastic, deadened cymbals, and a modified stool for me because I'm short. Stacks of manuscripts and odd drum parts line the room, with half-finished practice pads - circular bits of rubber glued onto a square slab of wood. His family would be going about their regular morning downstairs, the garbled noises of Saturday Superstore and the occasional smell of Bolognese wafting upstairs. I wonder if I'm going to miss seeing another band getting prank-called live on TV. It was surreal to watch Five Star asked why they were so fucking crap.

I sit there, clutching drumsticks, thinking how easy this will be. But first, there is the tour. The drum between my legs is the snare, the main drum to keep the beat or off-beat going and a driver for most rhythms. Next is the bass drum or kick drum, operated by a pedal with a beater and normally used by the right foot. The hi-hats are 2 cymbals on top of each other, operated by the left foot to give it that "scshh" sound and played with both hands for certain rhythms. Two tom-toms are mounted above the bass drum and a floor tom to the right. Surrounding the kit are crash cymbals and a ride cymbal, used for "riding" the beat.

Alan pushes his vast glasses up his nose. "Playing a rhythm is similar to tapping your head and rubbing your stomach simultaneously - All four limbs need to be doing something different, but in time", he says sagely.

Following my first go at a basic rock beat (think Billie Jean by Michael Jackson),

I am soon clenching my drumsticks in frustration. My lesson is an uncoordinated mess, much like everyone's first go behind a kit. I lean back and look up to make eye contact with Alan, airing my concerns. "It looks so easy on Top of the Pops", I whine shamelessly.

Alan smiles, "This time, play it slower and count out loud. Ready? One, two, three, four."

It will not take sixty minutes to be the next Buddy Rich, that's for sure. In the words of legendary Humble Pie drummer Jerry Shirley, 'If it don't swing, it don't mean a thing' - a phrase previously used to reference the size of someone's appendage, it's now the drummer's code of conduct. Luckily for me, Alan is a jazz/swing drummer and schools me in the old school grooves, riffing on tracks like "The Chattanooga Choo Choo", riding the cymbal with a "ting, ting ta-ting, ting ta-ting".

I get lambasted at school for adopting this technique as most other aspiring drummers wanted to show off by smacking the hell out of the kit. However, 'if it don't swing...'

In the first few weeks, Alan teaches me rudiments, rhythms, and solos, but more importantly, how to listen and improvise. Being more of a listener and less of a talker, this suits me rather well.

Memorizing the R.A.F. March Past still doesn't turn me off, so the tray and wooden spoons are replaced with drumsticks and a snare drum. This evolves into a gaudy purple and mauve second-hand kit purchased at Supreme Drums in Walthamstow. This "starter" kit has a bass drum bigger than me, and a snare drum made from the cheapest metal known to man. To practice, I'd put on headphones and play along karaoke-style (or drumaoke?) to records. Side two of Songs from The High Chair by Tears for Fears is a regular choice. Putting the headphones on and turning up the volume to eleven makes me feel like Marty McFly. There is a loud buzzing in my ears in-between songs as I wait for the next track to start so I can erupt into a beat. This is closely followed by the bedroom door swinging open to be told to use brushes instead.

I'm an easy option for Birthdays and Christmas (He needs a Cymbal bag, a cowbell, and some Random Percussion!) I even get the Ginger Baker Drum Book, his piratical face on the cover grinning back at me, arms folded, holding a pair of drumsticks.

Under Alan's tutelage, I go experimental with my style and use this to create alternative rhythms. The pile of exercise sheets grows with each week, I'm becoming more confident with every rhythm, beat and drum fill Alan throws at me, eager to learn more techniques, slapping my hands on my thighs to each song I watch on Top of The Pops, playing air drums in the car to Phil Collins and Status Quo. Things move up a notch when I start secondary school.

CHAPTER 2
SUFFER
& SERVE

Newport Free Grammar is an all-boys school based in a tiny village called Newport, midway between Cambridge and Harlow. Latin is still on the curriculum, throwing blackboard rubbers at pupils' heads commonplace. It is a dusty old place in parts, with cloisters straight out of Hogwarts and an extensive wood-panelled library full of ghostly portraits of previous headmasters. The school motto is *Suffer and Serve*. The teachers have nicknames like Stoat or Taff who are not afraid to dish out a dry slap. Teachers and pupils refer to each other using only surnames.

The school was founded in 1588, the year of the Armada. Some faculty still looks to be on standby should the Spanish invade again. A few of my friends from primary school have joined, but with no older siblings or familiar faces in my class, it's a scary and solitary start.

Lucky for me, the headmaster Mr. Hall, is a real fan of performing arts. He concentrates on growing the music and drama department and ensures the theatrical productions go above the norm. I am soon enrolled by the music teacher, a rosy-faced man called Mr. Partridge, to play the drums.

My debut performance is at a school concert, playing a swing beat along to the tune *Spread a little Happiness*, sung by three teachers. It is a simple "1, and a 2, and a 3" rhythm using brushes, with a piano accompaniment. Up until this point, my audience has been posters of Gloria Estefan or Alan. Playing in front of a packed school hall was something I hadn't prepared for.

With everyone seated, I am ushered into the hall with the rest of the musicians, banging and clattering our school chairs as we pick up the programme for the evening's entertainment. My eyes scan the running order, finding *Spread a Little Happiness* at the start of the night's second half. The programme quivers in my hand and I can feel my heartbeat reverberate around my eardrums. I can't replay the song in my head anymore. What if I drop my brushes due to my hands being so sweaty? What if I'm too loud, too quiet, too fast? Remembering the mantra *Suffer and Serve* doesn't help, and I sit there in a daze as the concert begins.

During the interval, I head outside and shiver in my white school shirt, pacing up and down the side of the hall. Mr. Partridge finds me and can tell I am in a state. He says, "Whatever happens, it doesn't matter". Shivering less and managing to choke back the tears, I return to my seat. After what feels like hours, it's time for my performance. "Mr Partridge checks the running order and proclaims, with Mr. Ryan and Mr. Berry singing, Michael on piano, Alex on drums, here is "Spread a Little Happiness".

I stand up and head over to the drums. I'm still small for my age, but the previous drummer wasn't. When I sit down, I can hardly reach the pedals. I stand up and try to look for something to make the stool lower. Nothing. I look underneath the seat; maybe I can lower the it? Nope, only Geoff Capes could loosen that nut. I hear shuffling in the audience as people wait for me to take my position. Some polite coughs here and there, the odd titter from the school choir. Only a matter of time before a paper plane flies out from the tenors, followed by a stern look from Mr. Hall. Mr. Partridge rushes over with a chair. This will have to do.

I sit down, pick up the brushes and hold them frozen over the snare drum, waiting for the pianist to start. Come on, Alex. Then it happens. Something takes over. The music and years of practice takes control of my arms, and I play the best swing shuffle you've ever heard. I am in the groove. The audience doesn't matter. The chair doesn't matter. Even the acoustics don't matter. I love it. Mr. Partridge looks over and makes pushing movements with his hands toward the floor - code for playing too loud. I compensate, calm the nerves down, and go lighter on the drum. The song ends in applause and a thumbs up from Mr. P.

From that moment on, I am the resident school drummer and have found my place as the short, quiet kid who can play loud. More drum opportunities start to roll in. I get taken to a Jazz Clinic run by two veteran jazz musicians, pianist Stan Jones and trumpet player Digby Fairweather. They spot me early in the day and ask me to join them for a jam in front of the audience. It's pure improvisation and riffing off each other with solos - Alan is so proud when he hears I had managed to hold my own with such an experienced duo.

I began to bond with school friends, especially Sam. He joined in the 2nd year so was entering a class of twenty-six boys who had already made decisions on who to stick with the year before. We've been sat next to each other, and soon enough our interest in The Blues Brothers, Eric Clapton and Prince makes us firm friends. Sam is taller than his years, with a layered stack of hair that adds to the height; he has a knowing smirk and the look of a bronze Adonis having spent the last few years living in Bahrain. Being of Italian origin, an evening spent around his home is vibrant, noisy, and full of good food and conversation. Between him and his three siblings and parents, I feel immediately at home and part of the family, something all Italian families I'm sure would wish to achieve with their guests.

I have a stint drumming for the local Operatic Society. The annual production would be something like kid's favourite "Bugsy Malone" or the Charleston orgy that is "The Boyfriend". I rehearse every Sunday afternoon in an empty school hall with the would-be Bonnie Langford and Michael Balls that market-town Bishops Stortford has to offer. All of us flirt outrageously with each other whilst learning our lines and rehearsing songs.

The production happens at The Rhodes Centre, a former 1960's hotspot that held The Hollies, The Who, Small Faces, Gene Vincent, and even David Bowie. During our show rehearsals, we cavort around the venue wearing our am-dram T-shirts, and dancing to Beats International during break times. Along with the yearly panto and productions, the centre hosts the notorious "Rhodes Disco" a manic free-for-all all packed with spotty teenagers in hoodies and baseball shirts throwing shapes to rave choon "20 Seconds to Comply" whilst choking on Benson & Hedges to look cool. The place soon becomes my second home, I get goosebumps every time I walk into the hall for rehearsals, seeing the empty stage, hearing props being shifted backstage and a piano tinkling as the lead actress rehearses her song. I'm starting to get used to the tingling nerves, and butterflies of trepidation, urging myself to perform and get into the groove.

CHAPTER 3

LET THERE BE ROCK

Still very much a product of mainstream pop, I am spending the late '80s listening to Terence Trent D'arby, Bros and Gloria Estefan. Needing more funds to buy records with, and bored of washing the car for a quid, I find a summer job helping at the local potato farm. I cycle over the fields on my BMX, arriving at a mud-covered metal warehouse, pallets stacked in every corner, with trucks trundling in and out, mountains of potatoes lolling about and colliding at the brim.

In return for a crumpled £10 note, my role is to grade the potatoes as they rumble by on a conveyor belt. Any green or mouldy ones are thrown away or used as projectiles. The whole place is dirty, and deafening, and smells of potatoes that have been kept in a warm cellophane bag for too long. One of the packers, with headphones that never leave his head, is the spitting image of Skid Row's Sebastien Bach. At lunch break, he asks me who I'm currently listening to. I nervously whisper The Pasadenas and Mike and The Mechanics. He shakes his head like I've offended his whole family. Lifting his headphones and placing them over my ears, he donates the next forty minutes introducing me to Poison, AC/DC and Motley Crue. Soon, multiple tapes are strewn across the table, as he fast forwards and rewinds to his favourite tracks, giving me a whistle-stop tour of hard rock. He shows me the front covers of each album, holding them there with a stern face, making me wonder if there will be a test later. I like what I hear, the energy, riffs and don't give a fuck attitude in the lyrics, a brazen, balls-out, here-to-rock mantra that captivates and pulls you in.

Hooked on this new sound, I discover a late-night music show called Raw Power, fronted by an excitable wild-haired presenter called Phil Alexander. I set the VHS to record each show, devoting my Sunday mornings watching Extreme, Warrant and Little Angels. Sensing a trend, my dad buys Hysteria by Def Leppard, and I am all in. I start growing my hair and get as far as a mullet before the teachers flag the no hair over the collar rule. I should have known, seeing as most kids have had to snip their rats' tails, a new style pioneered by footballers. Keen to play this new genre, I ended up having a jam with future super-producer to the stars, Paul Epworth. He is in the year above me and we spend an afternoon playing Faith No More and Guns' n Roses covers

7

in a stuffy room above a garden centre. We clatter through some attempts at "We Care a Lot" and "Patience". This is fun but nothing more than short-lived. Paul goes on to form a grunge band called Headswirl before he ends up producing tracks for Bloc Party, Baby Shambles and writing Skyfall with Adele.

I can't get enough of all these hard rock bands with their crazy hair, wild band names and drummers who stick their tongues out at the camera while twirling sticks around their fingers at blurry speed. By catching up on the founding fathers of hard rock, a real turning point is hearing the record "Houses of the Holy" by Led Zeppelin for the first time. Drummer John Bonham's style and power opened my eyes to what could be achieved behind a drum kit. I am a big fan of Keith Moon's showmanship and flair, as opposed to placid timekeepers like Charlie Watts and Ringo Starr. It feels like once I'm sitting behind the kit, I am no longer the friendly, mild-mannered Alex but more like Animal from the Muppets.

My parents take me to Talking Drums, a big store in Archway, North London to purchase a new drum kit for my birthday. I choose a nice white kit within the budget, made by a little-known brand called Juggs. Yes, really. The manufacturer obviously does not know bawdy British humour and its fondness for Carry On films. This proves to be a hilarious discovery for my first band and the crew, with the utterance of "Juggs" causing a guffaw on numerous occasions. A band certainly is what I want to be in, so I keep an eye out for something more regular.

CHAPTER 4
COUNT ME IN

During my fifth school year in 1990, it takes a mix tape from a friend to introduce me to alternative rock and shoegaze. He is a pen pal with Patrick Fitzgerald of Kitchens of Distinction, a trio from Ireland. They are in touch so often that Patrick has sent a demo version of a song called "Drive That Fast" to him for a preview. As I listen to the shimmering waves the guitars created, the driving beat and ethereal vocals, I am hooked. I sidle over from rock and metal to embrace indie bands like Happy Mondays, Stone Roses and The Charlatans. It is an exciting time for alternative music, with The Cure going mainstream after their punk beginnings, R.E.M. bringing their poetry to the masses and The Pixies with their loud/quiet dynamics. In the U.K., a poppier scene is growing, with "grebo" bands like Neds Atomic Dustbin, E.M.F. and Jesus Jones giving Jason Donovan and Kylie Minogue a run for their money in the charts. Mixtapes are traded, featuring songs by Irish rockers Power of Dreams, the ethereal Chapterhouse and anthemic crowd-pleasers James. Lyrics to "Terminally Groovie" by Neds would be scrawled on pencil cases in Tipp-Ex.

My parents show me a classified ad in the local paper towards the end of the year. It says, "local Drummer for indie band wanted for live gigs and demo recordings." I call the number and chat with one of the members, and they agree to pay me a visit to Stansted Mountfitchet to show them I can play.

One evening, as I wait nervously in my bedroom, they show up. I hear my Mum letting them in, multiple Doc Marten boots clomping upstairs. I smile as they file in and cram themselves onto my sofa bed. They've all got long hair, perfect teeth, baggy tops, dripping in denim with a standoffish vibe. It feels like I'm about to be kidnapped by The Wonder Stuff. They ooze confidence, but I can't tell who the leader is. I half expect lighters and cans of lager to fall from their pockets. The average age looks to be eighteen. Feeling admiration already, I offer to play a quick solo, and it gets a few heads slowly nodding. I swivel around on the drum stool and look at the kit. I can feel their eyes burning into my back, waiting for me to start. Don't screw this up. This could be cool. The drumsticks are shaking in my hands, I look up at the poster of The Black Crowes on my wall, nonchalantly staring at me with expectation. Come on, Alex. I'd been listening to The Charlatans recently, so I play relatively loose and groovy, then end with a John Bonham-style solo that thunders around the kit leaving parts of the furniture wobbling.

One of them speaks. "Thoughts on playing live, that OK with you?"

I bristle and say, "No problems there. Erm, if the drum stool can go low enough."

"What about playing gigs all over, like London or further?"

I nearly say I'd need to check with my parents first, but I stop myself and utter a casually laidback, "Yeah, sure." With or without permission, I was more than ready to travel the world.

The next thing to do is meet up for a proper jam, so they hand me their demo tape to memorize the tracks.

It's indie rock fare, with original songs "Fatman", "F.N.B.", and "Darling Blue". The songs are great and accomplished. The band consists of Matt (lead vocals & guitar), his younger brother Laurence (bass & backing vocals) and their friend Steve (guitar). A mate is managing them, also called Matt, with blonde hair. They have a roadie; his name is Gags, with a classic 90's curtains hairstyle. The previous drummer has quit because his girlfriend told him to. They were educated at Bishops Stortford College, a public boarding school that would one day have Charli X.C.X. as one of its pupils. The brothers live in a well-to-do area in Bishop's Stortford, where I head for our first jam on New Year's Eve. I'd normally be seeing in the new year at home, watching a Bond film and eating too many leftover Quality Street, so it's nice to be doing something different.

Blonde Matt and Gags pick me up, load my Juggs into their beat-up Renault 5, and drive over. The back seat doesn't seem to have seatbelts of any kind or a safety handle, so I desperately fish around for something as they hurtle around another roundabout. Matt turns and says, "What are you doing back there?"

"I'm just looking for something to hold on to" as another empty can of Heineken rolls towards me.

"Well, make sure you don't pull it off", comes the laconic reply.

We drive through a leafy estate. As we pass, I see shiny expensive cars parked in spacious driveways before large houses with names like "The Maltings" and "Forest Hall". Matt and Laurence's house is an impressive, imposing building set back from the road, with a driveway big enough for 8 cars. We unload my kit into their garage, a room bigger than my lounge. I half expect a maid to appear with coke cans on a silver tray or something. I didn't know what to expect, but it wasn't exactly this. Maybe a hippie commune or your typical three-bed semi. I'm a tad out of my comfort zone, but once guitars are plugged in and kit set up, I'm made to feel welcome, and we discuss which track we should run through first. I had listened to their songs repeatedly and written notes for each one - mainly to show I was efficient and well up for being their drummer. This was the second time I'd met up with the band, and I started to figure out the dynamics. Matt is quiet, driven, and tall with steel blue eyes and dark brown shoulder-length hair. I can tell a lot is going on inside his head. Laurence is the talker, always sharing opinions and up for a discussion on pretty much anything, mainstream indie bands and record labels being the popular topic. He looks different from Matt with a lighter complexion. Steve is affable and softly spoken with a mess of brown hair tied up with elastic bands. He normally has a fag on the go and wears a nice line in thick baggy cardigans. He learned classical guitar and is a talented musician. They all are. I will have to keep up with them if I want to stay the course.

We play through the songs from the tape. The song "Fatman" has a lot going on, with a fast vocal that Matt sings, making my drum part a tad tricky. "Darling Blue" has an up-tempo beat. I nailed it the first time, a lively boom-cha, bo-boom cha on the bass drum and snare. We even try jamming a few new tracks that will become songs for the next demo. It feels like a productive session in the West Wing, and we all agree it went well. A few days later I get summoned to a meeting in a pub. With smiles on their faces, as Blonde Matt speaks, he asks me if I would be up for joining the band. I don't need to hesitate and blurt out a combination of the words absolutely and yes, as I try to make eye contact with everyone across the table. Even though I've met them twice, it feels like I belong. I have a comforting sense I will be taken care of.

We celebrate the new line-up with a round of Snakebite and black (a Coke for me). I'm ready to tell the world I'm the new drummer for Three and A Half Minutes.

PART ONE

CHAPTER 5
SERIOUS
AS FUCK

1991

Hubble Telescope launched, New York Giants win the Super Bowl, Justify my Love by Madonna, Nevermind by Nirvana, Terminator 2, The Silence of The Lambs.

I've got some serious catching up to do. There are gigs booked, a new demo to be recorded and I still need to learn all of Three and a Half Minute's songs.

After playing the odd gig at the Rock Garden and a notorious party in Felixstowe (that keeps getting mentioned), the band have built a loyal following of school friends and local indie kids. The next progression is to write more songs, play more gigs, and see where things lead. I'm overwhelmed by this new demand upon my life, but in a good, nervous way, fuelled by anticipation. It feels like I have acquired three big brothers. At sixteen, I am the youngest, Laurence is about eighteen months older than me, and Matt and Steve are over two years older. I am made to feel welcome as much as any bunch of teenage lads would, i.e., an unspoken sort of acceptance that means you're allowed to mock each other once you've landed a good piss-take yourself. To avoid placing my foot in my mouth, I choose to be quiet. There is a quiet darkness about Matt, that can be misinterpreted as aloof or moody. It's hard for me to second-guess the atmosphere, seeing as I've only known these people for less than three months.

We rehearse often and write enough new material to fill a demo tape. Being in the band is a nice distraction from all the grim news about the Gulf War and it beats the drudgery of my paper round. The band borrows a disused classroom at a school in Bishops Stortford to record. The room is freezing, smells of cobwebs and has one bare lightbulb: proper Joy Division vibes. Being February, Steve's Ford Fiesta provides the heating between sessions. Songwriting is new, so Matt suggests rhythms and beats for the songs they are putting together. I quickly come up with some drum patterns that work, using my skills to detect where the riffs need loud accents or steady basic beats. I'm like a drumming magpie stealing beats and rhythms from Bonham, Moon, and Baker.

I get given some albums as homework - Nowhere by RIDE for the drumming, Come on Pilgrim/Surfer Rosa by Pixies for song structure and Disintegration by The Cure for when it rains. The band are all massive fans of The Cure. Until now, my limited knowledge of them was The Lovecats, big hair and lipstick and the gnarled face on the cover of their singles compilation. All of these albums have a profound effect on me, but the standout is Nowhere. Shoegaze as a genre mainly focuses on the guitar effects and vocals, so the drumming can get overlooked. But not with RIDE. Loz Colbert's drumming on songs like "Dreams Burn Down" and "Here and Now" are more akin to the style of John Bonham, hitting the skins as hard as possible but still managing to create beauty out of the sheer power behind the rhythms. I listen with goosebumps to those tracks and emulate the drum patterns, drum fills and style that Loz uses. I buy the Today Forever EP on VHS to watch him play. When I first hear Leave Them All Behind, I am blown away and listen to it endlessly on cassette single.

We compose seven tracks, all varying in style. It's an indie mixed bag, with searing anthems ("Blurred" & "S.T.A.I.N."), a bit of indie prog ("Phase 2") and jangly pop (a reworked "Darling Blue" and "Revisited"). The standout track for me is "M.C.D", it will turn out to be a live favourite due to its dramatic mid-way pause and mosh-inducing ending. "Darling Blue" and "M.C.D" I must learn, but the rest are all tracks we write from scratch, either in the classroom or the band's garage. The recording takes two days, technically overseen by blonde Matt with a tiny recording desk. There is zero compression for the microphones, so I do my best to play at an acceptable volume and keep a steady tempo but it's not without flaws. I hit the microphones placed over the drums a few times and completely lose my timing halfway through a middle section in "Revisited". To rescue this in the final mix, Blonde Matt needs to cut the offending section with some DIY editing. I feel embarrassed by this faux pas. It's not addressed by the rest of the band and a relief I'm not shown the door.

Once finished, we all decamp to Steve's car and listen on cassette. If it sounds good in his banger, it will sound good anywhere. And it does. Every part is audible, considering the analogue set-up we are working with. When my drums kick in on "Blurred", I beam with pride and feel like a proper musician ready to share their music with the world. I can't believe I've recorded a demo tape at the fresh age of sixteen. It is the first time I have heard myself playing. We call the demo "Sensible Hair". I love the tongue-in-cheek title of the tape, the sense of rebellion against the short back and sides crowd. I give out as many copies as I can to friends and family. Even my grandparents show interest, though I have to explain what the term "indie music" means. "No, it isn't for Indians and no, we won't be covering any Val Doonican songs for the time being." Tapes are sent out to the local newspaper and venues to get the ball rolling on reviews and gig bookings.

A Sensible Hair review from the local paper, The Herts & Essex Observer:

14

"After their somewhat muddled debut, "The Early Purges" and the slightly lacklustre "Paisley Crouton" Bishop's Stortford's answer to Blind Mice let rip again. Three and A Half Minutes put out demos as frequently as other bands play gigs, which affords us an almost unique glimpse at the development of an astoundingly prolific group, though also turning up a lot of deadwood.

While "The Early Purges" was a blurry hotchpotch of humorous experimenting and Paisley Croutons' redemption rested mainly on the excellent 72nd Address, Sensible Hair is far more focused and infinitely better developed. The songs are much stronger, with "Fatman" driving home the point that Three and A Half Minutes are more than just another indie guitar thrash machine and have something interesting to say. They have to be one of the most exciting new bands in the region. They have an aptitude for amusing, harmonic, quirky songs akin to The Wonderstuff, and a distinctive relentless guitar whine. That said, their potential is nowhere near realized, and we have to reconcile that when they happen upon the strong material they inevitably will produce, they will shake the world by its ears until it begs for mercy."

CHAPTER 6

SOUNDCHECK

We've got two gigs booked for March. My drumming debut is supporting the touring rock band Love's Young Nightmare at The Square in Harlow. The Square is a council-owned venue, providing live music for the area since the 1960s. It's opposite a multi-storey car park and adjacent to one of Harlow's eight-hundred-and-fifty roundabouts. It's an angular building, unimposing and long. Inside, all the walls are black except for a big The Square logo on the stage.

Everything is a new experience - loading in and setting up the kit, doing a sound-check, the backstage area/green room, and figuring out the setlist and stage times. Understanding what a rider is and learning the general etiquette of sharing gear. Discovering the smell of stale beer, gaffer tape and fags is intoxicating.

At The Square, the green room (or place where the band hides from their fans) is a portacabin behind the venue. I soon learn the "rider" is the drink and food you get given by the venue. This tends to vary depending on who the band is and what the promoter can be bothered to provide, but it's ordinarily several cans of beer and some sandwiches. Laurence tells me legendary tales of riders from the high echelons in rock, about Van Halen's famous stipulation of a bowl of M&Ms but with the brown ones removed. This odd request was to ensure their rider had been properly checked. Being a support band and not having much to consume, we live the next few years stealing or blagging other bands' riders.

I've been in Three and A Half Minutes for three months, so the tension to step up is predictably high. As I carry my drums into The Square, I feel it. The Fear. The band and all the other musicians will hear I'm a fraud, escort me out of the building, throwing my Juggs after me. I'm shaking and it feels like it's my first day at secondary school with all the older kids ready to scold me if I put a step wrong. I look over at Matt, Steve, and Laurence, busily unpacking their guitars. They seem quiet and reserved, too, giving me the impression I may not be alone in my nervous state. The big stage, lighting and speakers make me jittery, giving me imposter syndrome; no comparison to playing in a school hall. The sound check shows me how different things are going to be. The resident sound engineer is a chap everyone hates called Nic Foote. I assume this is the case as someone has scrawled "Nic Foote is a cunt" in the Gent's toilets. He wears a cap with a ponytail. I think it's to fool everyone he has a full head of hair underneath. Yep, he is bald as a coot; this is revealed to me once he's had a few drinks. I'm not sure whether to laugh or cry at the shiny dome. Nic diligently places microphones against each drum, over the cymbals and inside the bass drum, and then he asks me to play each section. The call and response between Nic and I go like this:

"Snare, please"

"bap. bap. Bap. B.A.P. BAP. BaP. B.A.P." The EQ and volume would change as Nic tinkers with the levels and settings.

"OK, hats."

"I'm sorry?"

"Hi-hats. Play the hi-hats" - the sigh from Nic is audible.

"Tik. Tik. Tik. TiK. TIK TIk. TIK tIK TIK TIK."

"OK, that's enough. Kick drum."

"Bomf. Bomf. BoMF. BOMF. BOMF."

Everyone is gawping at me, as I hit the bass drum like an automaton. It's a boring process so I guess I'm the only thing worth focusing on. I haven't grown much so I'm straining to look over the drums. I'm also behind the band from a fashion sense, with my tattered school shoes and a Captain Haddock T-shirt my parents got me for Christmas. I'm still growing my hair but it's at that in-between stage and resembles Ringo Starr circa 1965. I look like a foreign exchange student that's gate-crashed an indie gig.

"OK, all three together, please."

Summing up all my coordination and with sweaty drumsticks poised, I hit all three in perfect synchronicity. "BAPTIKBOMF".

"No, mate. I meant play all three in a beat, not all three at once".

Once the laughter from the other band, bar staff and Nic Foote has died down, on it goes, all around the kit. With my drum soundcheck done, we soundcheck the guitars, vocals, and finally do a run-through of a song. As we play, we listen for what we do or don't need in our speakers - more bass, less vocals, some guitar, etc. A massive speaker placed next to the drum kit provides me with the parts I need to hear the most. The speaker is on the left-hand side, and it remains there throughout all the gigs I play at The Square; it even becomes a habit to turn my head to the left whilst drumming, which I still do.

Soon, it is time to play our set. The venue is full, with excited fans down the front, ready to check out the new line-up and hear the new songs. Nerves bubbling, my goal is to focus and call on my experience of playing on stage. This time, there wouldn't be a pep talk from Mr. Partridge. We'd rehearsed the set list many times but playing in a music venue with stage lights heating up my shoulders and an expectant ticket-buying audience full of beer is a new challenge. With some words of encouragement from the lads, they help me hold my own on stage. Laurence makes sure I stay in time, nodding at me for the changes or mouthing one, two, three, four when needed. I survey the audience, scanning for validation, a smile, or a sign of encouragement. I glance up at the sound desk, Nic is standing there, arms folded, stooping to twiddle with the controls every now and then. Like Luke Skywalker in the trenches, I close my eyes for a moment. I mentally enter the zone and make the kit an extension of my body, listening to the guitar, bass, and vocals, with a conscious ear on the tempo. I pace myself, making sure I don't peak too soon and giving it my all for the last few songs in the set. Before I know it, the gig is over. We exit the stage to big applause, and I take a breather over by the drum cases, ears still ringing. A stranger in a Cure top comes over and claps me on the back, offering to buy me a beer. I tell him I'm underage and he makes a weird apology like somebody who's been lurking too near the school gates. I find Matt, who is beaming at me with a look of pride and relief. I've nailed it.

Two days later, we head into London to play our 2nd gig at the historic Camden Palais. Later renamed Koko, it has been a theatre venue since 1900. The popular indie disco "Feet First" is here every Tuesday night, playing floor fillers by The Wonder Stuff, The Farm, Happy Mondays, and James. For audiences of up to fourteen hundred, this was a complete change of scene from the small and intimate Square built for two hundred and fifty people. The gig we're booked for is a Gate Crasher Ball, a party for rich kids to get wasted on MD 20/20 and Thunderbird. I stand in the middle of the dancefloor and look around at the gilded balconies, plush carpets, and wide stage. The nerves make an unwelcome return, and I gulp as I take in the grandiose surroundings.

Once we're set up onstage and run through a few songs for the soundcheck, I feel ready. As this is a party, there is no pressure to impress anyone important in the audience. Laurence asks if we can play our demo through the venue speakers. We stand in the kiddle of the venue as lur music is blasted to every corner. Laurence throws me a toothy grin. It sounds bloody brilliant. The festivities begin. The band playing before us is a terrible covers band, killing songs like "Should I Stay or Should I Go" and "Jumping Jack Flash". At one point, the hapless bass player runs over to Laurence, who is on the side of the stage and shouts," I can't hear myself! I can't hear myself!" Laurence casually wanders over to the amp and pushes the guitar lead all the way in. Throughout the show, models strut across the stage and down a catwalk - it truly is an odd gig. Following an uncomfortable chat with the event manager, we find out we were supposed to be doing this gig out of the kindness of our hearts and we are told no petrol money or fee will be forthcoming. So, whilst we are waiting backstage to play, we wander around the labyrinth of hallways, stairs and corridors and stumble across a room full of brand-new, yet-to-be-plumbed-in toilets. One of them stands alone, separated from the white ceramic mountain that goes up to the ceiling. It sits there forlornly, resigned to a hundred years of piss, shit, and vomit. Hearing its clarion call for salvation, we decide to claim it as our payment. To deliver a fuck you to the organizers, our driver strides on stage during the set and places it at the end of the catwalk for the models to prance around. Deciding to leave right after we get pushed out of the fire exit, we take the toilet home, spray it with pink paint, whack on some band stickers and call it Graham.

Graham comes with us on tour, joining the band on stage while we play. We would sometimes put a smoke machine through his back pipe so it would emanate up from the seat. One of journalist Steve Lamacq's live reviews of the band starts with the legendary sentence, "There's a toilet on the stage" Graham is the first in a long line of items we "liberate" whilst on tour. With my gig cherry broken and the band still happy with my quiet presence, we arrange more gigs and start getting the word out to the local press.

23rd March - with Love's Young Nightmare, The Square, Harlow
25th March - Gate Crasher Ball, The Camden Palace, London

CHAPTER 7
WHISKEY BUSINESS

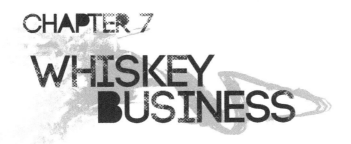

It's May, and Blonde Matt and Gags have moved on. We go into self-management mode and create some band merchandise. There are assorted yellow, green, and blue badges with our cartoon logo of a shaking alarm clock that has sprouted legs. We make bright orange stickers that riff off the Inspiral Carpets, saying "Serious as Fuck" instead of "Cool as Fuck". Similar T-shirts are designed with the clock and some psychedelic wording.

We do more gigs in London at the Amersham Arms, The Bull & Gate in Kentish Town, and the Powerhaus in Islington, supporting bands like Great Northern Electrics and Mondo Popless. A mate of the band called Andy regularly drives us in his Land Rover, the only stipulation being we listen to his beloved U2 for the journey. Luckily, "Achtung! Baby" is my album of the year, so that's all fine with me. It becomes a regular occurrence for a van or car to pull up at my house late afternoon, and then drop me off again around midnight or the early hours. My parents are OK with this, relieved that their good money spent on drum lessons, equipment and a decade of listening to me practising is paying off.

6th May - with Great Northern Electrics, The Amersham Arms, London
30th May - The Bull & Gate, Kentish Town, London
23rd May - The Powerhaus, Islington, London

I start a diary to record and track my busy calendar of engagements. I scribble in it to pass the time, when the TV broadcasts nothing but light entertainment fluff hosted by a pale, male and stale parade of presenters, from Des 'O Connor, Michael Barrymore, and Noel Edmonds to Terry Wogan. I use it to record how I'm feeling and log defining moments, a bit of a brain dump of my life. It proves to be a blessing and a curse.

As things start to gain momentum, I am hit with a bout of Glandular Fever. The virus refuses to leave for a while, but I won't let this fucker kill my chance of remaining in the band. Through symptoms of tiredness and fever, I must dig deep during the gigs and use every ounce of energy to keep the illness at bay. Still hooked on the album Disintegration, I would gestate in my room, hugging a pillow feeling weak and helpless. I'm sure Robert Smith would agree with this soundtrack to my virus. To help morale, we have a faithful entourage, and they follow us around in convoy to our gigs. One permanent fixture is wild-haired Ollie, all smiles, a machine gun laugh, wearing the brightest and baggiest of jumpers, with an immense love for Ned's Atomic Dustbin. Roger, a speccy chap whose car seems to fall apart every week. Impulsively, he lets us spray-paint his car in orange, stencil the clock logo all over it and put Serious as Fuck stickers on the dashboard. There is Simon, who seems to be constantly searching for ganja and a friend from my primary school, Kenton. Kenton is fully immersed in the scene, somehow finding time to see all the bands, like Pop Will Eat Itself, EMF, Jesus Jones, and Carter USM. It's nice to have loyal followers at every gig, willing to get the crowd going at the front.

We soon get friendly with Mac, the gig booker for The Square. He is a fan of our demo tape and is interested in managing us. Immediately noticeable by his immaculate rockabilly quiff, Mac is a former bassist of the Newtown Neurotics, The Pharaohs & The Skabilly Rebels and has all the right contacts to help us out. He's on good terms with bands like Carter USM, Senseless Things and punk legends UK Subs. Mac gives us coveted support slots at The Square whenever a big band is in town, so we open up for baggy scenesters Scorpio Rising, Sp!n (later known as Gene), the energetic Senseless Things and Aldershot punk-pop heroes Mega City Four. With the Mega's gig, I'm already a true fan and excited to be there, let alone support them. I feel more nervous going up to drummer Chris Jones to ask him about sharing kits than I do playing the gig.

In July, we take Mac on as our manager, after he gets us on the bill to support The Pogues at Harlow Town Park. The Pogues' gig is our most significant concert yet, and we're on first. We've devised an excellent start to the set, with Matt going on before us and chugging the guitar to get the atmosphere going. Steve joins and creates some feedback from his amp. Finally, Laurence and I walk on, take our places and I count us into his bass riff that starts "Blurred".

Tragically, one of Laurence's bass strings breaks at the top of the set. It's quick and easy to restring a guitar but a bass guitar is not so easily done. One of the other bands lends him theirs and we're back to the set as quickly as possible. Weathering the setback and a few apologetic words from Matt to the crowd, we blag our way through. There are some familiar faces in the crowd to help us muddle through. It feels odd playing outdoors mid-afternoon on a Saturday; our style is a bit more suited to dark venues with smoke machines. My parents come by to watch, although they don't share this until afterwards. Just in case my street cred gets ruined.

I wander aimlessly around the backstage area, pulling at my tight backstage pass that's been cutting off the circulation, wrapped around my wrist by an over-zealous member of security. I've been separated from the rest of the band, trying to find a way out into the crowd, before The Pogues start their set. I hear a snarling, raspy voice from around the corner, and nearly walk headlong into Shane MacGowan, making a beeline for the urinals. He's in a black shirt, messy hair and full beard with sunglasses, a cigarette dangling precariously between his fingers and a bottle of whisky swinging from his hip. He stops and stumbles back, before righting himself and focusing on me, as I'm frozen to the spot, not sure what to do next. "Here, watch my piss while I go for a drink" as he thrusts the bottle into my chest, droplets escaping from its neck and landing on mine. I couldn't help but marvel at the surreal situation I've found himself in. Here I am, holding the whiskey of the legendary Shane MacGowan, moments before the show is about to begin. The weight of the responsibility, coupled with the anticipation of seeing one of the most iconic bands in Irish music, made my heart race. It's my first encounter with a world-renowned rock star, even though I'm just a temporary drinks roadie. Minutes later, Shane returns, a mischievous grin etched across his face. He reclaims the bottle from me with a hearty pat on the back. I stay to watch The Pogues, with Shane MacGowan stumbling around the stage and slurring whilst the rest of the band roll their eyes with a tired "He's pissed again" look.

The stage has a moat separating it from the audience. Inevitably, the reveller's jump in, sparking a potential health and safety hazard for anyone near electrical equipment. I feel sorrier for the farm animal shelter 200 yards from the stage - we probably gave all the livestock tinnitus.

I have my first groupie experience when a girl I used to be in theatre school with, suddenly grabs me, pins me against an ambulance and sticks her tongue down my throat. This was unprecedented. Up until now, I had been spraying Rapport aftershave everywhere, donning a pastel jumper and writing love letters to girls I fancied. It was a long process, with hesitant phone calls to their house, hoping the dad didn't answer, followed maybe with a stroll in the park if I was lucky. Then the inevitable, "have you French-kissed yet" question followed by the clacking of teeth as we collided awkwardly, a stream of drool running down her chin as I rotate my tongue, trying to steer clear of metal braces.

But here I am, no longer the predator but the prey, mainly because I was onstage a few hours ago. It is a big boost to the ego. And as for the location, I guess we are conveniently located if my heart rate escalates. Her mate stands nearby, bored and waiting for the sweaty tryst to finish. I hear the cackles of Matt, Laurence, and Steve as they pass by, telling me the van is leaving. I pull myself away from the raven-haired temptress and join the band, feeling about 5 years older than I did yesterday.

The concert makes the local press with the headline "Whiskey Business". We're starting to get attention; extra gigs are booked, and more time spent is with the band. Right now, it looks like the band has potential to go far, but there's a small detail that I'm forgetting about. My education.

21st July - with The Pogues, Harlow Town Park
17th August - with Ratcat, The Square, Harlow

CHAPTER 8
CUTE

Matt has started a part-time job at Pizza Hut to earn some extra money and I decide to find one too. My first proper job is at a newly opened Tesco Superstore in Bishops Stortford, which seems to have recruited all my schoolmates as if the recruitment team had snuck into our school one day, carrying a massive net.

My section is the meat department, which involves re-stocking the aisles and cleaning dried blood off shelves. The other chore is "cleaning" the walk-in storage freezer for no apparent reason other than giving one of us something to do. Wasting an hour in a freezer room with a damp blue cloth wiping metal trolleys full of dead animals wrapped in plastic is an exercise in pointless banality. Everywhere is cold and grey; the butcher's room, the aisles pumping out cold air, even the rubbish disposal where all boxes must be flattened and tossed into a skip. The butchers are racist, misogynist morons. They dole out wedgies daily and get weirded out by my dyed black hair and undercut, a style favoured by Ned's Atomic Dustbin fans. It's a shaved head around the back and sides, keeping your long hair on top. I do not want this place to be my future. Absolutely not, no fucking way. The only perk is the discounted doughnuts you can buy at the end of the shift. Taking on a job means spinning plates for school, homework, working shifts, and playing gigs/rehearsing with the band. At some point, something has to give. I've been frog-marched into the patronizing Department Head's office one too many times for being late, so I decide to quit.

At this stage, I wonder whether there is any point in going back to school. The band is on the up, and Mac seems to think we've got what it takes. My parents ask me to stay nonetheless, visibly shocked by my suggestion that school is irrelevant.

September rolls around—time to return to school for my first year of Sixth Form. My GCSE results were shite, so I'm doing retakes. From this year and up, girls are allowed to attend. We'd spent the last few years wiping bogies on each other's shoulders, pointing at white dog turds, or asking who had just guffed, but we are now dousing ourselves in aftershave and combing our hair to become more attractive to the opposite sex. My twin sister Charlie also joins, having had enough of a catty all-girls school for the past five years. I've lost my best mate, Sam, as he's chosen to take his A-levels somewhere else.

Using our newfound freedom of driving to school, sporting long hair and paid jobs to buy beer, our independence leads to organising house parties, which become a focal point in our lives. It's not uncommon to be at a mate's house, with his parents away for the night or locked in their rooms, as we mosh to Kill Your Television by Ned's Atomic Dustbin on the family stereo at full blast. A trend of going on the rampage in the local neighbourhood starts, each of us trying to outdo each other. Dan stole a washing line. Sean found a fridge. Six of us picked up a Mini and turned it 180 degrees so it couldn't drive out of its space. At one party, we're walking along a country road with no streetlights, and we run to the side as a car approaches. I end up wading into a pond and sporting the host's tracksuit bottoms for the rest of the party. With the band acting as a comfort blanket, I feel more rebellious at school. I share an earphone with Steve Bailey as we listen to The Prodigy during Biology, dodging airborne blood clots that we've been lifting out of frogs. I don't even bother attending Double Maths anymore, deciding to chill in the Sixth Form Common Room and work on my next mixtape.

On my first month back, pop-punk band from Twickenham, Senseless Things are on the cover of Melody Maker, with guitarist Ben Harding wearing a Three and A Half Minutes T-shirt - another cheeky favour called in by Mac. Things are slowly ramping up with more gigs booked, and another session is planned to record our next tape.

Our six-track demo, called "Cute", is recorded over a couple of days at Von's Studios in Islington, London, a cool studio owned by a chap called Von. It has a massive fish tank and garish colours on the walls and groovy lighting to match. "Darling Blue" and "M.C.D" return to make the final cut, along with punkier, poppy tracks like "Feelings M" (short for "Mutual" fact-fans) with its ear-worm chorus and the brooding, sneering set-closer "Shake It Up". Track one is a jumpy Wonder Stuff track called "Lenthia Falls", and side two opens with a stop-start baggy tune called "Focus". This is a step up from the scrappy demo we'd recorded in the dusty classroom. Vons is a proper recording studio with a colossal desk, an engineer, and a sound-proofed recording room. Every inch of the drum kit has a microphone on it, meaning any mistake, cough, or rimshot will be picked up and the song would have to be recorded again.

The sessions go well as we are tight from playing so many gigs and rehearsing heavily. Only a few extra takes are needed; the meter is running, and we don't want to be handed a massive bill for studio time. The drums are a little cardboard-like on the tape, mainly because my Juggs are not up to the job. They've been manhandled too many times, bashed about a bit and are due for an upgrade. I need some Premium Juggs I can get my hands on and fast. We do an extended ending to "Shake It Up", fading out the squalling guitar noise and bringing it back again at max volume - an effective idea suggested by Mac. With cramps in his hands, Steve says "Thank fuck for that" right at the end. We give it the obligatory listen in Steve's car, and it sounds epic. We're happy with the finished product and can't wait to play more gigs and get some industry attention.

26th September - with The Fuzztones, The Powerhaus, Islington, London
28th September - with Mega City Four, The Square, Harlow
30th November - with The Family Cat, Colchester Arts Centre, Colchester

CHAPTER 9
ANYTIME, ANYPLACE, ANYWHERE

It's fair to say if I wasn't in the band, I would have been a fan - every track is a joy to listen to, and I play the tape constantly in the car and make copies for my friends. It's an excellent opportunity to approach girls I like at school and hand over a tape, which gives me an excuse to say hi to my main crush, Alice. From the moment she enters the Sixth Form Common Room, I am smitten. With her dark blonde hair, she looks like the actress Holly Vallance. There is a confident air about her, and she holds her own amongst the school's hormonal melting pot with a bohemian, free spirit energy. She scrunches her nose when she laughs. It takes me a couple of days, but I finally stride over, give her the tape, stutter something about being the drummer and march quickly away.

Tapes of Cute are sent out to the local press, and we get the occasional review and bite-sized bulletins on our upcoming gigs. In November, Mac takes me up to London to see Carter U.S.M. headline at the Kilburn National. Carter are well known for their frenetic live shows, and huge backdrop of lights on stage, raising the temperature to near tropical levels. Their line-up is two South London musicians, called Jim Bob and Fruitbat. And a drum machine. Supporting them on the bill are an up-and-coming trio from Hull called Kingmaker and Mega City Four. It's a memorable night, with my first experience of crowd-surfing and pogoing in the hot and crowded mosh pit down the front. Soaking our newly bought T-shirts in each other's sweat, we hoist each other onto the crowd to surf over heads and get passed to the stage without losing a shoe. Later, Mac introduces me to Wiz, the lead singer from Mega City Four, but I am bedraggled and gig deaf to communicate correctly. With Mac chaperoning, we wait outside for a cab, and he hands me my first joint. I look at it in wonder, the paper crinkling between my fingers, the herby wisps of smoke tickling my nostrils. I take a medium-sized drag and exhale, as the cool night air dries my soaked clothes and greasy hair. I enjoy being in the company of Mac with his sardonic wit and find it surreal to learn he had attended Newport. Mac and his wife Trudie take the Minutes under their wing and join us at many of the London gigs and are on hand at The Square when needed. They are an interesting couple, with Mac's broad smile and everlasting rollie. Trudie has messy blonde hair and a cheeky grin. She looks like she's been drawn by Tank Girl artist Jamie Hewlett, and always smells of coconuts. She and I have head-banging contests in the stairwell at The Powerhaus, trying not to fall down the stairs or whack our heads into some innocent bystander.

During this period, I'm unsure if I will ever sleep. With regular gigs, rehearsals, school, homework, the am-dram productions and hedonistic house parties, life is a constant whirlwind. It's been thirty years since the swinging 60's and it feels like the older generation has no real issue with us doing what they did; going to concerts to check out live bands, drinking alcohol and smoking cigarettes. Everything is affordable too, and if you can't get served at the local Off License there's an older brother or sister who is happy to oblige. With every pub closing at 11 pm, and shops shut on Sundays, there's little else to do if you're a teenager living in Hertfordshire and Essex. Being in a band fills that gap and I'd much rather be drumming and creating music than sitting at home watching Only Fools and Horses or reading a Fighting Fantasy book. Well… Ok, I confess, I did like the Fighting Fantasy books. But it was underwhelming when a troll didn't burst through my bedroom door after I turned to page forty-four.

On a regular basis, I stand eagerly at the front window, looking at the empty cul-de-sac, waiting for Steve or Matt's car to pull up and take me to the next gig, rehearsal session, meeting.

I've got used to the roles we all have in the band. Being the youngest and the last to join means few decisions are ever made or requested by me; I don't want to cause a fuss. Steve and I are easier going, but with Matt & Laurence being brothers, you get good days and not-so-good days. As with most siblings, they have a talent for pushing buttons, leading to a disagreement or a full-on bust-up. Laurence can be a squeaky wheel and is never afraid to offend or speak his mind; Matt tends to simmer quietly and twirl his hair, calculating whether to say something or let Laurence dig his hole. Steve is the peacemaker to keep tensions at bay but knows when it's time to go outside for a fag to avoid the explosion. Early signs of this happened during the Sensible Hair recordings when Matt was mute for most of the day, except for one tense exchange with Laurence:

"Matt, what is it? Say something. Or what's the point in us fuckin' being here?"

"Ooh, you're hard."

In time, the band forms a bubble (as most bands tend to be) with our coded language, Spinal Tap quotes, private jokes and assumed personalities - i.e., the moody one, the loudmouth, the pin-up, the baby. Being amongst the same people for so long, there's an expectation that you finish each other's sentences. It's more about knowing what mood everyone is in than band telepathy. Oddly, it seems to work when writing songs - there's a gut feeling you have when you come up with a rhythm or structure to a song you instinctively know everyone else will like. As for the hierarchy, we are all supposed to be equal and make decisions as a band. To be honest, it's a benevolent dictatorship nobody is brave enough to acknowledge.

We often come across as cold and opinionated to our audience and the music press - either on purpose or because we have been given that label due to our outspoken reputation. We are our most honest when speaking to fanzines. The band wants to define its sound/image and is frustrated by the constant pigeon-holing. It happens to every band, but a continual bone of contention with us. It doesn't help with Matt playing the strong and silent type with a scowl; he's often labelled a moody bastard on first impressions. But in our defence, journalists only see us for half an hour at a pub for an interview or watch us play before making their judgement - they don't see the other sides of the band, which at times is like a circus. It was not all doom and gloom. I have a picture of us bouncing on a bed in a hotel like kids in a bouncy castle.

In an interview with a local newspaper, we were keen to stress:

"There are massive contradictions in our image. Sometimes we come over as moody and arrogant. However, only the music is serious. None of us takes ourselves too seriously."

After being told we were aloof and arrogant on numerous occasions, I was worried this type of attitude might rub off on me, and I would become a moody, self-centred asshole. But then I had recently turned seventeen, so this was kind of the norm with every teenager.

CHAPTER 10

REACHING NIRVANA

While sitting in Steve's Ford Fiesta during a break from rehearsal, he pulls out a cassette with a blue front cover and asks me if I've heard it. Not recognising the name and image of a baby underwater, he gives a wry smile and slots the tape into the stereo. The first chords of "Smell Like Teen Spirit" blare, followed by Dave Grohl's epic drum intro, and I sit there in awe, feeling like I am discovering music for the first time. I can't believe the power of three musicians, playing heavy rock but with a distinct pop edge; it blows me away. This is the drumming I want to do, the only style to emulate. Up until now, I was a shoegazer, drawing influence from bands like Slowdive; inspired by Simon Scott's drums on Catch the Breeze, just a simple fill around the toms that gave the song that tumbling, spiralling rhythm. Another standout was Breather by Chapterhouse, with Ashley Bates providing its relentless driving force. I loved the backbeats and use of brushes by The Telescopes on their album Higher n Higher. And who can forget the electronic drum part that kicks off the epic Soon by My Bloody Valentine - a fantastic track. But now, I am ready to worship at the church of grunge and look out for more bands emerging from this new Seattle scene.

At the end of 1991, we cemented our "local band with a future" status with a barnstorming gig at the Football Club in Bishop's Stortford. This is not a Beatles at Shea Stadium set up with us playing to thousands on the pitch. The gig is inside the club bar on a floor space the size of an A4 piece of paper. All my classmates have come along, sporting Three and A Half Minutes shirts. I think Matt and Laurence are a tad freaked out by this clone-like tribe lining up along the front, but I'm in my element. After the soundcheck, Sam pulls me to one side.

"She's here."

"Who?"

"Naomi Campbell. Who do you think, you knob? Alice! Alice is here!"

This is the moment I've been waiting for. Time to play the best gig of my life and look good whilst doing it. No looking down to the left or leaving my hair matted over my face or gritting my teeth like a madman. I need to look cool like this whole drumming lark is effortless.

She's at the bar, laughing with some friends, doing that thing with her nose. She glances over and I whip my head around, nearly headbutting Steve in the process.

"Woah there, what was that?"

"Sorry. Someone's here."

"Well, yeah there's a lot of people here, Alex."

"No. I mean a certain someone. Don't look now. But she's over at the bar wearing a Three and A Half Minutes T-shirt."

"Everyone is wearing a Three and A Half Minutes T-shirt."

I snort casually and smile. Steve goes to tune up, and I try to look important and tune the drum kit. It's the first time I've ever done this, so I have no idea what I'm doing. But it looks professional. We've made the crowd wait long enough and emerge to play our set. I can't see past the first row, but I hope Alice has a good enough view. We play an epic gig. At the end of each show, we do a gradual stage departure, me first, followed by Matt & Steve then Laurence. This causes some confusion amongst my friends watching as they immediately wonder if I am OK. Hell yes, more than fine. I glide off stage to rapturous applause, sweep Alice off her feet and we kiss. We are an item from that moment on, writing schmaltzy letters to each other during English Lit and spending hours talking on the phone every night. Friday, I'm in love. She lives in a big creaky old house in a hamlet north of Saffron Walden, with undulating floorboards and dark, musty corners smelling of fireplaces.

We fool around in her large bedroom listening to Midway Still, a three-piece band everyone wants to be the UK Nirvana. They never reach those giddy heights, another victim of being chewed up and spat out by a record company. This was one of the regular reasons a band would split, along with having a crooked manager or an irreplaceable member of the band who also happens to be a dick. It's all the above if you were the Sex Pistols.

The band is on a new high followed by another successful Xmas gig at The Square the week after our Football Club show. The two local gigs had been branded as a face-off with another local band called Blind Mice, and Mac wants us to show them who are the rising stars in the area. We didn't take this competition too seriously, but we "win" in Mac's view.

A Readers poll for The Harlow Star and Herts & Essex Observer names us as the brightest hope of the year, Cute is voted 2nd best demo tape, and we are voted best live act. I've grown up quickly within short 12 months, spending many evenings travelling in a van and frequenting London venues. It feels like '92 is going to provide more of the same.

5th December - with Resque, The 'y' Club, Chelmsford
13th December - with Blind Mice, Bishop's Stortford Football Club
19th December - with Spitfire, The Powerhaus, Islington, London
21st December - with Blind Mice, The Square, Harlow

1991 - Mixtape

Smells Like Teen Spirit - Nirvana

One - U2

Even Flow - Pearl Jam

December - Teenage Fanclub

Throwing Things - Neds Atomic Dustbin

Breather - Chapterhouse

There's No Other Way - Blur

Catch The Breeze - Slowdive

Caught in My Shadow - The Wonder Stuff

High as a Kite - Kingmaker

Miles Apart - Mega City Four

Everybody's Gone - Senseless Things

CHAPTER 11
TOWN WITH NO TIME

1992

Rodney King & LA riots, Queen's annus horribilis, Church of England allows women priests, Achy Breaky Heart by Billy-Ray Cyrus, Copper Blue by Sugar, Wayne's World, Basic Instinct

It's 1992, and my hair is long. This ponytail is not for life. I'm saving up for a pair of purple DMs, and I'm wearing my grandad's golf jumpers which are three sizes too big for me. I have a growing collection of long-sleeved T-shirts from Scorpio Rising, Mega City Four and Kingmaker. Posters of Madonna and Kylie have been replaced with Toni Halliday of Curve, and Rachel Goswell from Slowdive.

With the constant drumming my fingers have blisters from gripping the drumsticks too tightly, and I never plan to make sure I have plasters at the ready. So, I use gaffer tape instead, and wrap the black or grey tape over the open sores until they lose all stickiness and fall off.

The year kicks off with another golden support slot at The Square with Senseless Things, to celebrate Mac's birthday. We do a rare surprise encore, playing The Only Ones' "Another Girl Another Planet", one of Mac's all-time fave songs. I even ask the DJ to play Alices' favourite song by the Pixies before our set to impress my girlfriend and give her the band setlist after we play. We are deeply in love, finishing each other's sentences and able to wind each other up in a way only a couple know how. My every waking hour is spent writing to her or making a mix tape for her. Everyone is visibly sickened by this gratuitous display.

7th January - with Senseless Things, The Square, Harlow
6th February - with Mondo Popless, The 'Y" Club, Chelmsford
29th February - with The Wish, Sugarblast, The Bull & Gate, Kentish Town, London

We are starting to make a name for ourselves on the Essex and London circuit. Throughout 1992, we will cast the net wider and play gigs up and down the country in venues of different shapes and sizes on the well-worn path of "toilet" venues such as

31

the Moles club in Bath, Boatrace in Cambridge and Duchess of York in Leeds, all pub/clubs with a dingy stage and a full calendar of gigs featuring bands that will become huge (Suede) and some that don't (Pop Am Good). Mac joins us on most of the gigs and always buys the sound engineer a pint to make sure we have a good sound mix when we play - I find out how important this little gesture can be; it can truly make or break your performance on the night.

The Herts & Essex Observer newspaper lists our whereabouts weekly and publishes interviews, highlighting us as the next big thing - mainly framed as an angst-ridden local band hoping to break out of a small-minded town, which is a provocative hook for the journalists and something we are vocal about. Our performances are emotive, loud, and intense. With Matt as our glowering frontman, we continue to impress audiences with our songs and energetic delivery.

Bishop's Stortford is a prosperous, historic market town. Its affluence has been maintained because of its closeness to London and nearby Stansted Airport. It's always been a bit full of itself. The fact Cecil Rhodes was born here, and the place is very Tory tells you all you need to know. Also, it is fucking boring. Like most market towns, the only source of entertainment would be to get pissed in the local pubs or down the park with Diamond White, go to the fairground when it was visiting, or start a band. The only famous act to have emerged from our region were the momentary jazz-pop outfit, Shakatak.

My surname has changed, it's now Alex "from Three and A Half Minutes" and I get used to the stares and double takes when wandering around Bishops Stortford with the boys. We become local heroes at The Boar's Head pub, pints of lager thrust into our hands as we hold court around our usual table and chat with fans of the band. At closing time, we wander over to Hong Sing House for a chicken chow mein, drawing more attention to ourselves as we talk loudly about indie bands, record labels and our next gig. My nights are finished with a last-minute dash to catch the last train home and watch The Word, a chaotic, unpredictable entertainment show with loud presenters and live bands (Mega City Four, Ned's Atomic Dustbin, Nirvana, you name it). There's something special about being in a band, that's hard to describe. You're surrounded by a collective aura, and it never feels complete unless all members are in the room.

In general, we're getting better with each gig we play. But one disastrous night at the Camden Falcon nearly derails the whole thing.

On the way, Laurence overindulges in too much beer with his friends. During our show, it soon becomes apparent he is playing all the wrong notes or the wrong songs. Then in a rock star moment, Laurence holds out his bass to the dwindling audience and, in true rock n roll style, puts his foot on the front stage monitor with the swagger of Gene Simmons. Unfortunately, the monitor is not secured to the floor, so he tips over. Luckily for Laurence, the stage is only about a foot high. This royally pisses Matt off, who leaves the building shortly afterwards in a huff, Laurence storms off in the other direction. Standing like lemons in the middle are the rest of us, waiting in the van with all the gear and some leftover food. They eventually return, and we have a stony silent journey home. I'm starting to get depressed with the fights and disagreements in the band, and I draw further back into my shell. I've never gelled with Laurence even though we are closer in age and the rhythm section. He has a passive aggressive way about him and can be judgmental. He also likes a debate as if he has something to prove. There's a dogged determination about him that sometimes gets focused on the wrong things. It's a battle of wills when it comes to preference, if I like God Fodder, he prefers Bite. If I like 101 Damnations, he prefers 30 Something. If I like Out of Time, he prefers Life's Rich Pageant. I'd be playing a tape in the van that I've chosen, and to air his disdain, he would simply ask "Who's this?"

"It's Madder Rose"

"Right, Madder Rose..." followed by silence.

5 minutes later;

"Who's this?"

I reply with the same answer again, feeling even more self-conscious and embarrassed that I'm making the van listen to something shit. I could be overthinking this. We didn't grow up together, we're not mates by choice – I've been enrolled and the dynamic between myself and the band doesn't go as deep as I'd like. I don't make this known, because I don't want to come across as weird, but clearly, I'm not a skilled sarcastronaut who's learnt to ride his ironicycle yet. Maybe I wasn't the drummer he voted for. Laurence and I click when we're not speaking. It's when he's trying new bass parts and I'm coming up with the beats, and we jam for hours on end, feeding off each other's energy.

The day after Camden, Matt picks me up for rehearsals. Noticing I am quieter than usual on the drive, Matt reassures me the band is more critical than bust-ups and to have faith. With his hand firmly on the gearstick and looking at me and then the road, he confides in me about how special the band is to him, and it makes me feel I am part of something exciting. Deep down, I think there is more going on behind the scenes than I'm privy to, but I hope these spats don't become worse, as we are about to invest much more time in each other's company on the road.

9th March - The Orange, Kensington, London
10th March - with Pele, PCL London

CHAPTER 12

GET IN THE BACK OF THE VAN

With our demo tape gaining interest and gigs getting praised, we attract some record industry attention. One of the first people we meet is Ben Wardle, from East/West Records. Ben is amiable and had signed a popular band called Five Thirty to the label but had missed out on signing indie shoegaze gods, RIDE. He comes down to Bishop's Stortford, we have a few drinks in a pub, questions are asked, and that is kind of it - this type of encounter ends up being par for the course with various record company A&R bods. We would meet for drinks/lunch, they'd pitch their label, promise to stay in touch - maybe even invite us to the office to blag a few free CDs. One perk is receiving the new album by The Cure, called Wish. Anticipation was high for the follow-up to Disintegration. On hearing the first single, "High" it was clear a more poppier, commercial sound was in store. I watch the music video, Robert Smith with tidier hair, climbing a tower and some spiralling piano added to the single version to make it more chart friendly. I check out the album's front cover, a psychedelic red and blue image, - could it be a moon or half a slice of grapefruit? Stalks with eyes, peering up at the sphere, trying to get close, trying to impregnate it perhaps.

As the first chords of "Open" come together, you can tell this album is going to be epic. Half the songs are over 5 minutes long. It's frantic, frivolous and fun.

Back to the record industry meet-ups; as a naive seventeen yr. old, I don't often speak up as I can't bring a great deal of conversation to the table, but it is clear our agenda is to be poker-faced until the right opportunity comes along. Sometimes, to keep us keen, they put us on the guest list for a high-demand gig.

Here, I am introduced to the culture of blagging and ligging. If you are blagging, it's getting free stuff, usually via the power of persuasion or using puppy-dog eyes. Ligging is getting access to gigs, parties, or travel i.e. "instead of touring, the band spend all their time arguing and ligging".

Things continue to go in the right direction with gigs: On 20th April, we play the Alternative Freddie Mercury benefit at the Marquee, an all-dayer with US:UK, Sugarblast, Sunshot, Sensitize, The Bardots, The Sandkings, The Godfathers, PWEI, and secret headliner Ned's Atomic Dustbin. Another legendary venue to be ticked off the list, The Marquee had changed its location a few times, but the name alone would invoke all the major rock bands from Queen to Thin Lizzy. I was playing on the same stage previously occupied by KISS, The Stone Roses, New Model Army, and Jane's Addiction. Because so many bands are playing, we have a fifteen-minute slot. Seizing the opportunity to play a short sharp set, we rip through a blistering show to a packed and receptive crowd. Mac is blown away by our set. I love the Marquee; we support Food Records band Sensitize there a month later, and I enjoy many a night moshing to indie bangers at the Feet First club night. It will one day become a Wetherspoons pub.

1st April - with Captain America, Powerhaus, Islington, London
2nd April - with Mondo Popless, the "Y" Club, Chelmsford
7th April - with Sofa Head, Princess Charlotte, Leicester
8th April - with Sugarblast, Monroe's, Workington
0th April - with Mondo Popless, Psychic Pig, Trowbridge
13th April - with Pop Am Good, The Wheatsheaf, Stoke
20th April - with Neds Atomic Dustbin, Pop Will Eat Itself, AIDS benefit, The Marquee, London
23rd April - with This Year's Blonde, Radiohead, The Mean Fiddler, Harlesden, London

We continue to play more gigs up and down the country and bring Murray Torkildsen, a local singer-songwriter from Harlow along for company. Luckily, we manage to avoid playing at the Sir George Robey in Finsbury Park, a notoriously rough pub where it's not uncommon to see a dog turd on the stage.

In May, a tour begins with Hull's three-piece, Kingmaker. We play big enough venues for both drum kits to be used, but one night at Manchester University, a smaller stage area means I must ask John Andrew if I can use his. John is an incredible drummer; one listen to the Eat Yourself Whole LP will show you how talented he is. So, it was to be expected when I asked him, he would oblige and said I could, but... I wasn't allowed to move anything. So, the cymbal stands, toms, and everything can't be adjusted for my height or style of playing. I just about manage it, but the weird angles mean I can't see above the kit, which is undoubtedly a different experience. The next day, we are told the tour is to be cancelled as Loz Hardy the singer has a back injury. I am gutted; I desperately wanted to get to know Kingmaker. I love all their songs and Loz is a brilliant frontman.

We play with a diverse bunch of bands, ranging from Sugarblast! in their hometown of Workington and the brilliant Bivouac at Manchester City Hall for "In the City" Festival. During their soundcheck, plaster begins to fall from the ceiling, so we had to turn the volume down for the gig. Other notable acts we support are Spitfire and Gallon Drunk in London, and Adorable & Back to The Planet in nearby Chelmsford.

We play a gig at The Mean Fiddler in London, supporting a band called Radiohead. At the Powerhaus gig supporting Captain America, we spot the actor George Wendt who plays Norm from Cheers in the audience. Ex-The Shout singer Leeson 'O Keefe has become one of our drivers and often opens for us as Genius Freak. He makes a killing with his Einstein-branded T-shirts. We share a love for Mega City Four and he regularly takes his hands off the wheel whilst driving, playing air guitar to songs from their mini-album, Terribly Sorry Bob. This is such a great time for me to be playing with some of my favourite bands and then watch them at the same show.

3rd May - with Big Fish, Little Fish, University of Nottingham
9th May - with Electric Sex Circus, The Bull & Gate, London
18th May - with A Band Called Jeff, The Falcon, Camden, London
21st May - with Strangelove, The Borderline, London
26th May - with Sensitize, The Marquee, London
29th May - with Kingmaker, Portsmouth Pier, Portsmouth
30th May - with Kingmaker, The Junction, Cambridge
31st May - with Kingmaker, Manchester University

Wearing a lucky cardigan that I've claimed from the Orange in Kensington, I pass my driving test. This means I take on the shared "driving to London" routine, where we park somewhere for free in Finsbury Park and head into Zone 1 for industry meetings, photoshoots, and interviews. Traversing the underground, someone (normally Laurence or Matt) will cheekily try to push one of us off the tube just before the doors close, giving a sad wave as the train pulls off. No wonder we were late all the time. We work for an afternoon with photographer Ed Sirrs, taking pictures of us at the base of Centrepoint in Tottenham Court Road, asking us to look moody, smile, look away from the camera, look up or into the distance. Any spare time is spent wandering around the cavernous HMV record store on Oxford Street. I am starting to discover bands for myself, like Buffalo Tom and The Telescopes, playing them constantly in my worn-out, second-hand Peugeot 204 as I drive to Alice's house. Getting there is sometimes up to the car, which I've called "Christine" because it has a life of its own. She only starts when she wants to. The new music video programme called The Chart Show proves to be a great addition to Top of The Pops for discovering tunes. I record music videos by the Boo Radleys and PJ Harvey, sitting cross-legged in the front room, my finger hovering over the VHS record button every Saturday morning.
It feels as if we are on the cusp of something tangible - a record deal and a single, if we find someone to front the cash. Luckily, we get a proposal which takes care of our predicament.

CHAPTER 13

SCARED HITLESS

Ben Wardle reaches out again, introducing us to two industry friends - Mike Smith and Andy Saunders. Mike started as an A&R scout at MCA Publishing in 1988, where he signed Blur, Levitation and scouted The Smashing Pumpkins. He then moved to EMI Publishing in 1992, where he would go on to sign acts such as PJ Harvey, Elastica, Supergrass, Teenage Fanclub, Starsailor, The Beta Band, The Avalanches, Gorillaz, The White Stripes, The Libertines, The Scissor Sisters, Arcade Fire, and Arctic Monkeys. Ben and Mike are old University mates and have walked the same career path in the music industry. They both met Andy while he was managing a band, The Honey Smugglers. Andy works for Emergo, a Record label from the Netherlands started by Roadrunner Records in 1986 for non-metal releases, including licensed releases from non-European labels - he handles UK indie bands like the Venus Beads and Sugarblast! They have clubbed together to start their indie label called Scared Hitless and pitched the idea of signing us to record an E.P.. An EP, short for "extended play" is a recording that contains more tracks than a single but fewer than an album or LP record. Publishing would be through EMI, the record distribution through a well-known company called APT. I like their dynamic, with Ben being the cheeky playful type with his Cheshire Cat smile. Andy is more stoic with the tendencies of a grumpy uncle and lofty ginger-haired Mike is the anchor and voice of reason on our decisions. I look up to all three of them, Mike especially - I am in awe of his music knowledge, and when he speaks, I always listen.

The band have some internal discussions and, in the end, says yes. Mike arranges a session for us to record and mix our first proper record in London. Around this time, things seem to be going quiet with Mac, and when I turn up for rehearsal one day, I get told he's been sacked. I'm not sure why, but I guessed it was because the band have outgrown him and the limited resources that he has access to. Still, it makes me feel sad, mainly because The Square is a regular haunt for me, and I consider Mac a friend and mentor. Most of the key decisions seem to be made without my knowledge or input. It makes me feel frustrated and isolated. Sometimes I see the guilt spread across Steve's face when he gives me updates on things he knows I can't change.

With our session booked at the EMI-owned studios off Tottenham Court Rd, we plan to record the PEEP E.P., so-called because it is a first proper glimpse of the band. We drive past the studio twice and curse the one-way system around Tottenham Court Road and Oxford Street, circumventing a few times until we spot the tiny entrance to Rathbone Place. Playing in a professional recording studio is a whole new world, with obsessive-compulsive levels of equipment set up to ensure a pitch-perfect recording. This involves tuning the kit and recording take after take with a click track in my headphones to help me play in time. Recording each part separately means I'd record the drums for a song first, then sit in silence at the kit, catching my breath as the rest of the band quickly listen back for any mistakes. After a short spell, a voice pipes up in my cans, with a "Just checking", followed by "That's a take" or "Let's do it again". The in-house producer/engineer is a guy called John Bell, who has us in stitches with his stories. John has worked with Bad Manners, The Waterboys, and many EMI artists using the studio. For the E.P., the opening track and lead single is "Feelings M", followed by "Shake It Up". Both have been finely tuned by now, "Feelings M" is faster and punkier, with its anthemic, catchy chorus. "Shake It Up" is doused in some reverse reverb and angrier, whilst retaining my relentless "boom-boom-ka, boom-boom-boom-ka" rhythm.

For the B side, we start with floor filler "M.C.D." John adds a drum machine-style intro and Matt says a tired "Go" to kick off the track, mainly for the irony. This is followed by "Sodium", a dark, grungy tune that segues into secret track "Shit Sells", a frantic 90-second punk diatribe.

We then set to work on the record cover, a concept using two mannequins. We take them over to Mike Smith's flat in Old Compton Street and while away the afternoon painting them and listening to The Lemonheads and Neil Young. Once completed, we head into the seedier parts of Soho with an American photographer called Melanie to take some pictures. Our picture for the cover looks great - a rain-soaked Soho Street with the mannequins standing lifeless outside the Raymond Revue Bar, the neon lights reflected in the wet pavement. Once finalised and vinyl pressed, the E.P. is set for release in August. Opening the first box and seeing all the 12" singles ready to be shipped is fantastic; I can't take my eyes off them. I'm thrilled to have been part of something so creative and it's a real step up from the DIY demo-tapes. We're a signed indie band and we're ready to blow everyone away - audiences, record companies, and other bands too. It's time.

CHAPTER 14
POPSCENE

An agency called Concorde, run by a live music veteran called Paul Bolton steps in to add us to their books, we are easily the smallest band on his roster, but he sees something in us, and we start to score some great gigs.

20th June - The Bull & Gate, Kentish Town
10th July - Marlborough Club, St Albans
23rd July - with Blur/Suede/Mega City Four, The Town & Country Club, Kentish Town, London
24th July - JB's, Dudley
25th July - with Ragged Jack, Moles, Bath
27th July - with Kinky Machine, Princess Charlotte, Leicester
28th July - with Kinky Machine, Psychic Pig, Trowbridge
30th July - with Adorable, The 'Y" Club, Chelmsford

In late July, we bag our biggest gig yet. The homeless charity Shelter has arranged a benefit gig co-hosted with the NME. We are first on the bill supporting Suede, Mega City Four and headliners, Blur. The venue is the Town & Country Club in Kentish Town, a large venue, housing up to 2000 people. This is a real "don't fuck this up" type of gig and we know it.

We all arrive in time for a soundcheck, but that doesn't make any difference. Suede vocalist Brett Anderson is late. He finally walks in, carrying some groceries in a Tesco bag, which ruins the look a tad. Despite the buzz around them, they are all calm and collected as they rehearse the intro to 'Metal Mickey' a few times. The music press has hyped them up in a massive way, calling them the best new band in Britain. Their glam image and sound are reminiscent of Bowie and T-Rex, a retaliation to the rockier grunge scene that has dominated the last year or so. The expectation is building for them at an immense speed, but there is no visible sign of pressure on Brett's beautiful bony shoulders. To me, they already look like superstars.

Being on first means we will sound-check last. It can make a real difference because if all the other bands take bloody ages (which Suede unfortunately do), things can get tense. It's not uncommon for a headline act to take so long to soundcheck it leaves the support bands with less than fifteen minutes to set up their instruments and soundcheck before the doors open. Even worse, if there's no time left at all, you must do a "line check", which means going on stage about five minutes before you play and quickly doing your soundcheck in front of the audience. This is something we have to do now, putting Matt and the rest of us in a nervous mood. Pre-gig activities vary between each member. Matt disappears with his girlfriend, and Laurence goes off with Ollie, Simon, and Roger. Steve sticks around and maybe goes for a cigarette or chats with some fans. I normally go for a wander or chill in the dressing room if there is one provided, composing my next love letter for Alice. Sometimes there is an interview with a fanzine or journalist to do or Scared Hitless take us out for a drink. These are the days before social media and the internet, so no peering idly at our phones. Some drummers practice before their gig - the Kinky Machine drummer has a habit of bringing his stool backstage and getting warmed up playing rudiments on it. I don't bother; I want to keep the animal caged so to speak. We all convene before our gig or get corralled by Ollie. Only then do we discover if anyone is a tad merry or has other issues. Sometimes we would do a band huddle, but on this occasion, the nerves are too high. We just stand in silence. Once I've got my beer and give the band a scare with my vanishing act, we start our set. We launch into the first song, and the lights dance around, mingling with the smoke. The onstage audio is booming, and I must focus my senses and ensure we stay in time. There is a sweet spot between giving it your all and leaving something in the tank for the rest of the set. As I play, I realise I have the best seat in the house. I'm not glancing down at guitar pedals or being distracted by someone trying to spill beer in the front row. Any projectiles need to be well-aimed to reach me. I'm sitting at the back, keeping the beat going and watching my fellow band members. Always checking for the odd glance where songs might need to change pace or anticipating a mistake. Looking out to the audience and watching the looks on their faces. Sometimes I connect with someone nodding approvingly, feeding off their excitement.

At this time, we have no idea this gig will be signposted as one of the defining moments in the history of Britpop. Justine Frischmann was a founding member of Suede but left the band and is now dating Damon Albarn. Everyone is there to see Blur and Suede duke it out. Mega City Four and we are the filler between the young glam upstarts and indie favourites. The main talking points from the night are Suede smash it, Mega City Four play a solid set, and Blur are drunk. We played well and probably got some new fans, but our set was early on, with the audience still trickling in as our set finished. Blur had returned from a stressful US tour, were facing burnout, and now all of them are plastered. Their temporary absence from the UK scene and being pitted against Suede might have been a reason to get pissed too. Lead singer Damon Albarn is so drunk he tells the crowd, "We're so shit, you should just fuck off now!" They'd released Popscene, their newest music since debut album Leisure, and opinions are mixed. Their label Food Records reads them the riot act in the aftermath, Blur sober up and write second album Modern Life Is Rubbish.

CHAPTER 15

SHAKE IT UP

PEEP E.P. is released on August 3rd and garners positive reviews, given Single of the Week in NME, and draws renewed interest from record companies.

"PEEP stands as one of the best debuts of the year - but on top of that, it marks a reprisal of sorts against recent conservative trends in both the indie and major mainstream (e.g. the inevitable Carter backlash, the return of pop snobbery). There is an overwhelming feeling of belligerence about it. Three and A Half Minutes are as bitter as hell. Currently, they present the best of what you could call the New Avengers (other groups to watch out for: the fast-improving Fretblanket from Birmingham and Reverse from Stoke on Trent) The Minutes, and their ilk, whip up a level of gut-feeling that sets the senses on edge. Arriving at their first record via some Kingmaker supports and a handful of London gigs, they sound precocious and awkward, searching out depths of feeling. "Peep" - the first release on the fledgling Scared Hitless label, catalogue number Fret 1 - gives an earnest, if not totally representative, picture of the foursome's promise. The demos of lead track "Feelings M" were better, but what the heck: "FM" is a frantic, teeth-gritting adventure into resentment and pride.

At times they lean into the old Neds/Cure comparisons, but they're already outgrowing the influences. I think the potential's all here. The big fuck off climax of "Shake it Up" and the intensity of "Sodium" tell me that, while in contrast, "MCD" is ridiculously pop, unpredictable."

Local hero and NME journalist Steve Lamacq is a fan. We meet him in a local pub called The Old Bulls Head and the band hit it off instantly. I'm drawn to his quizzical nature, and his thirst for new bands is wholesome and infectious. The band are still reticent about being compared to other similar acts. Still, I'm a fan of one such comparison: Fretblanket. I dig their songs - Steve Lamacq goes one further and does a prominent feature on us, Fretblanket and Reverse, labelling us the "Necks Generation".

"Three and A Half Minutes are causing a stir 'over there' as the latest Carter/ Nirvana/ Lush backlash intensifies. Harkening back to hardworking bands with voices (Wonder Stuff, not Senseless Things), Three and A Half Minutes throw it all back in our faces. Post-Smiths jangly pop with long hair and shaved sides. Grey days indeed when blando's like Catherine Wheel get a deal. Peep E.P. (Scared Hitless) is musical wallpaper worth covering your copybook with tunes that stick in your head rather than rot in Freebird's bargain bin."

6th August - The Ship Inn, Oundle

8th August - The Adelphi, Hull

11th August - with The Adventure Babies, The Duchess of York, Leeds

13th August - The Falcon, Camden, London

14th August - The Jericho Tavern, Oxford

15th August - with The Family Cat, Joiners Arms, Southampton

19th August - The Boardwalk, Manchester

26th August - with Family Go Town, The Wheatsheaf, Stoke

We make it onto the NME Singles of the Week compilation album, with "Feelings M" sandwiched between songs by St Etienne and The Tyrrell Corporation.

Another prominent journalist, Ian Watson from Melody Maker, interviews us for a regular article called "Advance", tipping us for the big time at any moment.

Food Records starts flirting with us, and it all begins to look positive. Their fresh-faced young talent scout Miles Jacobson takes us for drinks at The Good Mixer, a local Camden boozer, well known for being an indie band hangout. It wasn't uncommon to see Graham Coxon propping up the bar alongside market traders from Inverness Street. The pub goes on to become a local for Amy Winehouse, and an HQ for hyped-up Britpoppers, Menswe@r; a scrawny-looking bunch who seem to have the dress code of The Kinks but look like the cast from Oliver Twist underneath. With Miles chaperoning, we savour the surroundings playing pool before being summoned by David Balfe so he can scrutinise us for his label. David was the keyboardist for The Teardrop Explodes and started Food Records with acts like Zodiac Mindwarp and Voice of the Beehive. The label's biggest successes so far are Jesus Jones and Blur.

On our visit, it felt like being in the headmaster's office. I'm not sure we click, and the meeting is short-lived. We are given some free demo time at the Food studio, but the tracks we record don't see the light of day. One stand-out track was a country-rock song called "Sesame". It never gets played live. Anyway, conversations with Food soon fade, and after a few more lunches with smiley label manager Andy Ross, a contract deemed too low is turned down. I'm not sure why we've said no to a label with such a high pedigree and bands with a success rate; the consensus must be we are worth more.

In the meantime, we record more demos at The Square, including "Fragrance" a shimmering, driving track we use to open our set with and "Circus Classic", another moody Pixies-style number. Another poppy number called "Really" is written, named after me because I say "Really?" a lot. I'm not sure if this is a term of endearment or mocking on their part. The buzz is undoubtedly building - live reviews and the E.P. give us positive feedback and label us as one of the bright new hopes on the UK indie scene. We add a regular tune for our walk on, "Little Fluffy Clouds" by The Orb and invest in a smoke machine to flood the stage with before we play.

"Matt, lyricist, and Three and A Half Minutes frontman is already being tagged as a moody bastard. "I'm not a morbid bastard, and I don't go around being constantly depressed, but it is possible to obtain this kind of frustrating feeling from the record. This record is no normal record; this is, whether the band like it or not, one of the most promising debuts in history. Their average age is a tender 18 years, and they already have a bucketload of attitude (but not an attitude problem). The five-track E.P. is quite purposely called Peep and is released on a label called Scared Hitless, as bassist Lawrence explains: "It's called Peep cos all it is, is a glimpse of what we're doing. It's not supposed to be some masterpiece, and it certainly isn't. There are a lot of faults to it. It's on a label called Scared Hitless 'cos; unfortunately, that's what most people are now. They're running around saying to themselves, "Is it 'indie' or is it on a major?" Who cares? Why not just get into the music for fuck's sake? The band could unfairly be categorised as archetypal indie-pop. However, they have far more depth than that, as is shown in the E.P. "One of our qualities is that we're doing something different in the sense that most bands stick to one winning formula. We tend to diversify, and where Feelings M is like The Senseless Things, the others are nothing like it. I think we may even be prepared to sacrifice major success to carry on doing what we wanna do," says Laurence. Whatever you do, do not miss this record or this band, as both may be revolutionary.

Our outspoken views are still a refreshing tonic for journalists and indie fanzines, such as Between the Lies and Smitten. We don't hold back with our opinions. We want to ensure our shows and material are unpredictable. Matt takes umbrage at the indie pop label we are given and regularly sneers "fuckin' pop" into the mic before launching us into "M.C.D." There is a strict no-encore rule, and the average set time could be as short as thirty minutes. All part of the allure, I guess. We start playing further afield with gigs at the Adelphi in Hull, the Duchess of York in Leeds, and the Jericho Tavern in Oxford. The Adelphi is an excellent venue with a Tardis-like appearance. The front entrance looks like a typical terraced house until you go through to the back and find yourself standing in a music venue. The staff warns us not to answer anyone asking the time as it will reveal our southern accents and we risk getting our heads kicked in for being mistaken as posh students. Indulging Graham the Toilet's presence, Steve Lamacq continues to support us with vigour in the press, and it looks like there is an appetite to carry on with the Scared Hitless trio.

It's August, and we are playing another chaotic smoke machine-filled gig at the Camden Falcon. I like playing at the Falcon as there is a good kebab shop around the corner, and I tend to stroll over there for a bite, fresh off stage and soaked in sweat. The venue is small but has housed bands like RIDE, Pulp and Blur. A local scene has been invented called the Camden Lurch, with the pub as the focal point. It's apartments now.

The performance at the Falcon is not our best, with terrible onstage sound and Laurence losing count, a bass drum pedal that won't stay put and Ollie doing his hapless best, manually operating a stage light positioned behind one of our amps. Plus, we overdo it with the new smoke machine, and nobody can see us.

Afterwards, Mike introduces us to his plus one, Laura Ziffren - an American A&R scout from Hollywood Records. Laura is bubbly and charismatic, with perfect teeth and a California tan. She immediately sparks a schoolboy crush in me. Even though our set was not up to its usual standard, she is interested in the band and wants to stay in touch. Things proceed to a low point with a negative review of our gig in Melody Maker, written by an enigmatic journalist who only uses one name. Andy Saunders consoles us, me in particular as I get a mention in the review which is not pleasant to read. It looks like sides have been taken and NME will be extolling our virtues from now on.

The summer ends with Alice and I making the pilgrimage to the Reading Festival to watch headliners, The Wonder Stuff, Public Enemy and Nirvana. We navigate the weekend avoiding the mud, joining the fray, and contemplating her final year of Sixth Form. I take her to see Suede inside the main tent. The heat inside makes the grass sweat. Brett has the audience in the palms of his slender hands. They are stars in the making, and the crowd can tell this is a band with something special, an image and sound which paves the way for Britpop before Oasis pours lager on the whole thing in about 5 years. It rains overnight on Saturday, so by Sunday, it's a muddy marsh. Many festivalgoers decide to embrace the mud and, after several hours of frolicking in the swamps they create, are now entirely covered from head to toe. Seeing the irony, Mudhoney shows solidarity with the crowd and has mud smeared on their faces when they play. An all-female rock band called L7 throw a used tampon into the crowd. By the time Nirvana plays, we are tired and emotional, so we call it a night. I regret not scoring any weed, so we attempt to smoke the powder from a tomato flavour cup-a-soup instead. I squander the next hour hacking outside, watching the rain come down, causing mini rivers to the left and right of our tent. Luckily, our tent isn't swept away in the mudslides, but waking to the sounds of campers shouting, "Where the fuck is my tent" and "I wanna die" shows us how lucky we were to survive the mud bath.

On the 2nd of September, we return to the Town & Country Club in Kentish Town for another charity benefit gig, a series of concerts called "Viva! Eight". This is being recorded for a televised broadcast on Granada and a compilation CD. More new tracks such as "Parrot Fashion" and "Bled Me Dry" have been added to our set list, but we choose the 90-second "Shit Sells" track for the CD, joining Shonen Knife, Thousand Yard Stare, Moose and Blue Aeroplanes, amongst others. I am thrilled to be featured on the same album as my heroes, Buffalo Tom. Another TV broadcast comes in the shape of MTV's 120 Minutes, which is behind a series of gigs across London. We support

Luna2 at The Grand in Clapham. We're interviewed by Paul King (of Love and Pride by King) after the sound-check. With Hollywood Records now drafting a record deal offer and more touring planned until the end of the year, my school education needs to be addressed. Faced with leaving the band or ditching school is an easy decision for me - I mean, what would you do? Thankfully, my parents know if they prevent me from leaving school and quitting the band, I will never forgive them if the Minutes go on to become huge. It's agreed I don't return to finish my education. We are officially bona fide, full-time musicians pursuing our dream. If we don't burn out, we should be fine.

2nd September - with Kingmaker, Gallon Drunk and Shonen Knife, The Town & Country Club, Kentish Town
12th September - with Bark Psychosis, Esquires, Bedford
14th September - with Bivouac, Town Hall, Manchester
21st September - with Bark Psychosis, Wherehouse, Derby
23rd September - with Hyperhead, Princess Charlotte, Leicester
24th September - with Luna, The Grand, Clapham, London
29th September - UCL, London

CHAPTER 16
FREEWHEELING

We regularly rehearse in a local village hall and soon have the tracks written for our 2nd E.P. Our songwriting has become fluid, and each session provides the bones of a new song. We use most of October/November touring the country or meeting with lawyer Alexis Grower in New Bond Street to discuss the Hollywood Records offer. I love being on the road. The joking and band meetings in the van help the time go by, and each time we pull up outside a venue, I get that bubble of nerves. An apprehensive feeling, not knowing if the bands we're playing with are nice people, what kind of audience we'll have, if one at all. A short wander around the neighbourhood during the twilight time between soundcheck and gig, trying to eat as I struggle with the butterflies. The feeling of relief once finished, and the prospect of a long drive home in a dark van, playing shoegaze epic "Feel" by The Verve in my CD Walkman, sending me to sleep until I get prodded in the arm a few hours later. If we're too far from home, Ollie tries to find a helpful soul who will put us up for the night, rather than sleeping in a cold van. He would take the stage after our gig and ask the audience for help. Often, we are given a floor or spare bed by students and end up piling into someone's flat or student housing in the early hours of the morning. All the places we stay at blur into one, a constant conveyor belt of flats with mould on the bathroom walls and a kitchen that would need a hazmat suit for entry, displaying dried noodles, pizza boxes and plates from last Sunday, remaining there until the unspoken standoff finishes and someone decides to clean. Living rooms and bedrooms are plastered with posters of Eddie Vedder and Miles Hunt, Cindy Crawford and Courtney Love grinning over us as we sit on second-hand sofas in the jaundiced light. Ashtrays brim with butts and roaches, empty glass bottles line the skirting board, a black blocky stereo the size of a filing cabinet stands on a wooden table, festooned with piles of cassette tapes, the inlay cards covered in hand-written doodles, track listings and the odd squirting penis. On one boisterous night, our current host tells me the bedroom next door is free, as his flatmate is staying with his girlfriend. I settle into a cosy bed in a dark room, away from the others who are intent on staying up as late as they can. Hours later, I feel a hand pushing my shoulder. A silhouette of someone is standing above me. "Sorry, mate. You're in my bed."

I guess they broke up.

The next morning is spent gathering our things, drinking multiple cups of tea before we say goodbye to our new friends, and gifted a mixtape for the van. It's not unusual to get to the next town or city around lunchtime, meaning we have loads of spare time until the venue opens at 5pm. Great if you are in Edinburgh, not so much if you're in Swindon with six hours to kill.

By now, Ollie is the de facto Tour Manager and has enlisted various victims to help with the merch stand and van driving. There is a brother and sister, Charlotte on merch and Toby driving the van. But it's not just driving; Toby and Ollie have way more duties than taking us to the venue and back.

Here is a typical day in the life of Toby: Drive to wherever the van is being kept and leave the car. Pick everyone up - Steve from Harlow, Ollie, Matt & Laurence from Bishops Stortford, and then me from Stansted. Load in gear at each house - amplifiers, cables, drum cases, guitars, effects pedals, and merch. Drive for hours to the venue without a sat nav or phone, using only a road map or directions faxed and printed out by a helpful promoter, or stopping to ask directions. The only hard work the band had to do was decide whose turn it was for the music on the stereo. We would jump from R.E.M. (Laurence) to The Jesus and Mary Chain (Matt), to Alice in Chains (Steve) to Thousand Yard Stare (me).

Getting there on time is crucial, as you risk screwing up the soundcheck schedule and may not get one at all. Spotting the venue from the wrong side of a dual carriageway in a ludicrous one-way system was commonplace. I'm talking about you, Princess Charlotte in Leicester. More than once, we ended up in the bus depot. Being new to visiting these cities and towns meant making an illegal U-turn or parking nearby. Once the venue was located, everything gets removed from the van. Thankfully, most venues are on the ground floor. Still, if you're playing at the Krazyhouse in Liverpool or the Venue in New Cross, you face several flights of stairs to lug everything up.

Once unloaded, unpacked, and set up on the stage, it's time for the soundcheck. Toby and Ollie guide the in-house engineer on what sounds right and help with levels as they know what we prefer. I remind them to give the sound engineer a beer before we play. During our set, they re-string and tune guitars in the dark, having barely one song to restore the guitar to a playable fashion. As tempting as it might be to get royally smashed on free beer, Toby has to abstain from alcohol, and once we're finished, all the gear is disassembled, packed, and returned to the van. Ollie finds the promoter and gets paid. Sometimes we have company for the return trip - liberated objects, cans of beer, or a random person. If we've played in London, we stop at The Happening Bagel Bakery in Finsbury Park for a Salt Beef bagel. Then it's a drive home through the night. Ollie puts on ambient tunes, and when we're a few miles out from our respective houses, plays our homecoming tape, The Best of Dr Hook. Finally, Toby returns the van and drives home. Roadies and drivers are unsung heroes.

We register our songs with the Performing Rights Society. Signing up means we receive royalties if our music is broadcast on TV and radio and when we play at PRS-registered music venues. In the olden days, royalty percentages were allocated in favour of the songwriter and vocalists, but ours was equal. We have detailed discussions with booking agencies, music producers and P.R agencies. One PR company we meet is Bad Moon, a well-known agency owned by Anton Brookes. They have recently acted as publicists for Nirvana. We visit their cramped office near Portobello Road. Anton looks like he could be in a band with shoulder-length hair and a faded T-shirt. He warns us about Hollywood Records, saying they are a joke record label. This only adds fuel to the rebellious fire as we press on with a recording contract with Hollywood Records and an E.M.I. publishing deal.

We are booked for a string of dates supporting Sultans of Ping F.C, a rowdy indie punk band with an added slice of British humour to their lyrics and image. They'd hit the charts with their irreverent debut single, "Where's Me Jumper?" and continue to grow with more singles such as "Stupid Kid" and "U Talk Too Much." The onstage persona is striking, with both guitarists clad in black latex and standing stationary for the whole set, the drummer in a football kit and lead singer Niall cavorting about in whatever he likes. Their fans are lively, too, and every gig is rammed. We're on the Northern part of the tour, playing to a packed house every night. It's a good opportunity to collect more fans. If it wasn't for the band, I would never have had a reason to visit somewhere like Buckley, a small town in North East Wales. I look out at houses, buildings, people going about their lives, things I'll never play a part in. Some might think I wasn't missing much, but I love seeing new places as it fuels my wanderlust and curiosity.

Tours can be weird - you only tend to see the band you're supporting at each venue during the soundcheck. Once complete, both bands disappear into a green room. And you don't see each other again (unless you watch their set) until the next day when you do it all again in a different town.

The separation means it can be hard to click with a band - for instance, it is only by the final night of the tour in Bradford when we grab some quality time with Sultans of Ping in their dressing room. We would have stayed longer, but Toby wants to get home, so we have to relent.

2nd October - with Sunscreem, Southampton University
5th October - with Sultans of Ping F.C The Adelphi, Hull
6th October - with Sultans of Ping F.C, Lancaster University
7th October - with Sultans of Ping F.C, Buckley Tivoli, Buckley
8th October - with Sultans of Ping F.C, Krazy House, Liverpool
9th October - with Sultans of Ping F.C, Queens Hall, Bradford
10th October - The Falcon, Camden
11th October - Notts Polytechnic
18th October - Rat Hole, Tamworth
21st October – The Boat Race, Cambridge
22nd October – The Clay Pigeon, Eastcote
23rd October - with Love Battery, Jericho Tavern, Oxford

CHAPTER 17
NOT SLEEPING AROUND

I celebrate my 18th birthday with a raucous gig at the Bowes Lyon in Stevenage. We are supporting a U.S. band called Love Battery. The drummer is a brilliant, friendly guy and goes on to form The Presidents of the United States of America. Backstage, I meet Chris Evans, singer and guitarist from a local band called The Herbsmen. From being plied with birthday beers and shots the moment I arrive; I'm amazed I can even play; I am so drunk. The whole audience sings Happy Birthday to me, which is nice. I make our entourage drive to Alice's place for a house party she's holding in my honour, which is a tad further than expected. I've sobered up by the time we get there. The throbbing bass of "Killing in the Name" reverberates through the living room, where the party is in full swing and reaching its chaotic zenith. The air is thick with the mingling scents of cheap beer, cigarette smoke, and charged hormones. In one corner, a group of gate crashers huddle around a makeshift bar, passing around a bottle of something suspiciously potent. On the sofa, a couple engage in a passionate snogging session, blissfully unaware of the hubbub around them. Flannel shirts and torn jeans are the unofficial dress code, reflecting the grunge spirit. The room buzzes with unbridled energy, a mix of teenage rebellion and the exhilaration of breaking free from societal norms. In the kitchen, someone fumbles with a cassette tape, trying to switch the soundtrack to something even more hard-edged. The floor is sticky with spilt drinks, and the flickering neon lights from a lava lamp cast an otherworldly glow on the scene. Amidst the debauchery, an old school friend stumbles into the hallway and up the stairs, his face turning various shades of green. Not making it to the bathroom in time, he opens the first-floor window. The vomiting sounds splashing to the concrete meld with the music, creating an oddly harmonious cacophony. Amidst the chaos, friendships are forged, hearts broken, and memories etched into the fabric of teenage existence. Unfortunately, Alice has to endure my growing ego, petulant antics, mood swings and the constant coming and going. I don't even thank her for the soirée and decide to be aloof and cold, walking around the party as if I'm Bono. I'm very hungover and shamefully quiet when Alice drives me home the next day.

25th October - with Love Battery, Bowes Lyon, Stevenage
26th October - with Love Battery, The Old Trout, Windsor
27th October - Players, Bath
30th October - The Mauritania, Bristol

The growing adulation from girls has been a boost for me, and after every gig, there are girls waiting outside to meet the band. Walking into the Boar's Head always causes a hot fuss and after a few bottles of K, flirting with wide-eyed girls becomes a regular occurrence. Finally, the inevitable happens at another house party thrown by friends of Matt and Laurence. I'm in a small village near Bishop's Stortford, milling about and not knowing anyone. I feel isolated and sit outside on a garden bench, staring out at the massive garden and Essex countryside, as I work my way through a pack of Silk Cut. An elfin girl with a cheeky grin and a glint in her eye wanders over and hands me a bottle of Becks. She sits down next to me, talking about the other people at the party and who else I know. I shrug nervously, letting my hair fall across my face, nearly singeing the ends with my cigarette. She giggles as I flap my hand at my fringe, fag ash falling onto my palm. She helps me brush the ash off and puts her hand on my leg, leaving it there as she sips from her vodka and lemonade. Everything I say makes her laugh and with every instance, she moves in closer and warms my leg with her hand. As another empty bottle of Becks is added to line up by my feet, the garden spins a tad and I have to focus my vision and control the slurring. She turns to me, drooping her eyelids and flashing another flirty smile. "So, tell me more about Alice".

"Well, we've been seeing each other a while now. She's brilliant. Like a best mate too, you know? We wind each other up a lot. Write each other tons of letters".

"Sounds very sweet. Where is she?"

"She wasn't invited - this is more of a band party, so she's at home".

"I'm on my own too. Shall we keep each other company?"

I raise my eyebrows, feeling both pairs of hands on my thighs tightening their grip.

"Come again?"

"I'm OK with that," she says, burrowing her head into my chest and laughing at her joke. I snigger, smelling her hair and perfume for the first time, the warmth of her body making me tremble. She stays there for a while, before raising her head and bringing her mouth towards mine. I lean back.

She moves her lips towards my ear and whispers, "She's not here".

I look around, checking for spies and see the band inside the house, laughing and drinking. Steve spots me and gives a thumbs up, something I wrongly translate to be a sign of approval. The devil on my shoulder takes hold of the back of my head and slowly turns it to meet hers. Before I can stop to think, I'm in a tight embrace, locking lips with a girl who isn't Alice. I can blame the booze, the girl, and the fact I think I'm someone special. But there's no excuse. I'm an idiot. I stay in her company for a while, before making my excuses.

I walk home from the party, all eight miles of it to punish myself. Worse still, I hid it from Alice and wrote the confession in my diary.

Off the back of some more dates with Love Battery, another gig lands on our lap for the Cambridge Corn Exchange. We are opening for Ned's Atomic Dustbin as part of their "Are You Normal" tour. I can't believe it. I've gorged myself on their albums God

Fodder and Are You Normal, and now we get to share the same stage! This was a big deal. They'd asked local bands to open each gig on their tour, labelling these acts as "Thirdies". We are all buzzing and can't wait to get to Cambridge and play in such a hallowed venue with one of our favourite bands on the scene. It's a win-win: playing the gig and seeing Neds. But when we arrive at the venue to see the main support band sound checking, our faces drop.

Kinky Machine are a glam indie band we played a few dates with before they morphed into Britpop hopefuls Rialto. To win over the crowd, frontman Louis has a habit of rocking out; his top will be off, and his foot on the monitor by the 2nd song in their set. We scoff at this in an interview with Steve Lamacq, saying we would prefer not to go on stage after a band like that. We also slag them off in a zine called Between the Lies, saying they were NOT glamorous and were a bunch of fucking wankers. Our short stint touring with them didn't forge long-lasting friendships, and I think the band name is terrible. Anyway, I guess they found out about all this, as they purposely take a long while with their soundcheck and leave us with no time to set up. As we file to the side of the stage with our gear, Louis puts his foot on the monitor and chuckles with the rest of the band. Fair play. We have mocked them in the music press, so maybe we deserve this. Still, they can't stop us from performing, and we know this could be another chance to win over a room packed with indie kids. Our set-opener is the riff-heavy "Parrot Fashion", starting with me playing a beat. My intro lasts a few minutes longer as Laurence experiences last-minute problems with his amp due to the limited soundcheck. Another sabotage by Kinky Machine, or is it karma? But we rescue it and play a robust set in front of the entire Corn Exchange. Afterwards, I join the mosh pit, joining Alice and my mates to watch a stunning set by Ned's - I have to pinch myself; I can't believe we've supported such a great band!

"3½ Minutes are destined for great things; they have a following after supporting the likes of the Sultans of Ping, Mega City 4, Suede, Ned's & Kingmaker. They offer a jolly impressive range of catchy guitar grooves and instant pop-picking melodies. I'd put a tenner on 'em making it big and deservedly so. Atmospheric, gloomy aggression."

6th November - Kent University
7th November - University of Westminster
13th November - Arts Centre, Norwich
14th November - Army & Navy, Chelmsford
18th November - Fleece & Firkin, Bristol
26th November - with Ned's Atomic Dustbin, Corn Exchange, Cambridge
30th December - The Monkey Club, Swindon

CHAPTER 18
ALL APOLOGIES

The music papers have become our first port of call when reading about trends, news, and gigs. Every Thursday, when I pop around the band's house, I see Laurence idly flicking through a new copy of Melody Maker or NME. Both titles have been going since the 1950s and are essential reading for aspiring musicians and bands and their fans. By the '90s, there was a lot of bandwagon-jumping with the editorial team, creating scene after scene - some of them resonate with the readers, whilst some don't last a week. Like all British Media, there is a habit of building 'em up and knocking 'em down; plus, a real "them and us" attitude between who the NME likes and who Melody Maker has taken a shine to.

I love scanning through the gig guides and searching for our listings, and each time we are given coverage, I get a little dopamine hit. My mum adds the clipping to a scrapbook. If I still didn't have that in my possession, this memoir would be short, so thanks, Mum.

I become a music mag junkie and buy copies of Select, Vox and the comic/magazine, Deadline. I want to have a constant connection with the music community, and I love reading album reviews of bands I'd never heard of and taking a punt on their new album the next time I visit Our Price. It's how I discover bands like Catherine Wheel, Revolver, Airhead, Curve, and Levitation. On one visit to the band HQ, I find Matt in his room, rediscovering his vinyl collection and playing a 7" single over and over. It's Head Like a Hole, by Nine Inch Nails. I'd been aware of them but not paid much attention until now. I've never heard something sound so taut, angry and intense and for all its drum machines and industrial sounds, I am drawn in by vocalist Trent Reznor's emotive lyrics and anthemic chorus. We both listen in silence. Matt stands up and goes to the record player.

"I'm putting it on again."

I'm no longer at school, but Alice still is. On Tuesdays, I pick her up when I know she has a free afternoon for a study group. Even though it's a few villages away, we go back to my house to chill. Out of the blue, I see my parents' car pull up. They've decided to come home for lunch. Panicking, I send Alice upstairs to hide because although my parents like her they'll question why she's here and not at school. Better to avoid any awkward scenarios. With Alice quietly sitting in my bedroom, I chat with my folks, we have a sandwich, and finally, they leave. As the car pulls away, I breathe a sigh of relief.

"The coast is clear," I shout.

Silence from upstairs. I expected a "whoop" or a laugh to acknowledge our lucky escape.

"Al?"

I hear footsteps from the bedroom. She appears at the top of the stairs, stony-faced. I wonder if this is one of her wind-ups. We have crafted this into an art where we tell each other elaborate stories, trying to get the other to fall for them. She treads slowly downstairs. "I've been reading your diary."

My life contra-zooms, my face turns red with a hot flush, and any smiles or light from my life suddenly snuffed out. "Shit".

I'm angry that she's picked up my diary, but how can I object? I've let her write it in before, so I guess it didn't seem out of bounds. I've written my drunken divergence down for her to read. It's not based on rumours or hearsay. Now I have no way to salvage the car crash I've created. Words fail me and I squirm as the silence hits a deafening level. Slowly, she picks up her school bag and leaves without a word, no doubt walking herself to the nearest train station.

In the days that follow, I become a pariah, snubbed by her friends, and have to explain to my parents why Alice never calls anymore. I write her a letter and try to call, but no reply. Days are spent wallowing in self-pity as I sit and weep on my bed, trying to smell her scent on my pillows and listening to Slowdive on repeat. I try to figure out why I did what I did, what made me shun a lovely girl's attention in favour of somebody else? Was it because I was still seeking validation? Is this the norm when you're in a band and people want to be a part of your life, no matter what the cost?

Charlie comes home from school one day with some news. "Have you heard about Alice?" I'm expecting news of a new boyfriend, so I attempt to act indifferent and shrug, nodding my head.

"She's been in a car crash".

A cold wave flushes through my skin and I sit upright, eyes widening as I look at Charlie.

"What?" I start welling up, picturing Alice lying in the hospital, broken bones, with life-changing injuries or worst still, on life-support.

"Yeah, she was driving her dad's van and it toppled over on a sharp bend, then slid along the road. She's fine, just in shock. Thought you should know."

I rush to the telephone, dialling the numbers as fast as I can on its off-white rotary face.

Shit, why does her phone number have so many zeros in it?

A voice responds down the crackly line. "Hello?"

Its Alice. I breathe a sigh of relief that she's answered and sounds OK too.

"It's me," I say.

We talk. I ask her if she's OK. She's fine, a bit shaken up. I make her laugh. She makes me laugh. I tell her I'm sorry. She tells me I'm a fool. I send her another letter. I get one back. We speak a few more times.

Then, even though I don't deserve it, she gives me another chance.

CHAPTER 19
HOLLYWOOD RECORDS

We are ready to record our second E.P. with John Bell producing again, this time at Matrix Studios in London. Former occupants of this recording studio have been The Clash, The Rolling Stones, and Prince. The band using the studio next door are The Fall; they wander around first thing in the morning, drinking from cans of Special Brew. The session takes five days, and we lay down four new tracks. "Bled Me Dry" is the new single, another infectious pop song with a quiet/loud format and a grunge chorus. "A Little Howl" is a darker number, with heavy use of the toms and an absolute favourite of mine to record. "Parrot Fashion" is the third song. The last number is a woozy Velvet Underground-style track, "The Spellbinding Mr Benn's Trauma Parlour". The song is a change of direction for us with gentle percussion, and some tinkly piano added at the last minute. By late November, the record deal with Hollywood Records is still being finalised. Out of the offers from Food and Chrysalis, Hollywood Records proffered the best option. Matt & Laurence have become disillusioned by the U.K. record industry; I think the constant pigeon-holing and cynical press coverage has gotten to them, so we are full steam ahead with the U.S. label.

Before email and Facebook, bands communicated through the post and so we create a little mail-order newsletter called Hydrant Drone, listing tour dates, news, and contact details for merch. Here's a quote from one:

"The end of '92 was spent in America talking to record labels who have a healthy attitude, compared to British ones who just want to sign the next indie giant or the band on the front cover of last week's N.M.E."

The 5-figure record deal is completed by Alexis Grower, our bulldog of a lawyer. Laura has signed her discovery from the smoke-drenched gig in the Camden Falcon. Previously, she'd found Smashing Pumpkins but wasn't allowed to sign them. They became massive, so Laura was given a free pass on any new bands she liked, being us four. Also, Hollywood Records have recently bought Queen's back catalogue for $10 million. Freddie Mercury dies soon after, providing an unexpected income reaching $95 million over four years, giving them cash to burn. Anyhow, our collective lightbulb flickers. We request to go and meet with our U.S. record company before signing the dotted line. Happily, they fly us over to Los Angeles, along with Ollie. We all sit separately on the plane, and I end up in a window seat next to the guy who owns a clothing brand called Mossimo. Once he realises, I'm in a band, he gives me a pack of stickers and a Mossimo dog tag. Not even off the plane yet, and I'm already blagging merch. On the tiny TV screens, I watch a movie called Singles - it's a tribute to the Seattle scene with a grunge soundtrack, thinly disguised as a romantic comedy. When we land, a driver greets us in true Spinal Tap style with a card saying "3.5 Mins". Our hotel is the well-known Mondrian on Sunset Boulevard. We share two rooms, Matt, Laurence, and Ollie in one, Steve and I in the other. Laura is our chaperone the entire time, taking us out to diners, burger joints and Asian restaurants. She has a great itinerary planned.

It is my first ever visit to the United States; I love the California sun on my face, the giant billboards and how polite everyone is. The portions of food are massive. On the first night, we go to see EMF at The Roxy, which is random - a U.K. band in the U.S. watching another U.K. band? I would've preferred Nirvana or Pearl Jam. Walt Disney Corp owns Hollywood Records, so we get to experience a day in Disneyland, taking free rides on Splash Mountain and jumping the queues. Laura drives us back in her open-top car. The drive takes us along the palm-lined streets of Anaheim, gradually transitioning from the pastels of Disneyland to the bold, vibrant hues of Sunset Strip. The radio, now playing "Winona" by Drop Nineteens, provides a soundtrack that echoes the changing landscapes. The conversation gets on to favourite bands. I mention my latest obsession, Nine Inch Nails. "You like Nine Inch Nails? I know Trent Reznor! Let me call him." I go numb as Laura dials the number on her brick-sized car phone and waits for an answer. Am I about to have a conversation with Trent Reznor?? After some silence, she leaves a voicemail. "He never picks up", she says. As we cruise through Los Angeles, the iconic landmarks began to emerge. I spot the famous Hollywood Sign standing on the distant hills. I couldn't help but feel a sense of awe as we passed the legendary Capitol Records building, an icon of music history. The car rolls down Sunset Boulevard, the strip coming alive with the neon pulse of billboards and the glow of nightlife. The iconic Whisky a Go Go, its history embedded in the very fabric of rock and roll, beckoned with promises of legendary performances. Maybe ours one day. As we pulled up to The Mondrian, I couldn't help but marvel at the beauty of a city that effortlessly dances between dreams and the dazzling lights of the Sunset Strip.

The next day, we meet Label President, Peter Paterno at the Hollywood Records office, set among the leafy Walt Disney studios plot in Buena Vista. Peter has a big frame, a thick moustache, and a firm handshake. He used to be Guns 'N Roses' lawyer. We sit in his cavernous office and help ourselves to cookies with chocolate chips the size of your fist. Lunch with Laura is in the staff canteen, with all menu options named after Disney films - I go for the "That Darn Cat" chicken sandwich. As I walk past an employee's office, I spot the Oscar statuette from Snow White in the cabinet behind him. We meet the rest of the Hollywood Records team and check out posters of their other signings, a band called Motorpsycho, Natural Life and of course Queen. Back at The Mondrian, we chose not to kill our televisions by throwing them out of the window but take some lovely photos instead, wearing branded caps given to us by the marketing team. I venture out onto the strip and find a store where I can load up on Twinkies, Ding Dongs, and Hershey bars.

Finally, the main event is a record label showcase gig at the famous Roxbury Club, over the road from our hotel on Sunset Boulevard. We weren't told about this until the last minute and I'm a tad jittery about performing in font of our new employers. On the bill, there's us and label mates The Fluid and The Boo-Yaa T.R.I.B.E. The Fluid are a garage rock band previously signed to SubPop and produced by Butch Vig. The Boo-Yaa T.R.I.B.E are a gangsta rap outfit. Pretty eclectic. I'm already tipsy from the free bar, and as I'm underage, I have to get Ollie to pass the bottles to me under the table. Our set goes down well, and considering the jet lag, beer, and nerves, I still go nuts on the drums, flailing my arms and hair about, with wild abandon. Our set finishes in clouds of smoke, white noise, and the usual moody storming off stage. I storm off stage left, staggering through a crowd of onlookers. I find a corner, where I can stop and catch my breath. A colossal guy comes up to me, blotting out all the light. I'm ready for a comment, question or even compliment.

"Yo, man," he says. "You stepped on my foot, man. On my sneakers."

It's one of the Boo-Yaa T.R.I.B.E. He menacingly looms over me, and I have no idea what to say. He's stepping from left to right, squaring up to me, clearly annoyed some little punk has left a mark on his white sneakers. His fists are clenched, and his head is nodding with pent-up anger. The L.A. riots had happened earlier in the year, sparked by the footage of police officers violently beating a black man called Rodney King. There was still much tension in L.A., so I guess a white kid stomping on a rapper's trainers was not the best thing to do. So, what do I do now? I'm a shy kid from Essex, just turned 18 and utterly new to a confrontation like this. Does he want me to buy him a new pair? Get on my knees and clean it with my tongue? He repeats the same line with a bit more irritation. I'm scared this could escalate into something violent. Steve comes over, puzzled.

The man remembers where he is and stomps off, nodding to himself in frustration, kissing his teeth and swatting his hand like he would a fly. I choose not to watch their set by the side of the stage. We get the offer to stick around a bit longer in L.A. It's nearly Christmas, so we decline. We enjoy our last morning at a diner (more coffee, Hun?), a brief shopping spree in Tower Records (I buy Broken and Fixed by Nine Inch Nails on cassette) followed by a short tour around Melrose, and we fly back home. After the 11-hour flight and ninety-minute drive back home, I call Alice immediately and arrange to see her straight away. I brush away the jetlag, I missed her like crazy and can't wait to see her and share all the amazing things that have happened on the other side of the Atlantic.

CHAPTER 20

HANG ON TO YOUR EGO

I still need to work on communicating correctly with the band. I've given myself imposter syndrome, fearing that anything I overshare or suggest will reveal me as a simpleton or liar. Naively, I think it better to stay schtum. I develop a nervous tick sucking the ends of my hair; once they've dried and formed a sharp point, it stabs at my cheeks. As I mature, I become braver on stage, and open up a little, but I still find it hard to release myself completely. I've become so used to being mute that it is a challenge to break out of it, like a brain stutter that prevents me from saying something right when it needed to be heard. I'll just take things in, digest them, bottle them up, or spill them onto the diary.

On a personal level, the casualties are starting to pile up. With all the attention I am getting and the lifestyle of being in a band, I've started to become a self-centred rock star wannabe. I've let true friendships crumble away, with friends like Sam now fully in the background.

Plus, I'm taking constant risks with the petty thieving at venues too. Nothing is sacred, and it doesn't matter what it is. I want to nick it. Give, give, give, me more, more, more. I'm growing entitled, using my home as somewhere to sleep and eat, ignoring any issues my family happen to be going through. Luckily there are none, but if someone did make an announcement of serious importance at the dinner table, I would probably be thinking about when my next gig is.

To end the year on a high, we have a New Year's Eve party in a flat in Bishops Stortford. U2 Andy arrives with the booze, but he's left it so late, the only things left on the shelves are cheap, warm bottles of vodka. The drinking games commence, and we take shots whilst playing Mousetrap. After 2 hours of this, I'm beyond wasted. The room starts spinning the moment I stand up. Holding me up, I pose for a photo between Laurence and Roger, then fall forward in a heap the moment they let go of me. If this was today, my green face would be all over Instagram in seconds, but lucky for me, it would take another few weeks for someone to bother getting the photos developed and printed. What follows is a manic, vodka-fuelled freak-out episode. Screaming and shouting nonsense as I hug the toilet, vomiting profusely as the vodka burns my throat on its journey back out. Eventually, I pass out. I regain consciousness and look around. It's all white and clinical. Luckily, it's not a hospital. I'm in the bathtub. The flat is deathly quiet. I've been stashed there to sleep it off, and everyone has gone to the pub. I get to the Boar's Head just in time to see in 1993, the band amazed that I'm walking and talking so soon after my wild episode. In another act of self-harm and needing attention from someone who notices me, I snog a random girl, and then go back to the flat to sober up. While everyone sleeps, I watch the launch of Carlton TV.

1992 - Mixtape

A Good Idea - Sugar

Sheela Na Gig - PJ Harvey

Hey Jealousy - Gin Blossoms

High - The Cure

It's a Shame About Ray - The Lemonheads

Taillights Fade - Buffalo Tom

Dollar Bill - Screaming Trees

Fait Accompli - Curve

Wish - Nine Inch Nails

You Set My Soul - The Telescopes

World Around - Levitation

Leave Them All Behind - RID

CHAPTER 21

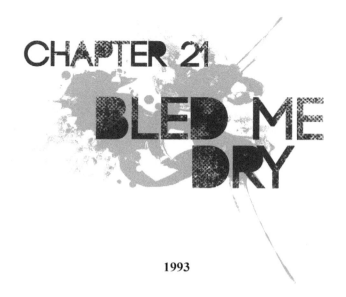

BLED ME DRY

1993

Waco Texas siege, The Maastricht Treaty takes effect, formally establishing the European Union, River Phoenix dies, Informer by Snow, Siamese Dream by The Smashing Pumpkins, Jurassic Park, Indecent Proposal.

We start the year with another mail-out from the band zine Hydrant Drone, featuring the message:

"The gigs in '92 were hard work because we were constantly trying to lay to rest ghouls and ghosts created by journalists already labelling the band. We can't tolerate this ignorance - every band has influences, and journalists should learn to give bands room to develop their own sound/audience. That's why we're much happier with the new record, which is much more in the vein of Sodium/Shake It Up. but has, in typical Three and A Half Minutes style, a classic A-side in Bled Me Dry - a "pop" song spiked with cynicism."

22nd January - with Jamiroquai, Imperial College, London
23rd January - Esquires, Bedford
28th January - University of Loughborough
30th January - Coventry Polytechnic
3rd February - with Senseless Things, Lancaster University, Preston
4th February - with Senseless Things, Krazy House, Liverpool
6th February - Kingston University
8th February - Middlesex University
13th February - Sussex University, Brighton
18th February - Brunel University, Uxbridge
23rd February - Moles, Bath
26th February - Army & Navy, Chelmsford

One of our longest tours coincides with the Bled Me Dry E.P. release, set for March. We kick things off with the Senseless Things as they headline a few gigs and then head off on our own tour, where we play for the first time in Scotland. The first night in Greenock gig is hard work. We choose to bring a punkier vibe to the seemingly hardened audience and keep the talking to a minimum. We bring a camcorder to record shenanigans, ending up with shaky footage of the band in various dressing rooms, and stranger's bedrooms or aimlessly wandering around Edinburgh. Rehearsal footage from March 3rd shows us at Princess Charlotte in Leicester as we jam some new songs for E.P. number three. Watching it back weeks later, I can see the cracks are starting to show. I am becoming the butt of private jokes and facing jibes about my music tastes and general demeanour. If I mention Airhead, The Lemonheads, and even Mega City Four, it's met with derision. It seems everything I do or say is not correct. I start to feel like a burden, the stupid one with stupid ideas who should shut up and drum. The weird thing about being in a band is it's a cross between colleagues, friends and family. You're bound together with something more potent than your mate next door or the friend you sat next to in Geography. To create kick-ass music and perform each night, we rely on each other to show up every day. Record companies, managers, and the press are all looking to us for what might be next. They depend on us to get along and be a functioning unit. I think they forget how young we are. Sometimes, the pressure can be too much, and like a whistling kettle, someone in the band lets off steam.

Back on home turf, The Army and Navy venue in Chelmsford sells out. It's the first notable sign of our constant gigging paying off, with a jam-packed audience there to see the headliners; us. Toby has to act as security, pushing off the pissed-up stage invaders who are taking too long to jump back into the fray.

The contract with Hollywood Records is signed in mid-February. The deal has a £40k advance to record the first album with another £7500 for new equipment. Gone are the Juggs, now replaced with a shiny white Premier A.P.K. kit with Zildjian cymbals and a Ludwig "Black Beauty" snare drum. We buy a mini-bus and pay ourselves per diems, a daily stipend for everything an 18-year-old might need. A session is booked with professional photographer, Paul Rider. He has done photo shoots for The Stone Roses, Manic Street Preachers, The Smiths, and New Order. We allocate a day posing in his London studio, wearing various styles of alternative street clothing and the odd silk shirt. On previous photo shoots, I've made the faux pas of turning up in another band's t-shirt and getting it in the neck. There are some photos where it's obvious I'm wearing a top inside out. What can I say, I like band T-shirts. Things come to an awkward head when we are asked by Paul to sit a certain way or place our hands in a specific position - taking control, Matt moves my arms and hands for me like I'm some toddler who doesn't understand instructions. The red mist rises, and I flip out, shouting "Stop treating me like a baby" instantly causing an air of uncomfortable silence in the studio.

"But you are" smiles Matt, to lighten the mood. Is he trying to help, or just being a control freak? I don't know what to feel sometimes.

Thousands of copies of Bled Me Dry are released on 8th March - this time on cd single and vinyl. On the front cover is a girl with accentuated features holding out her hands. Mike and Ben had overseen the photo shoot, we added a few extra images to the back of the cover, including the quote "There's virtue and there's creed, in duality we believe".

Again, the buzz of holding it in my hands is fantastic, more so because it was an actual compact disc that can be played anywhere! We sit in a pub whilst on tour, ready to hear the single broadcast on Radio 1's Evening Session. We get played right after "Sex Type Thing" by Stone Temple Pilots. It is genuinely surreal to hear Mark Goodier announce us. We sit in silence, all grinning - I visualise our Top of the Pops appearance and put my faith in the record selling enough to receive an invitation from the Beeb. Unfortunately, things go downhill in the music press. Our single review in NME is branded as vaguely pleasant but hopelessly derivative. Reviewing our single in Melody Maker, Everett True pours more cold water, requesting that we be shot. Fun times.

3rd March - with Dr Phibes and the House of Wax Equations, Princess Charlotte, Leicester
4th March - Longton Leisurebowl, Stoke
5th March - Nice n Sleazy, Glasgow
6th March - The Subway, Edinburgh
7th March - Cafe Drummond, Aberdeen
8th March - Twa Tams, Perth
10th March - with Bang Bang Machine, Duchess of York, Leeds
12th March - Ship Inn, Oundle
13th March - Penny Theatre, Canterbury
18th March - Hallamshire, Sheffield
19th March - with Mint 400, Powerhaus, London
23rd March - Moles, Bath
24th March - with The Auteurs, Fleece & Firkin, Bristol
25th March - with Orange Deluxe, The Joiners Arms, Southampton
26th March - The Forum, Hatfield
27th March - with Echobelly, University of Westminster
15th April - Four Alls, Taunton
16th April - with Zu Zu's Petals, Madeira Hotel, Brighton

We finish touring at the end of March and attempt to film a music video for Bled Me

Dry in Bishop's Stortford. It doesn't go to plan. Using the loudest generator in Essex for power and located in a disused water fountain, the idea is to film a Cure-style video where we are all gothic caricatures of ourselves. My drum kit is transformed into a miniature toy version. I'm getting told what to do again, but I'm bored of listening and doing my own thing instead. It is a cold night, and the filming process is dull. The final cut doesn't impress. I guess a whole night spent filming a non-existent music video is called "suffering for your art".

We received a message from Laura telling us "Bled Me Dry" will be used in a film soundtrack. As Disney owns Hollywood Records, this was easy to arrange. The film is called Son-in-Law, a Pauly Shore comedy about a flamboyant party animal who becomes a fish out of water when he visits a small farm town. Our song can be heard during a scene in a college dorm. At the time, this is an interesting bit of news, but once the P.R.S. cheques start coming in, with details of everywhere the film has aired, it's a nice little boost. I still get about £25 every three months from the P.R.S., which is nice. In terms of sales, the E.P. does OK, but not enough to propel us into the next tier of bands who can sell out a London venue or get on the cover of N.M.E./Select/Melody Maker.

We have a band meeting to discuss our image, what style we should emulate and how we can get around being pigeonholed. We needed an angle. No good trying to be original, as nothing is original anymore. A focal point was needed, a direction to send the journalists off on, rather than lazy tags as another angry young band. I was crossing my fingers for "Bled Me Dry", but the next single will be the breakthrough we need. I'm hopeful these discussions bring us closer together as a band without a hierarchy. With no other prospects, they are all I have.

CHAPTER 22

ROCKFIELD

With Scared Hitless moving out of the picture and Hollywood Records calling the shots, it's time to hire a full-time manager who can oversee all the business and admin while we concentrate on making music. As recommended by Mike Smith, we meet with Tim Paton. Tim is a professional photographer and former manager for The Milltown Brothers. He is easy-going and quiet-natured and makes a real effort to get acquainted with the band and all our quirks. There was some deliberation, but we ultimately choose Tim to become the new manager.

We need to write new material, and a house in the middle of nowhere in Norfolk is booked for a few days - viewed as a retreat for the band, it's a chance to get away from it all and create. We just about manage to squeeze the drums, amps and gear into the rustic front room and set about composing new songs. Being a self-catering situation, we have to improvise once the pot noodles have been consumed. A moment of levity is had with Laurence, as he and I do our version of late-night cooking show, "Get Stuffed". We attempt to cook a stew, consisting of a can of stewed steak and one can of spaghetti in tomato sauce. The orangey-brown concoction tastes pretty good on toast. It's been good to bond with Laurence for a change and I sometimes wonder if his outspoken devil's advocate nature is just a younger brother's defence mechanism. Take a look at the Gallaghers, who's the loudest?

We manage to last about two days before all-night SEGA Megadrive tournaments on N.H.L. 92 or Streets of Rage 2 take over. Then another twenty-four hours before the freeloaders and friends show up, ready to party somewhere parent-free.

With our new songs sketched out, the plan is to determine where we should record the third E.P. and who would be a good producer. I'm out of the loop on decisions like this, but after passing on Stephen Street, they pick Hugh Jones. Having worked with Echo and the Bunnymen, The Charlatans, James, and The Icicle Works, he is deemed a good fit. The recording studio requested by Hugh is the iconic Rockfield Studios in Wales.

We've written two new tracks from jamming in between tours and time in Norfolk. The next single, "Idyll" is a fast-paced, Joy Division-style track. "Yellowish" is an epic 8-minute-long opus with Spanish guitar, and the same gothic tones as "Idyll". Turning up at rehearsal one day, I see a drum machine has been set up next to it. It makes me hesitant to play second fiddle to a machine, and the paranoid voice in my head wonders if this will be my replacement. I can play in time, but ensuring I stay in sync with a drum machine whilst playing a complex rhythm is a chore. Up until now, the drumming has been fun. This feels more clinical and restrictive.

Producer Hugh Jones is easy-going and diligent. We book a day in a rehearsal studio in Ongar, getting acquainted and recording demos of the song. Then we drive down in our minibus to Monmouth Valley to stay at Rockfield to work on the E.P. This is a rich experience for me, staying in a top-of-the-range studio and having our plush sleeping quarters, and food laid on every day by the staff. Being there is a dream come true.

Everyone has recorded here - Queen, Motörhead, The Cult, Simple Minds and in the future, Oasis, Coldplay, and Paul Weller. I spot the graffiti in the vocal booth: "Lemmy '77" sprayed in white on the wall. We record my snare drum part in the corridor for acoustics, in true Martin Hannett Joy Division style. We get "Idyll" and "Yellowish" recorded in good time. There is still time to put together the third track, which ends up being another laidback acoustic track similar to "Spellbinding Mr Benn's Trauma Parlour", with some conga parts from me.

Matt comes up with a name for the new E.P. - "Despotic Operatic" he proclaims, with a flourish.

We relax in the residential building between takes, playing our beloved SEGA Megadrive games. I pine for Alice and call her from my room. We are still limping along, best mates in love. Certain people in our entourage are still keen for me to take advantage of the procession of females we come across on tour at house parties, and I do my utmost to keep the temptation at bay.

Post-Rockfield, more sessions are booked at the Roundhouse Studios in Camden to record some string parts. It takes a few more glacial weeks for Hugh to mix the E.P. Even though I never get to listen to the final version in full, the rest of the band is less than impressed. I hear a snippet of it at the Band mansion before Laurence takes out the tape and tosses it across the room in disgust, saying "Hugh can't mix for shit".

By this time, musical directions are changing, with Neds and Carter being replaced by early Bowie, Velvet Underground, Bauhaus, and Tori Amos. I mean, Bowie and that is all fine, but I'm not up for emulating it. And "change in musical direction" is the last thing a record label or manager wants to hear. It feels like bitterness is constantly rising to the top. Radiohead get jealously slagged off because their best-selling LP Pablo Honey is "basically the E.P.s".

The master tapes are sent to Hollywood Records, who are surprised at the dark tonal shift in music and a clear departure from the songs they have signed us for.

Matt and co want to pursue a more stark and electronic direction, but it doesn't sit well with me.

CHAPTER 23

GOODBYE, MR. M.C.D

Returning from a two month break in gigs, we plan a highly anticipated headline appearance on the 24th of June at the Mean Fiddler in Harlesden. This is the biggest headline London show yet and could pave the way for our next step up the ladder. Located in North West London, the venue has been open since 1983. It's where you have to go to collect your Reading Festival tickets if you don't want to risk mail order. Eric Clapton, Paul McCartney, Johnny Cash, and Nick Cave have all graced the stage. All we need is one excitable live review by a prominent music journalist; that will be enough. Dressed in black and with an electronic drum set now bolted onto my kit, we wander onto the stage and open our first gig in months with three of the new, downbeat songs. The headbangers at the front stand with confused faces, and it isn't until we play the older tracks that they jump back into life. By the end of the set, it's clear we've started to alienate the fans, and it's up to our manager and the record label to step in before things get weird. Tim comes down to Bishops Stortford, and we meet in a pub called The Wheatsheaf, a stone's throw from where we recorded the Sensible Hair demo. Tim says there has been a request by the label for the band to come up with the same kind of material as before or to meet halfway. The mood is stubborn from the band's point of view, even though I agree with Tim, who becomes visibly frustrated and suggests that maybe we go the whole hog and add some candles to the stage. We have been compared to The Cure in the past, which is high praise, but that reference was more to the early punkier songs of the band, not Seventeen Seconds. I'm happiest playing the crowd-pleasers and not keen on being upstaged by a drum machine at everyone's behest.

The meeting ends with Matt asking Tim to believe in us, but for me, some proper soul-searching is needed. Matt has always been passionate about the band, but watching things go in this direction breaks my heart. I don't know what to do. I've left school for this. What will my parents think if I decide to call it a day?

I know I do not influence Matt, Laurence, and Steve, so convincing them to write M.C.D. version 2 is not up for debate. If I stick around, it's more electronic fuckery and a re-brand that isn't my cup of tea. But if I leave, what do I do? No A levels, no specific skills other than drumming, stealing things and being the last man standing after a game of Minesweeper.

Dear Reader, I know what you're thinking. Is this 18-year-old signed artist about to walk away from a £40k record deal? The problem is, I wasn't happy anymore. Being in the band had already negatively affected the people around me. Plus, after two years of being the last one to know or being told what to do, how to play, what music to listen to and whom we should point and laugh at, I was at a point of no return. I sit down with my parents and tell them of my dilemma. I had been hiding the fact that being in the band wasn't all sunshine and roses, mainly because they had let me put my education on hold to make this work. Up until now, I couldn't bring myself to tell them things weren't all they were cracked up to be. So, I remained in a dark mood, making the atmosphere at home even worse. They blamed my petulant attitude on puberty, lack of sleep, and ego; they had no idea it was killing me not to share how miserable I had become and how trapped I was feeling. Following a long and heartfelt discussion, their primary advice is to leave if I'm not happy.

On the 1st of July, I head to the big house for what should be a regular rehearsal. Laurence is already talking about new songs and ideas.

The mood is light and upbeat, a weird contrast to the current identity crisis I assumed we were going through. The positive vibe makes it harder for me to pluck up the courage and speak my mind. I sit down at the kit, searching for the words. I glance at the drum machine, blinking at me like some annoying padded robot. Fuck it. I have to say something important, something for me. A thing I've not done in the last two years. Come on, Alex. I clear my throat and speak at a volume that is louder than usual, causing my voice to break a bit.

"Can we just stop for a second? I need to talk to you all" An air of confusion fills the room, and they look at me differently for the first time. A bit like, "Where is our quiet drummer, and what have you done with him?".

With trembling hands and voice, nerves rattling, I say unless we go back to something similar to before, to the music we are known for, I don't think I can continue. The room goes icily quiet. Steve shakes his head in disbelief; Matt sits there, not saying much and twirling his hair. Laurence takes control before things get awkward and says dryly, "Well, if that's your decision.".

My inner voice starts screaming inside, of course, it isn't. You're like brothers to me, and I want a fucking hug.

Maybe if I had said that things would have worked out differently. We all have baggage and issues in our life no ordinary young adult should be dealing with. But in the end, there is no real effort to convince me to stay. I should be shocked, but it's no surprise. There will be no love lost, it seems. I'm no longer part of their vision. I slowly pack up all my stuff and leave. I wait for a phone call or some sign from them that maybe they've been a bit hasty, and we should talk things through. But nothing materialises. Letters are exchanged between record companies, lawyers, and publishers. Then it's all over. My time is up.

I live the next few months in limbo. Plenty of soul-searching and crying on Alice's shoulder. I wonder if I've been monumentally stupid in walking away and dashing all hopes of making it big with Three and A Half Minutes. It drives me mad, flying from "Yes, you are a fool", to "No, they can mould someone else now" on a daily basis.

I have more time with Alice, so we go to Reading Festival, and I mope in the tent; only breaking cover to watch Bivouac and Rage Against the Machine - don't judge me, I've just walked out on the best job an 18-year-old could ever have. I sign on for unemployment benefits. My name is now Alex "who used to be in Three and A Half Minutes".

Eventually, I get a temp job packing computer games into envelopes at a mail order store in Sawbridgeworth. It feels weird having structure, a line manager, shift work and a payslip handed to me in a small brown envelope each month. As I stuff another train simulator game into a Jiffy bag bound for Colin in Exeter, I have to check my face from the hard landing. Falling on a bruise.

I head up to London to clear my head, wandering the streets, popping in and out of record shops to spend my royalties. Taking a few back streets, I meander past the campus of Kings University. I spot a dead car, abandoned, covered in orange paint, with "Serious as Fuck" stickers and daubed in clock graffiti.

Instead of being on the road, my evenings are spent in front of the TV watching "Stars in Their Eyes" with my family. I take the dog for walks with my dad, something I've not done in ages. The colour comes back to my cheeks. I'm not existing on Pot Noodles and cans of Boddingtons, with a side of Marlboro Lights. Sam comes back on the scene. I had distanced myself from him while I was off being a trainee rock star. It's good to be out with him again, seeing his wonderful family and sharing our latest music discoveries.

It is a stark lesson in humility. But I'd nearly made it. The Top of the Pops appearance was in my grasp. Whilst this had been a downbeat ending to a (mostly) fun two years, I wasn't ready to give up. I'd had a taste and I wanted more. Much more. Joining another band was something I started to entertain. I wonder if Mike Smith could help. Then I get a phone call from someone else that takes things in a different direction.

PLAYING MY FIRST KIT (CREDIT: BOUCHER FAMILY ARCHIVE)

PLAYING THE JUGGS . . . (CREDIT: BOUCHER FAMILY ARCHIVE)

LOOKING TO THE LEFT AT THE SQUARE (CREDIT: UNKNOWN)

GRAHAM AND MATT (CREDIT: UNKNOWN)

POP CONCERT

SUNDAY JULY 21st
6.00 p.m. — Show Starts
BANDSTAND HARLOW TOWN PARK
Licensed bar and food available

THE POGUES

COLOR FACTORY
THE TENDER TRAP
THREE AND
A HALF MINUTES

All artistes appear subject to
exchange of contract

Admission £6.00
Harlow Leisure Card £4.00
(C-Category — FREE)
No Alcohol or Glass Containers to
be brought on site.

For more details contact
Leisure Services, 1 Adams House Tel. 446411/2

HARLOW

THREE & HALF MINUTES

[pow'er:ha(u)s]

on stage 9pm
SEPTEMBER 26

CUTE

THREE & HALF MINUTES

Town with no tim
for 3½
Minutes

XMAS RAVE

FOURTH AVENUE, HARLOW,
ESSEX ☎ (0279) 417029

THE SQUARE

some very VERY **special guests**
with **THREE & HALF MINUTES**
and **BLIND MICE**

...It's tough being a woman in a man's world.

IF YOU'RE A SANTA THEN THAT MEANS MY PARENTS DON'T EXIST!

ONLY £2.50 WITH THIS FLYER
OR WITH STUDENT I.D.

SATURDAY 21st DEC

Angry young band tha[t] beat off the boredom

It's a sly, knowing bill. Choose [yo]ur weapons, pop-pickers, it's [Sw]eat versus Swoon as the [ho]nest toilers take on the [wo]rkshy fops. May the best men [wi]n? On this evidence, merely [try]ing hard is simply not enough. [3]½ MINUTES set something [of] an ominous precedent, [su]bsequently endorsed to a [ce]rtain degree by all who [fol]lowed, in that they're from the [so]uth-east of England, they're [ma]le and they like to whinge. [...] Lead whinger Matt [su]perficially suggests a [tu]mescent Miles Hunt but that's [ma]inly down to his mates' [fr]enzied yet dour clatter on crap [er]satz Stuff like 'MCD'. No, strip [...] 3½ Minutes' reputation

[...]L SCREAM'S 'SCREAMADELICA'[...]

MELODY·MAKER

BOWIE

[Mach]ine in [Los] Angeles

GUNS N' ROSES LIVE!

READING 91

FOUR PAGE SPECIAL

BETWEEN DAYS
The Cure and CD

Mallet of the gods!

[THE] SENSELESS THINGS HAMMER IT OU[T]

nutes: precocious and bitter as hell — and they've never watched Eldorado either . . .

SINGLE OF THE WEEK

INUTES: PEEP (*Scared Hitless*)

t me, or is everyone waiting to see which member of *lorado* cast will be the first to make a single? Judging by te of this week's single pile – and the recent buzz-bands ress – the majority of critics/producers/labels have pending too much time in front of the TV and not h time retuning their ears to the World Outside.

ty per cent of new Brit-pop bands are just *Eldorado* in se anyway – purpose-built, expensive and badly acted 'hich makes this record all the more challenging and as tant as a pop record can be. 3½ Minutes show some tion for a change; some desire and determination to people.

self, 'PEEP' stands as one of the best debuts of the year – top of that, it marks a reprisal of sorts against recent rvative trends in both the indie and major mainstream e inevitable Carter backlash, the return of pop ery). There is an overwhelming feeling of belligerence it.

Minutes are as bitter as hell. Currently they present the best of what you could call The New Avengers (other groups to watch out for: the fast-improving Fret Blanket from Birmingham and Reverse from Stoke-On-Trent).

The Minutes, and their ilk, whip up a level of gut-feeling that sets the senses on edge. Arriving at their first record via some Kingmaker supports and a handful of London gigs, they sound precocious and awkward, searching out depths of feeling.

'PEEP' – the first release on the fledgling Scared Hitless label, catalogue number Fret 1 – gives an earnest, if not totally representative picture of the foursome's promise. The demos of lead track 'Feelings M' were better, but what the heck: 'FM' is a frantic, teeth-gritting adventure into resentment and pride.

At times they lean into the old Neds/Cure comparisons, but they're already outgrowing the influences. I think the potential's all here. The big f— off climax of 'Shake It Up' and the intensity of 'Sodium' tell me that, while in contrast 'MCD' is ridiculously poppy, unpredictable.

Why don't you switch off your television and go and see something less boring instead?

½ MINUTES, Hertfordshire heart-toppers, are playing more peepshows at he Falcon, Camden, tonight (Thurs-ay); Jericho Tavern, Oxford, tomorrow Friday); a lunchtime gig with the Fam-y Cat at Joiners, Southampton, on Sat-rday, and The Broadwalk, Manchester, n Wednesday. The band, whose name s on everyone's lips, were cryptically lugged on the front page of Monday's Guardian wherein a British Olympic of-cial moaned that while this year John Major had spent 3½ hours talking to ompetitors, "we never got 3½ Minutes om Margaret Thatcher." Which is un-erstandable, really.

Churlish indie guitar gods 3½ MINUTES were, undeniably, the local success story of the year, with their de-but "Peep" being praised as Single of the Week in the NME by local scribe Steve Lamacq; playing at the NME's birthday bash and the NME spon-sored Viva Eight gigs before, so rumour has it, jetting off to the States to be wooed by a US label.

KINGMAKER
31/5

XCP.

BACKSTAGE

METROPOL

AFTER

CARTE
7 NO
KILI

METROPOLIS M

ACCESS ALL A

KINGMAKER
29 MAY 1992
PORTSMOUTH

OPPOSITE PAGE: SINGLE OF THE WEEK, NME (PHOTO: ED SIRRS) / GIG INFO IN LOCAL PRESS
PEEP EP: FRONT COVER - SCARED HITLESS RECORDS/ PEEP EP COVERAGE AND GIG NEWS

THIS PAGE: BAND PHOTO AND FLYERS (PHOTO: MELANIE COX)

LET'S CLOCK!

ON ON ON

...ck around the clock! *On* burrows ever ...r for new superstars and digs up THREE & A ...MINUTES, stroppy new rockers from ...p's Stortford, and THE BADGERS, Norfolk's ...r to the Sundays – with chainsaws!

Time for action! The Three & A Half Minute heroes

...ld Bull's Head ... a piece of ...p's Stortford ...re. One day, in ...t of mild ...ation-come- ...ness, the ...ordshire ...lry, bored by ...st of ...ation, decided ...lare itself an ...omous state.

...revels, unofficially, ...e name The Isle Of ...ned after a ...ing viking maybe?). ...aside, by the fireplace, ...ES are in a pretty ...nous state. ...ves. ...re the first group from ...tortford destined to ...e charts since ...k. Now *there's* ...y for you. They are no ...y new guitar band! ...oursome sit hunched

over two Guinnesses and two cokes, unsure about life in general. They represent everything a band of their stature should be about . . . musically aggressive, lyrically ambiguous, and, attitude-wise, slightly difficult.

It is almost a year to the day that they played their second London gig at the Bull & Gate, where they were unmitigated crap. Twelve months on – having just completed a handful of supports on the recent Kingmaker tour – they've honed their heat-seeking guitar sound into something raging and beautiful.

There are elements of early Cure/Neds/Only Ones/Wonder Stuff and other stuff. Yet essentially, it has a mind of its own.

"I've seen so many bands who walk on and announce the name of the song . . . and no-one gives a f——," says singer Matt. "I hate all that. We haven't proved anything to

anyone yet . . . so what we try and do is leave them with a taste in their mouth.

"It's more important what they take away with them from a gig than what they get out of it at the time, I think."

The overall impression is good. Minutes' songs are bitter, but with an underlying positive touch (like possible first single 'Feelings M', with its uncompromising air of self-belief, a classic mix of pride and rejection).

Lyricist Matt is already being tagged a moody bastard:

"Backstage at the Marquee, we'd just come off and some guy I'd never met before pushed past and said 'Get out of the way you you miserable f——er'. I said 'WHATT?!' 'You, you're a miserable f——er aren't you?' "

You are!

"Well yeah, but he didn't even know me."

The gigs recently have been

patchy. While Lawrence and drummer Alex have been finishing off exams, Matt and guitarist Steve have been left, frustrated and marking time. The result has been a couple of duff London shows, followed by three superior dates with Kingmaker – including a wilfully spiteful night at Cambridge.

The Minutes, I'm sure, have captured that ability to make songs which provide a release of energy and emotion. On

form, they make your veins swell to boiling point (going from the intensity of 'Sodium', to the poppier 'MCD', complete with ragged harmonies and rifling, uptempo drums).

Lawrence: "Everything we've done has always been serious at one point, even if something like 'MCD' sounds a bit happier – but that's my ideal song, one that can sound nice but you know it's about something or someone."

BLUR NME SUEDE
GIMME SHELTER
PARTY
MEGA CITY FOUR
3½ MINUTES
THURSDAY 23 JULY 1992
Doors 7.00pm
Advance £10.00

1484

t&c 1 8-17 HIGHGATE ROAD,
KENTISH TOWN
LONDON NW5 1JY

METROPOLIS MUSIC
ACCESS ALL AREAS

KINGMAKER
2 9 MAY 1992
PORTSMOUTH

Alex facing The Future - Blind

PPOSITE PAGE: NME COVERAGE (PHOTO: ED SIRRS) / CAMDEN FALCON GIG LISTING, 1992 / AIDS BENEFIT LINE-UP AT THE MARQUE

HIS PAGE: MAIN IMAGE: BIG FEATURE ON US BY STEVE LAMACQ (PHOTO: ED SIRRS) / TICKET FOR THE LEGENDARY BLU
UEDE GIG FOR NME AND SHELTER / KINGMAKER BACKSTAGE PASS / MIKE SMITH CATCHING THE MOMENT CREDIT: MIKE SMIT

RIVERMAN PRESENTS

THERAPY
LEATHERFACE

THE FALL
CATHERINE WHEEL

URGE OVERKILL
Polvo

luna ②
3½ Minutes
THE GRAND
THURSDAY 24th SEPTEMBER

THE JOYRIDERS

IAN McNABB
WITH FULL BAND
THE GRAND
SATURDAY 26th SEPTEMBER

120 MINUTES

the lemon trees
THE GRAND

PAVEMENT

MUSIC TELEVISION

MUSIC FESTIVAL 1992

MELODY MAKER

Xfm

NME

THE SPASTICS SOCIETY

Anniversary 1992

PRESENTS

viva! eight

AY 1st SEPTEMBER
CK CAVE
E BAD SEEDS
OOSE
ROCKINGBIRDS
7PM TICKETS £8 50 ADVANCE

WEDNESDAY 2nd SEPTEMBER
KINGMAKER
GALLON DRUNK
3 : Minutes
DOORS 7 PM TICKETS £7 ADVANCE

THURSDAY 3rd SEPTEMBER
THE BLUE AEROPLANES
GREEN ON RED
A HOUSE
DOORS 7 30PM TICKETS £8 ADVANCE

FRIDAY 4th SEPTEMBER
EDWYN COLLINS
VIC GODARD
FIVETHIRTY
DOORS 7PM TICKETS £8 ADVANCE

DAY 5th SEPTEMBER
AD II
FGANG PRESS
E CORPORATION
PM TICKETS £10 ADVANCE

SUNDAY 6th SEPTEMBER
JAH WOBBLE
GARY CLAIL'S
ON-U-SOUND SYSTEM
CABARET VOLTAIRE
7PM TICKETS £12 ADVANCE

MONDAY 7th SEPTEMBER
THE BUZZCOCKS
REVOLVER
THE HIGH
DOORS 7 30 PM TICKETS £8 ADVANCE

TUESDAY 8th SEPTEMBER
Buffalo tom
EAT
THOUSAND YARD STARE
SKAW
DOORS 7 PM TICKETS £8 ADVANCE

TOWN & COUNTRY CLUB
9/17 HIGHGATE ROAD LONDON N.W.5
BOX OFFICE 071 284 0303 T&C STATION(CREDIT
CARD HOTLINE) 071 284 1221 PREMIER 071 240 0771
STARGREEN 071 734 8932 THE TICKET SHOP 071 323 5481
ROUGHTRADE 071 240 0105 & 071 229 8541
& ALL USUAL AGENTS

SEPTEMBER
1 - 8 -

METROPOLIS MUSIC

BACKSTAGE

GIMME SHELTER

2 8 JUL 1992

NME T&C

Riverma

DATE 24.7.92

VENUE Grand

ARTISTE LUNA

ACCESS
ALL AREAS

OPPOSITE PAGE: MTV 120 MINUTES GIG POSTER / VIVA! EIGHT LINE-UP FOR TELEVISED SHOWS AND CD COMPILATION

THIS PAGE: GIMME SHELTER BACKSTAGE PASS/ BACKSTAGE PASS FOR MTV GIG WIH LUNA/ POSING AT DISNEYLAND (PHOTO AUTHOR) / #29 THREE AND A HALF MINUTES PHOTO SHOOT 1992

DISNEY EMPLOYEES (PHOTO: AUTHOR)

AT THE MONDRIAN (PHOTO: AUTHOR)

PLAYING TO OUR RECORD LABEL AT THE ROXBURY CAFE

MESSING ABOUT IN THE HOTEL (PHOTO: AUTHOR)

THREE HALF MINUTES

SODIUM
REALLY
CIRCUS CLASSIC
FEELINGS M
SHAKE IT UP
FRAGRANCE
MCD
SHIT SELLS

WITH LAURA ZIFFREN WHO SIGNED US, AND OLLIE (PHOTO: AUTHOR)

MATT AT THE ROXBURY CAFE)PHOTO: AUTHOR) / INSET: BAND SETLIST

LAURENCE AT THE ROXBURY CAFE (PHOTO: AUTHOR)

PROMO SHOOT (PHOTO: MELANIE COX)

THIS PAGE: BAND (PHOTO: PAUL RIDER) / BLED ME DRY COVER (CREDIT: SCARED HITLESS RECORDS) / BAND ZINE 'HYDRANT DRONE'

OPPOSITE PAGE: TOUR DATES / BATH MOLES GIG LISTING/ BORDERLINE PRESS INFO

OCTOBER

2nd	**SOUTHAMPTON** University	
5th	**HULL** Adelphi	(Sultans of Ping)
6th	**LANCASTER** University	(Sultans of Ping)
7th	**BUCKLEY** Tivoli	(Sultans of Ping)
8th	**LIVERPOOL** Krazy House	(Sultans of Ping)
9th	**BRADFORD** Queens Hall	(Sultans of Ping)
10th	**LONDON** Camden Falcon	
11th	**NOTTINGHAM** Polytechnic	
18th	**TAMWORTH** The Rat Hole	
21st	**CAMBRIDGE** The Boat Race	
22nd	**MIDDLESEX** The Pigeon Ballroom	
25th	**STEVENAGE** Bowes Lion	
26th	**WINDSOR** The Old Trout	
27th	**BATH** Players	(Cum-Cum Club)
30th	**BRISTOL** The Louisiana	

NOVEMBER

5th	**KENT** University	
7th	**LONDON** University of Westminster	
13th	**NORWICH** Arts Centre	
18th	**BRISTOL** Fleece and Firkin	
26th	**CAMBRIDGE** Corn Exchange	(Ned's AtomicDustbin)

Because of a serious lack of money,on many of the dates (especially the ones with the Sultans) we will have to sleep in the van or in tents.So if anyone's feeling particularly generous or mad and have got space on their floor/table/roof/**bed** for about 5 or 6 friendly people then approach us at the gig or look for a man in a rainbow jumper.

Bye

3½MINUTE

Music **MOLES** **Dance**

WED AUG 18th WHY NOT! **PROMISE**

THUR 19th **APACHE DROPOUT + SHED 7**

FRI 20th **DES'REE**

SAT 21st **SLEEPER** **3 1/2 MINUTES**

MON 23rd **THE OVER YELLOW** **THE SEESAWS + THE PIER**

TUES 24th CLUB 303 **ACID SPECIAL** Special DJ Line-up Featuring: TECHNOSAURUS, SNOOPT & POSTMAN'S BUM

COMING SOON: HOWARD JONES (26TH) SENSATION (28TH) (DISOUL FAMILY SENSATION)

225 333448 14 George St.

Lick & Promise ©

"GAMES FOR MAY" DOUBLE HEADER
THURSDAY 21ST MAY

3½ MINUTES

Hailing from Harlow, they have supported the likes of MEGACITY FOUR, THE S THINGS and MIDWAY STILL amongst others – and are now taking off in their o "3½ MINUTES play a gorgeously brash set which shows how much they've i over the last six months from parochial pretenders to contentious contende ...Steve Lemacq, NME

STRANGELOV

A five piece from Bristol that includes ex-members of LEVITATION and THE AEROPLANES – featuring twin leadguitars and unique vocals.
"The music flies unrestrained and exhilarating... The singer's so intense you c at him all night, as he gets more possessd and the guitars get deeper and underwater and it all seems to last for ever and you don't care'cos ther so much going on..."
...Ian McGregor, MELODY MAKER

£2 OFF WITH THIS FLYER.
£3.00 with flyer, £5.00 on the door.
Doors open: 8.30pm. Running order decided on the night.
First band on stage at 9.00pm. Tickets from the Borderline box offic
Watch press for future Lick & Promise Club nights.
The Borderline, Orange Yard, Off Manette St, London, W1
Telephone 071 287 1441

The Borderline

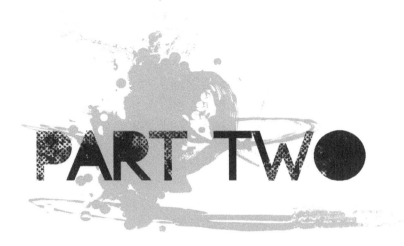

CHAPTER 24
WINGLESS

In the wake of the band unceremoniously dumping him, I am surprised and nervous to hear from Mac. However, I soon relaxed as he sounded cheery on the phone and interested in what I was doing. I'm currently watching Kilroy in my pyjamas, eating a bowl of Kellogg's Start but I don't tell him this. "Would you be up for jamming with me and Chris?" he asks.

Chris is a singer and guitarist I once met - formerly of The Herbsmen, a band from Stevenage and Ware.

We meet for rehearsals at The Square or Burnt Mill School in Harlow, and the same studio Three and A Half Minutes uses in Ongar. I look over my shoulder whilst there, nervous about bumping into them.

Mac describes our ideal influence as similar to Husker Du and being a fan of Bob Mould's new band Sugar, this suits me. Chris is enthusiastic, chatty, and upbeat. Mac has mastered comic timing with his dry wit and stories about his earlier punk rock days and running The Square. His style could be foreboding to some with his rockabilly quiff and intense stare, but we click and enjoy making music together. The three of us have a knack where overthinking stays outside the door. Chris or Mac have a riff, I quickly find the right tempo and drumbeat, jam it out and add structure, and then boom, we've got another song.

Quickly finding our flow, we write more than enough songs to play a set with. Rumours of our new project make the local press, and because of Mac's handy black book, we soon have two gigs lined up - our debut supporting Canadian punk band D.O.A. at the Garage, and a support slot for Skyscraper at The Square.

We call ourselves Travis Cut (short for Travis Bickle's Hair Cut). Chris and I have similar tastes in bands like Buffalo Tom and Levitation, so the musical direction is more collaborative than the later Three and A Half Minutes music. I love Chris' self-effacing nature, the bravery to wear a T-shirt on stage that says, "tiny penis" and to not take everything seriously. It was a world away from the intense silences in Three and A Half Minutes, where you could almost taste the vehemence in the air.

19th November - with D.O.A. The Garage, Highbury, London
26th November - with Skyscraper, The Square, Harlow

With some industry contacts still keen to help and off the back of a good debut at The Garage, we soon find ourselves back at the E.M.I. studios recording a demo with John Bell. Because of a contractual stipulation with E.M.I., Mike Smith is obliged to give me some studio time, which is nice. He'd also been to the D.O.A. gig with Steve Lamacq in tow, so everything seemed to be going in a great direction.

The recording with John is a bit haphazard. It isn't his vibe, and he seems to be doing the production under duress. We don't click with John the same way as the Minutes did, and as Mac can be a little gloomy and guarded at times, it affects the mood. We are unprepared and still need to find our sound, so we leave the session with mediocre songs that seem flung together and awkward. Perhaps only being together for six weeks is a bit hasty to rush into such a high-level recording studio.

The end of 1993 is upon us, and I hope this New Year's Eve is not as messy as the last one. I plan a house party at home as my parents are away for the night. Alice picks me up from work, and we head back to set everything up. She can tell I'm hiding something. I'm quiet and distant. I can't keep doing this to her, I love her too much to carry on with this charade. We've been here before, and my guilty conscience always gets the better of me. "There's been a couple of flings I need to tell you about," I confess, breaking down in a pathetic state of tears, blubbering dramatically in a vain attempt to pull on her heartstrings to forgive me. But not this time. Her face is hard; she is tired and fed up. "No more chances," she says.

I consider coming up with several lame excuses to put the blame elsewhere, but it's all on me. I am an absolute shit who struggles to be faithful. So, minutes before our house party begins, I cancel it, and drive Alice home for the last time. Pulling up at her house, I try to think of something to say, maybe I can still salvage us from the wreckage I've caused. Before I get the chance, she's out of the car, a downbeat "bye" uttered as the door slams shut. Trying to maintain a stiff upper lip, I reach down for my tape case and choose "Let Me Come Over" by Buffalo Tom. I slowly reverse out of her driveway for the last time. And cry the whole way back.

I sit down with my diary, trying to understand what I've done and who I've become. Being unfaithful in Three and A Half Minutes was ego-driven, feeling untouchable and privileged. This time around, there was resentment. I was bitter and down about life, upset that the taste I had of fame was abandoned. So, in a moment of drunken rebellion, I wanted the impulsiveness to return, having a "I do what I like" mantra and fuck the consequences. Well, congratulations Mr Self-Destruct, you've broken her heart, and your own. From this point on, I vow to be a better person.

1993 - Mixtape

Cherub Rock - Smashing Pumpkins

Perfect Blue Buildings - Counting Crows

Crank - Catherine Wheel

Slow Emotion Replay – The The

Lazarus - Boo Radleys

Animal Nitrate - Suede

Creep - Radiohead

Fade Into You - Mazzy Star

Feed The Tree - Belly

I'm Allowed - Buffalo Tom

From Despair to Where - Manic Street Preachers

CHAPTER 25

WAKING HOURS

1994

Nelson Mandela is elected President, France – UK Euro Channel Tunnel opened, Jeff Bezos founds Amazon, The Downward Spiral by Nine Inch Nails, Definitely Maybe by Oasis, The Lion King, and Forrest Gump.

It's 1994. My hair is short. I'm a broken, tired, single man. I've been let go from the job of stuffing envelopes and have found a new poorly paid job at the local indie record store, Discus Music, in Bishops Stortford. I say indie; this is a record store for the more discerning music listener.

The managers wear a nice line in patterned jumpers and play The Division Bell by Pink Floyd on heavy rotation. Regulars come in to moan about the price of the new Roachford album. But on the plus side, it is a record store. What better place to spend your working day than listening to music and dealing with idiots? This is where I first hear Supersonic by a band called Oasis. The manager gathers us around the turntable and sets the needle down on the record. The drumbeat comes in, followed by Noel's riff and Liam's nasal vocals, with those self-assured lyrics. I stand there in silence, thinking how special this band will be. I'd not heard so much swagger bottled in one song for a long time.

Chris works in Our Price, so we have similar battle scars from dealing with pedantic customers trying to buy a single they heard on the radio without knowing the artist or song title. I am jealous that he gets to wear a funky Our Price top and lanyard, whereas I am cajoled into wearing the kind of clothes that would have a Werther's Original left in the pocket. I wonder if Chris has to clean the shelves like I do, making sure no dust is left on unsold albums, like the overpriced double cassette album by Extreme, in the vain hope that today would be the day somebody would bring it to the counter.

Laurence stops by the shop, half-pissed with some cronies tagging along for the free beer. He slurs that he has a lot of respect for what I did by sticking to my guns and quitting the band. Three and a Half Minutes have already recruited a new drummer and changed their name to Poloroid. It's a bit too close for the well-known photography brand's liking, who ask them to change it, so they came up with another name: Inaura. So, while Inaura seeks to surf a second wave with a new music scene dubbed Romo (Romantic Modernism), I am gigging with Travis Cut and composing two-and-a-half-minute punk pop anthems. With my Mike Smith credit used up, and more punk-oriented songs coming to the fore, we're ready to make 1994 the year of The Cut.

To get over my Alice heartbreak, I find solace at The Square, which has become a real hub for Travis Cut. We rehearse there, meet there, and leave our gear stored in the office Mac works in. It has become my local, and I visit most evenings and weekends, socialising in the bar and choosing songs from the best jukebox the world has ever seen. Someone puts on a Three and A Half Minutes track now and then, pointing at me with a wink. I go to the gigs, and we have impromptu band meetings over drinks. I get asked to judge the Rock Contest and consume too much free beer. Jamie Oliver, another friend from school has formed a band called Scarlet Division and plays there a few times whilst he juggles a new job in cheffing.

The Square was always awash with blue, yellow, and white posters, featuring a grainy black and white image of a band, their tour dates and support bands listed beneath. Stickers were fair game, plastered over the toilet doors, on old posters and the sound desk, some peeling off or with upturned corners, the whole building a scrapbook for ambitious bands keen to make a dent in the local scene.

I'd always find Mac on the pinball machine out the back, a pint on the go and ably flicking the buttons with a fag in his mouth. There was always a quiet mystery about Mac, a sense of trepidation as I wondered which Mac I would be getting today. Trudie has gone, replaced by regulars at The Square, who would sometimes join us in the van for a Travis Cut gig, sitting silently as we spoke our own band language and finished each other's sentences.

Time is spent winning hearts and minds up and down the country and supporting the likes of U.S. punks Lagwagon at The Square (complaining about how sore their fresh tattoos are), or hot band of the hour Mint 400, and ex-five thirty act, The Nubiles. I am in a daze, on autopilot, back in a band and back on the road, rehearsing, driving, gigging, recording, rehearsing, driving, gigging, recording. It's like that new movie Groundhog Day, where Bill Murray's character lives the same day over and over, his alarm radio playing "I Got You Babe" by Sonny & Cher, but instead, I'm hearing "Ska Sucks" by Propagandhi. I've gone nocturnal again, arriving at venues as the sun sets, and returning home a few hours before sunrise. I am thinking about starting a guidebook on service stations, ranking them on their toilet facilities, choice of snacks and customer service. Most of them have just one member of staff working in the dead of night, the only way of communicating is through a strengthened window as you talk into a microphone, using a metal tray to process the transaction.

With friends now thinking about what to do once they've finished secondary school, I am still doing all I've ever known for the past three years - playing the drums.

Luck seems to be on Travis Cut's side. We secure a support slot for The Meat Puppets in London, who are enjoying their renaissance from the Nirvana Unplugged album. Then, on the day of the gig, Kurt Cobain takes his own life.

The tragic news naturally overshadows the support slot win. From being a huge fan since my first listen in Steve's car, this affects me more than I realise. I feel like everything needs to stop so I can take the time to process the news and reflect on the music world's loss. Nirvana resonated with me on many levels - their songs, Dave Grohl's rhythms, carefree identity, and rebellious nature. I think back to watching Kurt singing "Smells Like Teen Spirit", an octave lower on Top of The Pops. Mainly as a fuck you to the stipulation bands are required to mime instruments on the show but sing the live vocals. It's a real "where were you when you found out" moment. Their impact on music, how bands communicate with fans and Kurt not being afraid to talk about personal issues through songs and interviews created a watershed moment for young people who only recently had Bon Jovi and Guns N Roses to adulate. Watching it on the news before I left for The Meat Puppets gig will forever be etched in my brain.

11th February - with Lagwagon, The Square, Harlow
1st April - with Jawbone, Powerhaus, Islington
7th April - with The Meat Puppets, The Garage, Highbury
9th April - with The Nubiles, The Falcon, Camden

CHAPTER 26

PURPLE RAIN

With some songs that deserve to be recorded, we decide to find a studio catering more to bands of our persuasion. So, we book a session at Purple Rain studios in Great Yarmouth.

The studio is located at the furthest southern end of the beach, behind a nondescript door on the edge of an industrial estate. I guess we're not in Rathbone Place anymore. The set-up is similar to Rockfield in that you could stay in the studio too. Opposed to a fully staffed residential studio and a jacuzzi in your room for the likes of The Stone Roses, this comes with a fridge, a tiny kitchenette, and a raised platform crawl space above it to throw your sleeping bag on. There are two recording rooms and a spacious studio with the obligatory sound desk that goes on for miles.

In the recreation area, there's a sofa and a T.V. I bring my Megadrive. The vibe is homely, and owner/engineer Richard Hammerton is a marvellous raconteur with wild blond hair and a pure Norfolk accent. He'd been in an indie band called Stare and had tasted a bit of the "hot signed band" experience similar to mine. Rich had worked with bands like Catherine Wheel and The Suncharms, before recording punk and hardcore bands like Goober Patrol and Lovejunk. My favourite story of his is about having an arrogant up-and-coming band recording in the studio. They kept talking about hash and getting stoned as if they were the Rolling Stones working on their next platinum record. Fed up with their attitude, Rich promised to make them a joint in the room next door while they listen to their demo. He goes to the other room, closes the door, reaches down to grab a handful of pubes, and liberally sprinkles them into the joint.

With the E.M.I. sessions now a beautiful mistake, we record tracks for our first 7" single. The A-side is a track called "Waking Hours", a finely crafted power-pop number with some catchy lyrics. Other tracks are "Wuss (Theme from Travis Cut)", a fast instrumental number, and "No Static", an instrumental with tones of early Goo Goo Dolls, and Chris growling about guns and flowers in the final section.

From using a click track during recordings with Three and A Half Minutes and under pressure in the presence of legends such as Hugh Jones, I was prepared to use this experience fully and get my drum tracks recorded quickly. Travis Cut are cash-poor, so this saves valuable time for the rest of the sessions and any final overdubs needed.

Luckily this is a switch I can turn on with every recording, giving us ample time to work on the other parts and for me to get more beers in at the local pub.

The nearest pub is The Gunner, and it's like entering a 1970s time warp. It's a proper Norfolk local pub, and we get the classic cowboys walking into a saloon silence whenever we visit. It feels like we've entered a lock-in that's been going on for four months. The barman has a stern Mos Eisley air about him and if we had droids, they would have remained outside. Things are made more surreal for them when our driver Andi joins us. He has about 18 piercings, 12 of which are on his face. They look at him like a being from another planet. One of the regulars approaches and slowly reaches out to twiddle the crowbar stuck through Andi's nose. Andi is no stranger to this kind of intrusion, and it makes for a good icebreaker.

The dynamic is working well at the studio, with my quick drum recording, Chris nailing the vocals and guitar parts, and Mac bringing all his virtuoso talent to the sessions both in the booth and with Rich at the mixing desk. Happy with the final cut, we make the well-worn trek to Porky's Mastering Service in Soho to have the single printed. For any vinyl aficionados, if you take a close look at the smooth bit before the label, sometimes there is a message engraved in the wax. The owner, George "Porky" Peckham, would have his records branded "A Porky Prime Cut" - we decide to slag off ex-girlfriends or etch random comedy quotes in the run-out grooves instead.

It's nice to be a founding band member, our decisions are made collectively, and all creative ideas seem to be on the same wavelength. Mac and Chris's interest and knowledge in U.S. and U.K. punk music are leagues ahead of mine though, and when discussing bands and record labels, it sometimes feels like they are talking in a different language; I am dipping my toe, whereas they are fully immersed. I still have Chapterhouse and Pop Will Eat Itself tapes in my car. Nevertheless, I like our songs and the band's personality. A three-piece setup suits me for some reason. Mac writes and sings songs too, which means we have a nice dual vocal style in our repertoire. With 500 singles designed using art from my favourite anime comics, and some help printing the sleeves through my dad's business, we package them and brand them with our label, "Incoming!" With a minor distribution deal secured with Southern Records, we hit the road for the single-release tour with the U.S. band, Down by Law.

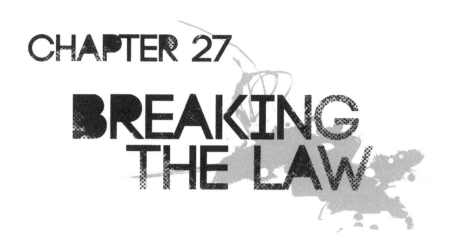

CHAPTER 27

BREAKING THE LAW

t feels good to be back on the road, in the back of a van, listening to Green Day and chewing the fat with Chris and Mac. Our tour is supporting Down by Law, a Los Angeles band led by Dave Smalley. He is a punk legend, having fronted All and Dag Nasty. His new band has been signed to Epitaph, a label about to have the year of its life when Smash by The Offspring is released and sells like crazy.

The first gig is in Preston, where we almost don't get paid and nearly lose our 7″ singles. The young promoter, who looks like he learnt to speak yesterday, has fucked up the numbers and seems to think crying will solve this crisis. Bad news, Dave Smalley and Co didn't fly halfway across the world to suffer fools. Luckily, the payment is resolved, and we relocated the record box too. The Down by Law drummer Hunter is excellent. Watching him soundcheck is a truly spellbinding sight to behold. It's like he's got three arms or something.

Not wanting to lose all band-on-the-road traditions, things are being liberated earnestly. We find the first item of a new initiative, "Travis Cut Arts Ltd", by stealing a street sign. In other news, O.J. Simpson has offered a reward for evidence of his wife's killer. I hope someone comes forward; I loved him in Naked Gun.

As we flick from album to radio in the van, it's hard to understand why Love is All Around by Wet Wet Wet, is STILL number one. Our next stop is Leeds. The support band Dirty Pictures are your typical local aloof band, with a superiority complex and one brain cell between them. It doesn't matter, as we are bonding with Down by Law. We share the same Zen approach to gigs and have a few veterans in both bands who know how to pace themselves on tour. As for free items, we've collected two gnomes, a roadworks sign, a planning permission card, and a hair treatment sign. It must be a record. Our young roadie Paul is taking this rather seriously. Due to the other bands being idiots, I've been playing angrily, so my arms hurt every night.

Off the back of playing Leeds and Harlow, we pay Down by Law a final visit at their London gig. An exciting night ensues at the Dublin Castle in Camden. Chris has a drunken conversation with a member of Madness. Chris is convinced he is not a member of Madness. He must have forgotten it was The Dublin Castle where Madness earned their live reputation about 20 years ago. It's also the last place Bon Scott of AC/DC was seen drinking before he died.

Seeking enablers for our ongoing liberation spree, we persuade one of Down by Law to steal something from the pub. A brass plaque is quietly removed from the wall. So far, we've had a good experience with a U.S. band, but when Sloppy Seconds comes over to take us on their tour, the difference is night and day.

19th July - with Down by Law, Preston
20th July - with Down by Law, Duchess of York, Leeds
22nd July - with Down by Law, The Square Harlow
July 26th - Army & Navy, Chelmsford
29th July - The Venue, New Cross
4th August – The Falcon, Camden

CHAPTER 28

A BIT OF A BLUR

"Waking Hours" is doing well - Steve Lamacq gives us a few blasts on his BBC radio show, the Evening Session. Fanzines are giving us positive reviews, likening us to N.O.F.X. and Husker Du. We are more niche than Three and A Half Minutes. Still, it means our audience is easier to connect with, and is supportive and enthusiastic. The U.K. Punk scene is thriving, influenced by bands like Green Day, Rancid and The Offspring.

A certain D.J. called John Peel also gives us a spin on his little show. Some people may have misheard our band name as someone asked for the new single by "Trappist Cult" at Rough Trade records; good name for a prog-rock band, though.

With our next tour on the horizon, we grab another session at Purple Rain to record the follow-up single, "Had A Gun". This time, we ask local hero Ant Chapman of Collapsed Lung, to help produce the tracks. Ant has been a regular at The Square for aeons, and despite the huge success of "Eat My Goal" remains fully grounded. He's a big gentle bear of a man and always innovating and sporting a swish pair of trainers every time we see him. He brings his technical flair into the single, adding a gunshot sample at the start, and a line from Denis Leary from Sylvester Stallone film `Demolition Man' to finish.

We record a gruff B-side track written by Mac called "Acceptance". The third song is "Theme Park", a frenetic track we use to open the set. "Had A Gun" is a poppy, Nirvana-esque track that is a joy for me to play. A University campus in Nottingham puts the song on heavy rotation for its club nights, and it becomes a popular floor-filler. When we eventually perform at the Notts venue, the crowd jumps to life as soon as we play it.

Our inner circle has grown with the regular addition of Paul, a lanky wide-eyed regular at The Square. He becomes our tour manager/roadie/butt of many jokes. We also have Senior Aircraftman Ian McKellar reporting for duty, or "Squaddie" as he's affectionately known, driving us in a rental when Andi has to repair his dilapidated van.

A gig at the Joiner's Arms allows us to air the new tracks. The local punks, known as the S.T.E. collective, had seen us support Down by Law in Harlow and were keen for us to play on their home turf, Southampton. The collective is a great bunch of lads who ensure all gigs are well-organised and provide bands with a place to stay. I like the Joiner's Arms and its high stage. It's always been a favourite venue for me. Every band has played here, from the Arctic Monkeys to The Verve.

13th August - with Huggy Bear, The Joiners Arms, Southampton

Our gig is supporting "Riot Grrl" act Huggy Bear, a shouty chaotic band who are the current media darlings. The lead singer, Jo, is going out with Graham Coxon from Blur, and he is at the gig. I'm not brave enough to say hi or attempt to talk about Food Records or the time we played with Blur when they were pissed. Chris takes the initiative in a somewhat different way than I do. Similar to the awkward conversation where he was convinced the bloke from Madness wasn't from Madness, Chris starts to push Graham's buttons, dropping Blur lyrics into the conversation and generally being contrary. This goes on long enough for Graham lose his rag and pin Chris up against a wall, followed by a mini wrestle on the pavement outside the venue. Luckily things end amicably, alcohol is blamed, and Graham scribbles some notes down for The Great Escape album (probably).

CHAPTER 29

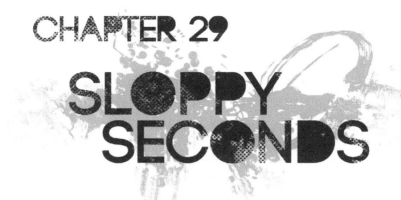

SLOPPY SECONDS

It's time to join Sloppy Seconds for their U.K. tour; ten dates in a row, from Glasgow to Brighton. The band have had trouble getting the tour arranged. Because their bass player is so obese, they need to book two seats on the plane just for him. Ultimately, they save their money and replace him with someone thinner!

It becomes clear we would not bond with them as we did with Down by Law. The band are stand-offish and uses one-word answers in conversation. They are using our backline and sharing the same tour van. Luckily, this is where headphones come in handy. My knowledge of who they are is limited. It turns out Chris and Mac aren't massive fans, either. The vocalist has a nasal, whiny tone and every song sounds the same. Their other gimmick seems to be they are all overweight, except for the stand-in bass player who looks like Where's Wally if he'd grown his hair out and dressed in black. Unfortunately, unlike the band, the audiences are not big. We've picked a cult U.S. punk act with which to spend over a week. But the tour has its highlights. We witness a true feat of strength in Glasgow, concerning Mac's bass cabinet. This is no ordinary bass cabinet. You could fit a small child inside, and it weighs a ton. We call it the Beast, and you have to dig deep when lugging it out of the van, up some stairs and onto the stage.

On this occasion, the sturdy engineer at the Cathouse in Glasgow takes one look at the cabinet and says, "Is this tae go in?"

We nod, ready to grab one end, but he hoists it onto his shoulder and bounds up the stairs with it, leaving us gobsmacked. The next surreal moment is seeing Evan Dando of The Lemonheads in the club. We spent the evening trying to put Travis Cut stickers on his back.

Being so far North and needing somewhere to stay overnight, Andi has conveniently pulled a Glaswegian lass who is into his piercings. She offers to put us up. Chris, Mac, and Paul are not sure this is the best idea, but we have nowhere to stay and kipping in the van is an uncomfortable and cold experience. We listen intently to her directions in a thick Scottish accent, not helped by the stream of consciousness that's interspersed: "Aye, go left here and then I said to my flatmate you would'nae believe the piercings on this fucker's face, straight over, so I told her there's space on ours floor, right? Sorry no, not a direction, don't go right, just keep going darlin'. Anyways so I says we can help yous, just need to get the speed in and some bevvies, turn left."

We finally pull up at an estate with high-rise flats. It looks like the place Taggart would be seen the morning after a murder. We reluctantly take some of our equipment out of the van, and look up at the grey edifice, necks going back as far as possible. She beckons us over to the entrance, so we lug our gear towards a piss-stained metal lift covered in graffiti and surrounded by empty crisp packets and crushed cans of McEwan's Export. The lift can barely hold four people. We attempt to get all our gear and the Beast up to the 20th floor, but Chris, Mac and Paul soon give up and retreat to the van. Lucky for me, Andi's friend has another friend. I'm invited to stick around. She has the same Glaswegian brogue as her flatmate, and I have to politely ask her to repeat herself on several occasions. I blame it on the loud gig.

She hands me a drink, we talk, take some speed, dance to Bon Jovi, and have an enjoyable night. There are no expectations here, just two people, taking advantage of our impulses as we collide for one night only. I wonder if we are part of a conveyor belt of traveling musicians that they prey upon, like vixens in the Cathouse. Then I realise the amount of trust needed on both sides to enter each other's lives for 12 hours with the positive faith that no one is about to fuck the other person over. Maybe the speed is an insurance policy, to make sure nobody falls asleep and disappears into the night. The following day is met with a physical and metaphorical, frosty reception.

The rest of the crew have had a rough night slumming it in the van, with Paul branding Andi a "fucking liability". I am exempt from this rant as I am apparently 'the talent'.

 We say our goodbyes, but phone numbers are not swapped. Just a polite but uneasy, "Maybe see you next time you're in Glasgow". Paul gets the roadmap out and we chart our course for the next stop on the tour.

Kleptomania enters a new phase with my time in Travis Cut. Though we never steal a toilet, the highlight is a glitter ball we found last night. We take all the mirrored squares off, leaving a plastic ball and stick all the pieces on the dashboard of Andi's van. This proves to be an error when the sun is shining because it produces a cascading beam of light around the cabin, and Andi is momentarily blinded. Between this and the van constantly breaking down on busy motorways, it's a miracle we never crash.

I endure the next day in Edinburgh fighting an epic hangover and a speed come down. I phone home feeling tearful and homesick. At this point, I wonder if things will improve somehow. Most people would be grateful to be on a tour where you are experiencing sex, drugs, and rock n roll. But I'm missing Alice terribly. I can't let her go.

The next stop is Darlington, home of our portly booking agent Ian. By this point, we are living on crisp sandwiches and playing to hardly anyone. Sloppy Seconds are too alternative even for Darlington punks, it seems. The tour becomes increasingly sordid with Sloppy Seconds' lack of hygiene and interest in deviant porn mags they picked up in Germany. The tour bus stinks to high heaven, and I beg to be up the front, away from the nose-stinging body odour and acrid beer farts. The van becomes our bed, as we refuse to stay in the dirty punk communes our US guests are invited back to.

The final straw is in Birmingham, with a support band boldly announcing, "This is a song about backstabbers. It's called Backstabbers!"

It's good to get home finally and shower.

15th August - with Sloppy Seconds, Duchess of York, Leeds
16th August - The Cathouse, Glasgow
17th August - Venue, Edinburgh
18th August - Darlington
19th August - Liverpool
21st August - Fleece & Firkin, Bristol
22nd August – The Wheatsheaf, Stoke
23rd August - City Tavern, Birmingham
24th August - The Wherehouse, Derby
25th August - Princess Charlotte, Leicester
21st September - The Boatrace, Cambridge

We repeat the same process for our 2nd single, "Had A Gun", printing a few hundred more under the Incoming label and designing the front cover: a black and white photo of Robert De Niro in full Travis Bickle mode. For the back cover, we do a D.I.Y. photoshoot backstage at The Water Rats, each taking a word from the single title. "Had' is scrawled on Chris's palm, "A" on my bare chest with a black marker pen and Mac with "Gun" written on his hand placed across his face.

As with "Waking Hours", we hit the road to sell the single and win more attention. There are no tours this time, but the constant there and back again every other night is taking its toll on our lives, with little financial return. On the plus side, the steady gigs turn us into a tight band, and each night is a success from the band's technical viewpoint. I notice, worryingly, the songs are getting faster and faster and I end up gasping for air between each song and finishing the set with aching forearms.

On other occasions, we are lucky to make it to a gig because Andi's van is still a lottery draw each time he turns on the ignition or stops at traffic lights. The inevitable happens when we get halfway to Brighton, and the cam belt breaks. We waste a good few hours trying to find a way to the gig, but eventually give up and call roadside assistance.

We do a big push for the single, supporting China Drum, for a bonfire night gig at the

Water Rats in London. A three-piece from Northumberland, China Drum are one of the bands we play with that I really like; I always love watching the vocalist and drummer Adam Lee. We have some issues getting paid as this is one of those "bring your own audience" setups used by promoters. Even though we sent flyers advertising the gig and brought a coachload from Harlow, we don't qualify for payment, so Paul has to get shirty with the promoter.

Steve Lamacq makes "Had a Gun" single of the week on the Evening Session, and we get some nice reviews comparing us to the Manic Street Preachers (must have been the marker pen photos) and The Clash.

From the N.M.E.: "On a more aggressive front are Travis Cut, Harlow's answer to something extremely pissed off. Their new single is called "Had a Gun", which is kinetic, slamming effort doused with an innate sense of haziness thanks to some smartly muffled vocals, The kind of record that makes you drive fast.

We do another gig put on by our friends at S.T.E., only to break down again on the way home near Hertford. He's a nice guy, but the band are losing patience with Andi. The constant worry of getting stranded before or after each gig is a reality. The final straw is on the way back from Leicester when the headlights stop working halfway home. We pull over and sleep in the van in a car park until sunrise. We try to amuse ourselves for the night, waiting until it's light enough to drive. A stray cat is the only distraction, enough for me to mutter "It's Travis Cat" as I fall in and out of slumber. We call on Squaddie and a friend of Chris's also called Andi, to drive us in a more reliable vehicle for future gigs. Even though my 20th year on this planet wasn't the year to hit the big time, Travis Cut have impacted the U.K. Punk scene, and the well-known label Damaged Goods ask us if we'd like to record an album.

1st October - The Monarch, Camden
5th November - with China Drum, The Splash Club, Kings Cross
12th November - The Joiners Arms, Southampton
13th November - The Wherehouse, Derby
9th December – with China Drum, The Underworld, Camden
17th December - The Joiners Arms, Southampton

For New Year's Eve, I decide to meet up with Sam in his home town of Saffron Walden for a coffee. We've slowly but surely got back in touch again and amongst all the touring and recording we have found the time to meet. He's been enduring my heartbreak all year, so spending the one-year anniversary of losing Alice with me is a kind and supportive gesture. I did think about lighting a candle in the local church to commemorate our lost love, but I reckon that's a bit too weird so I write a poem instead.

"Sustained"

I sit at the table
Pen in hand
Look for inspiration
Inside a troubled man
The coffee steams
The music plays
The weather changes
It's the view that stays
The phone never rings
The post is weak
I grow ever solitary
With my invisible streak
"I'm there when you need me"
"Call me some time"
If there's laws in friendship
I've committed a crime
As hope decays
And time loses faith
I look in the mirror
And try to feel safe.

It's a cold fresh day, as I stride through Saffron Walden's cobbled alleyways towards the cafe. I turn a corner and nearly bump into someone. It's Alice. What are the chances? My heart skips a beat and for a second, I have to check if I'm dreaming. I manage to blurt out a hello, how are you, trying desperately to reign in the shivers. She's clearly in a hurry, looks nervous and glances away from me as she tells me she's fine. I'm lost for words but decide this is not the best time to fall to my knees, professing my undying love and bitter regret. We stumble over some more pleasantries, and I manage to get a smile and a scrunched nose before we go our separate directions, after an awkward "Good to see you".

In a daze, I float to the cafe on a cloud and slump down in front of Sam as he stirs his cappuccino. He takes one look at me and instantly knows something monumental has happened.

"Guess what," I say.

"What?"

"I saw her."

"Who?"

"Claudia Schiffer. Who do you think? Alice. I just saw Alice. Exactly one year since we broke up! You know what, I think it's a sign".

Sam's face falls and he rolls his eyes, knowing the next forty-five minutes will be a therapy session for me and not a good chinwag about music and films.

I barely notice the waitress has been standing there for a while, so Sam orders for me.

1994 - Mixtape

Slide Away - Oasis

Nutshell - Alice in Chains

Basket case - Green Day

Closer - Nine Inch Nails

Do you still hate me? - Jawbreaker

Self-Esteem - The Offspring

Why Should Eye - Bracket

Sabotage - Beastie Boys

Screamager - Therapy?

Babies - Pulp

Love Spreads - The Stone Roses

CHAPTER 30
SERIAL INCOMPETENCE

1995

John Major is re-elected, PlayStation is released, O.J. not guilty, I Should Coco by Supergrass, Different Class by Pulp, Goldeneye, Se7en.

It's been nearly two months. Definitely not a sign. With the self-loathing now in check, I have listened to enough Nine Inch Nails to (temporarily) get over Alice. I'm in a relationship with one of The Square regulars, a girl called Kerry. She has a nose ring, an undercut and smouldering look. She is a girl of few words, with a permanent grin and a rebellious nature; befitting of somebody who has grown up in Harlow, with a social life exclusive to The Square. All the other girls close to the band seem to be called Kerrie or Kelly, which can sometimes get confusing.

Mac's birthday is always a good excuse to put something special on at The Square, so the year kicks off in good company with an all-dayer featuring Snuff, Wat Tyler, China Drum, Reverse, Shutdown and Goober Patrol.

7th January - Punk All-Dayer, The Square, Harlow
13th January – with Big Boy Tomato, The Garage, Highbury, London

I need to be back in the right headspace for the album recording. An album. This is what I've been waiting for - an actual long player with numerous tracks and maybe a secret one or two at the end. We are back at Purple Rain to record, but the sessions will take longer, this being an album. Fine if you are in the middle of London but having heaps of spare time in Great Yarmouth in winter can be a tad soul-destroying.

Even though Kerry is a welcome diversion, I am still recovering from a self-inflicted broken heart, trying to endure Mac's mood swings, and having a creative conflict with the band versus my own interests. Both previous singles are featured for the album, and new songs, such as "Not To Blame", "Just A Girl", a cover of Screeching Weasel's "Totally", and Mac's love letter barnstormer "Mailage" and brutal set-closer "Open Letter". The day before our session, we travel up to Purple Rain for a fresh start the next morning. Packing a van with equipment and people is a bit like Tetris, ensuring there are enough places to sit and positioning the heavy gear so it won't crush you if the driver hits the brakes. We get stoned on the way, arrive at the studio, and settle into our sleeping quarters.

Ant Chapman is back for the album on producer duties. Mac is in one of his moods, so the vibe is grey. From his brief time managing Three and A Half Minutes, I looked up to Mac as a person of authority and a mentor as he showed me the ropes at gigs, recording studios and dealing with fans. But now we are fellow musicians, the relationship has changed, and we are on the same level. It takes me a while to get used to the new hierarchy but with Mac set in his ways on many things and a darker cloud above him than there was in 1991, I find it hard to get close.

The drums are recorded first to create the backing track for the guitars and vocals. I get four songs recorded; "Totally", "Mailage", and "Open Letter", plus the album opener, a Fugazi-inspired instrumental called "Electric Retarder". Ant is a great producer and shouts "Um Baba" each time a song is completed. We nail it before last orders, so I head to The Gunner for a poor excuse for a pint; the lager looks like the "water" they serve in The Goonies. Last time I checked, lager doesn't have a vintage. I lose some money on the fruit machine and decline an offer by the shifty locals for a game of darts in case I win and end up getting strangled in my sleep.

I stride back to the studio in freezing coastal conditions that takes my breath away. The last time I was here I sprayed Alice's name on the beach wall. The graffiti is still there, a bit weathered and holding on. Like me. We stay up until late, reminiscing about old Children's cartoons and T.V. shows.

As the sessions continue, Mac remains grumpy. I say remains; he is grumpy, and I'm not sure of an expiration date here. Any attempt to ask why, is met with a silence so cold and stony the person asking needs to add another layer of clothing. It's another late start for day two, and I finish drumming by mid-afternoon. The songs completed are "Waking Hours" and "Not to Blame". Following a depressing visit to the cash point, it's clear I need some more money in the bank. This is an even more stark reality when I visit the amusement arcades and have no choice but to watch the games. I return to the studio and watch one of my favourite films in the world, Withnail & I – we're using some dialogue as a sample on one of the tracks. I think I've seen this film 50 times. We've come to Great Yarmouth by mistake!

I think somebody up there likes me. The next day I check my bank account I'm pleasantly surprised to see funds have been added - thank you, P.R.S. and the TV channel that broadcast Son-in-Law. With some money fresh in my pocket, I go shopping because I'm a spendthrift fool. I've finished my drum takes on "Just A Girl" and "Schism", and there's only one track left to do. With cabin fever now growing, Mac is officially getting to me. It feels like this doesn't matter to him. Thank God there is only two days to go.

As a drummer, there's a lot of sitting around because more work goes into getting the vocals nailed, as singers don't have infinite energy to sing their hearts out, for take after take. Adding lots of guitar parts is also time-consuming. My job is almost done, so I'm now only here for moral support.

On day four, I finish the drum parts in the morning for the extra non-album song "Summer of Hate". All that's left for me now, is some tambourine on "Waking Hours" (acoustic). Mac has been in the best mood so far, making the studio feel more upbeat. We end up sitting on the floor in the booth and recording unplugged acoustic versions of "Waking Hours" and "Mailage". To celebrate, we start on the beer, and our descent into childhood continues with Paul phoning shopping channel Q.V.C. to ask them to define a quibble. There's a one-upmanship game on who can say "I would" to stuff and still make it funny.

We go out to Great Yarmouth's centre for Ant's birthday. I have a tenner left. It's a real concern how broke I am. I need to get a hold of my finances; it's doing my head in. How to control your finances is not something they teach you at school. We do a pub crawl, dance in an empty nightclub, and then get pissed on wine in a restaurant before we all stagger back to the studio, stopping to ask girls if they "touch fish".

We also remove boards from some takeaway shops. I'm surprised the police aren't called out to monitor our rampage of the Suffolk riviera.

Day five is a recovery day. From drinking a lot over the last few years, my liver may finally be OK with it. Either that, or I wonder if I'll be dead by 30.

I don't do anything for the morning; only little things left to tie up that don't involve me. The albums going to be great. It's a real sense of achievement to record an album, I'm thrilled to be working with Chris and Mac on the track order and listening back to the final version.

Finished and satisfied, we leave the studio at about 7.30, and I'm back home by 9.30. It will be nice to get my privacy back. In the studio, when having a shower, the only thing between the rest of the crew and me is a mouldy curtain. I'm looking forward to a soak in the bath with some of those new-fangled bath bombs from Lush. But we're not done yet. One more visit for a final mix at the studio, and then it's complete.

Back up in the studio, I do hardly anything to begin with. Ant samples my snare drum, I add some vocals and more attempts at "Waking Hours" and "Mailage" (acoustic), then we watch Norwich v Coventry on the telly (3-1)

The following day, Chris and I go to a greasy spoon. Two punks in a room full of truckers, reading The Sun and leering at today's page 3 stunner, as they drip egg over their tattooed forearms, wiping the yellow goo on their bellies. We chat about the album, where we should play next, and Mac. Due to their mutual love for Arsenal FC, Mac and Chris have more time together at the matches, but I can tell from Chris's face our endurance of Mac is taking its toll. We're not up for firing him, as the band was his idea, and he's a talented musician. Plus, the fallout from letting him go would be too much to bear. Damned if we do, damned if we don't.

I head to the arcades again, as Ant hasn't shown up yet. It dawns on me I'm probably doing nothing today. Ant finally arrives, and he mixes some songs. Mixing is an art because you have to decide what needs to be higher or lower in the mix and if certain effects should be added here and there. They all sound so cool. I love hearing the bones of each song and the other parts from each of us as they are added in. We end the day making a start on the studio fridge and drinking many cans of Fosters. By 1:30am, Mac is stoned and ends every sentence with the phrase "sanitary towel dispenser". A typical day in the life of Travis Cut. Just a little more mixing and sampling to go.

Ant completes the rest of the album, Withnail & I samples and all - right at the end of "Open Letter", Withnail barks, "right you fucker, I'm gonna do the washing up".

I hold back a request to make the drums louder, but I'm happy with how the album turns out. We've added the single B-sides and two secret tracks for the CD format. You will need to wait fifty-five minutes until track 68 reveals an acoustic version of Waking Hours and Mailage with a tambourine, organ, sung with a Brian Jonestown Massacre vibe.

We name the LP "Serial Incompetence" and have it lined up for an April release. The front cover features a simple blue background with three images - a gun, a heart, and a wine glass with a bottle. The back cover is a photo of us in a Stevenage skate park, the blur of a skater whizzing behind us. It should have been the front cover, to be honest.

Serial Incompetence press release:
Having toured up and down the country several times, the debut album "Serial Incompetence" was recorded, produced by Big Ant of Collapsed Lung, and thrust onto an unsuspecting market last May. Reviews from fanzines and independent magazines flooded in, while the mainstream press remained blissfully unaware of the band's existence. A German reviewer declared that the L.P. gathers together "all the ingredients which turned punk rock into the most beautiful music in the world," whilst in this country, reviews heralded the band as "one of the U.K.'s most promising melodic hardcore bands", "a mix of Fugazi/Green Day and Snuff", and "nods to all that is seminal from the annals of melody edged punk" that the L.P. gathers together "all the ingredients which turned punk rock into the most beautiful music in the world"

whilst in this country, reviews heralded the band as "one of the U.K.'s most promising melodic hardcore bands", "a mix of Fugazi/Green Day and Snuff", and "nods to all that is seminal from the annals of melody edged punk."

In a career that only began at the end of '93 with support to D.O.A, Travis Cut has been compared, quite favourably, we think, to bands such as Husker Du, All/Descendents, early Moving Targets, Green Day, The Parasites, Lemonheads, and Face to Face.

Another single is scheduled for release at the beginning of October, followed by the band's first jaunt abroad from some Swiss, German and French Dates, and then a full-length tour of the U.K. in November before settling down to write and record L.P. number two".

Things are looking up with the album in the can, a healing heart, and an ever-changing social life. If I can get a grip on the finances, all will be well. But something else taunts me: an urge to try something completely different.

CHAPTER 31

UPSIDE DOWN

After a string of doomed relationships with should-be Alices, I am trying bachelorhood, and it seems a nice place to be. Socially, I am starting to lead a strange double life. On certain nights, you can find me playing at a scummy venue somewhere in the country, bashing out forty minutes of fast power punk. Other nights, I'm in my silk shirt, smart trousers and shoes in a nightclub, dancing to Strike, Livin' Joy, and Baby D.

It feels like Travis Cut is a full-time job, and clubbing is my chance for escapism. From all those years watching chart music on Top of the Pops and spending most of the 80s in the company of S-Express and Yazz, I still have a deep connection with all things pop.

With boy bands Take That, Boyzone and Let Loose in the ascendance, it feels natural to keep a close eye on these new musical trends. I often idly daydream about what it would be like to join an act like that. As if my thoughts have been answered, an unexpected opportunity presents itself when my sister shows me an ad posted at her Drama college. Pre-dating Simon Cowell by a decade, a T.V. production company is planning to put together a boy band and will be filming the whole process for a documentary. I am compelled to give it a go, mainly as a push back to the punk lifestyle I am struggling to fall in love with, but also to see if being at the front of the stage is more fun.

The first step is to submit a photo and send it off. I get a nice letter, stating that out of 40,000 boys who have applied, I'm one of the 200 that have made it through to the next stage. I have to learn a song and attend an open audition in London. For Dutch courage, I meet up with some mates the night before and fantasise about pop stardom over a few drinks. It is one of those evenings where the beer is going down rather well, the conversation flowing, and every tune on the jukebox is a banger. By closing time, we have solved the world of its problems and cried on each other's shoulders. Walking home, one of my mates decides to have a bundle and drunkenly pushes me sideways into someone's hedge. But not some ordinary hedge. This one has thorns.

As I emerge, parts of my cheek and lips feel wet, and when I get home, there are streaks of blood all over my face and down my front. Post clean, it looks like I've gone ten rounds with a rabid cat. Paper-thin scratches are scattered across my cheek, chin, and mouth.

In the morning, it looks drier and better. I attempt to conceal it with talcum powder. I call in sick (hungover, so it's convincing) and head into the big smoke with the audition info in my hand. I soon find the address in a West London borough and join a queue of young lads all dressed in tight tops and white jeans, doused in pints of aftershave that I detected from a kilometre away.

The audition process is like herding sheep, leading us into a reception area, a second waiting room and finally into the audition room itself. The two songs we had to choose from are the soppy ballad "Love Me for A Reason" by Boyzone, or Rick Astley's 80's hit and viral sensation, "Never Gonna Give You Up". I chose "Never Gonna Give You Up" as it is closer to my vocal range. We all get allocated numbers, and the butterflies get worse with each one called out. I start to doubt myself. What am I doing here? I'm in a punk band that likes me, with a growing and devoted audience, and here's me, hoping to be the next Mark Owen. Am I turning into a fame-hungry whore?

This sudden existential crisis isn't helping, so I head to the gents to take a few breaths. I look in the mirror at my pockmarked face, bestowed with lumps of congealed talcum powder. I do my best to smooth it back in and around the cuts. I hum the song for a bit and psych myself up. Well, I'm here in London with a scarred face and stinking of Stella. I've pulled a sickie. I might as well go through with it and then head to the record shops. I go back to my seat and hear "number 64" being called out. I look down at my blue raffle ticket. 68. Not long to go. The rooms are quiet; all I can hear are the muffled audition noises coming from behind a closed door. Sensing the air of competition, nobody wants to make friends and chat. Maybe we are all as nervous as each other, desperately trying not to lose control of our bodily functions. Thank God I didn't choose white jeans.

"66". How many of these dudes are actual musicians? They're hard to spot when it looks like we're all about to go clubbing. I spot a guy with long hair and ripped jeans, giving off a "me in 1992" vibe. I wish I'd come dressed as a member of Travis Cut instead of boy-band cosplay. Something more genuine might have put my anxiety at ease.

"67". I sing the song in my head: We're no strangers to love. You know the rules, and so do I. Got to hit that high note, or I'm toast. I hope my face looks OK. Maybe I could be the rugged band member, the scarred "bad boy" all the fans hate to love. A girl wearing a headset opens the door and calls out, "Number 68? Alex??".

I stand up and give her the thumbs up, instantly regretting it. This is not an audition for Crackerjack; what was I thinking with the thumbs? I show her my sweaty ticket, and she turns swiftly and says, "This way".

I'm led into a small room with a low ceiling. One wall has a white backdrop and a camera on a tripod placed in front of it. Five men are sitting behind the camera on chairs. They look very corporate and clean cut, nothing like my music industry peers from previous bands. I guess this is the culture when it comes to mainstream pop.

"Alex, is it?" One of them says, glancing at me, my photo, and then at me again.

I sweat a bit, realising the photo features me without thorn trauma. And long hair.

"Yes, that's me. Hello."

"What are you going to sing for us today?"

"The Rick Astley one. I mean, Never Gonna Give. Sorry, Never Gonna Give You Up by Rick Astley."

He raises an eyebrow - not the popular choice, it seems.

"OK, thanks for that. Can you stand in front of the camera, please?"

I do as I'm told and try to smoulder a bit. The crew are inspecting their monitors, checking me over. God, I hope my scratched face isn't showing up. Maybe I can say I was mugged on the way. Or I fell onto a bottle of talcum powder whilst kissing a rat. Oh, Christ, what if they think it's cocaine? What if someone saw me go into the toilet, reckons I've done a couple of lines, but in a panic attack, I've dumped my face in it? I start sweating, worried they are judging me as some drug-addled vandal who has fought with someone who uses tiny knives.

"OK, Alex, the song is all cued up, so ready when you are."

"Thanks, I'm ready."

I nearly hold up my hands to click the sticks four times, then remind myself. The famous Stock, Aitken, and Waterman intro kicks in, and I realise I didn't rehearse any dance moves. I'm standing there like a lemon. Rookie mistake. The crew are watching me, some of them shifting in seats, the odd whisper here and there. I try to sway a bit and end up doing an Alan Partridge-type dance, the sort of moves you see your sixty-year-old Uncle do at a wedding. I wait for Rick's voice as an indicator to sing, but Rick's voice isn't there. This is a backing track. They want to hear my voice, not Rick's. I quickly catch up and rush in, singing,

"We're no strangers to lurrve (I give the word love my own Barry White spin) "You know the rules and SO DO IIII" - I point upwards on the high note like I'm some kind of pound-shop Michael Bolton. "A full commitment's what I'm thinking of; you wouldn't get this from any other guyyyy" I crack a smile and feel one of the cuts open up.

One of the men stifles a yawn. I gently touch my face to make sure I haven't started bleeding. I blag it to the chorus, and the man waves at me. As the music fades, I sing a half-hearted acapella, my voice trailing off as the waving continues.

"Thanks, Alex. We'll be in touch."

I nod excitedly as the headset woman opens a door leading back onto the street. It slams behind me with a kind of "See ya" retort.

The audition went by in a flash, leaving me with a regretful feeling about all the things I could have done better. A sense of failure washes over me during the long trip home. Unsurprisingly, I don't get selected. The documentary is shown, and a boy band called Upside Down is born. They then vanish into obscurity.

CHAPTER 32

BOARD STUPID

As if to remind me of the advantages of being in Travis Cut, we are invited to appear on Channel 4's Board Stupid. This is a mad-cap Sunday afternoon snowboarding programme hosted by Normski. I have no idea how we've blagged this, but I am up for being on T.V. again.

With Mac in yet another of his foul moods, we head up to the Snowdome at Tamworth and are told to set up our gear at the bottom of the slope. This gets added to the list of the weirdest places I've played the drums; we must find ways to prevent the gear from freezing or sliding away. Makeshift adjustments are done, and cameras are in place, so we wait for our moment. The main guests on the show are soon-to-be one-hit wonders Stiltskin, who have been successful with the song "Inside" from the latest Levi's ad.

Chris delights himself by playing the opening riff during their interview and provoking considerable ire! When it comes to us, Normski does a bit to the camera from behind an inflatable desk. Proclaiming, "Here's Travis Cut with "Wuss".

He then bounds over and jumps about as we play. We get given a box full of merch, ski hats and branded tees, and a free snowboarding lesson which was a nice perk.

17th March – with Bracket, The Old Trout, Windsor
20th March - Duchess of York, Leeds
22nd March – with China Drum, Bracket, The Garage, Highbury
23rd March- The Joiners Arms, Southampton
24th March - Dublin Castle, Camden, London
26th March - The Boat Race, Cambridge

As you may have gathered, the band's happiness and general well-being are dependent on Mac's mood. During the '90s, if you had issues or mental illness, it was waved away with the person being "difficult" or "crazy".

It would be a few years before Mac is diagnosed with bipolar disorder and other conditions requiring counselling and heavy medication. But during this time, Chris and I are on eggshells, having to navigate through each recording, tour, and meeting with an air of uncertainty. The three of us have some great times, but sometimes it is a constant grind and pressure on our mental health to cope with Mac.

I decide I need a holiday, and call on Sam, Peter, Charlie, and her flatmate to join me. We scour through Teletext Holidays to find a last-minute deal and book a week in Crete. It's a well-deserved break, getting some sun and catching up with dear friends outside of the maelstrom. With batteries fully recharged, it's time to promote the album and head back on the road.

CHAPTER 33
NICE & SLEAZY

"Any work in the past two weeks?"

I shuffle in the grey plastic chair and shake my head, attempting to look frustrated as I say "No, unfortunately".

We both know there will be no work for me. My CV screams creative arts, and the only jobs listed in the Job Centre are for a Warehouse Assistant or part-time receptionist. We're both going through the regular ritual; the adviser asks me the same question before scribbling a signature in the little booklet so I can get the Jobseekers Allowance. She asks me if I would be interested in an interview for a telesales role and shows me the card with the job specification. It has all the buzz words, like "can-do attitude" and "not afraid to roll up your sleeves" with lots of sales jargon that's making me throw up in my mouth. I ask about jobs in the Music Industry again, knowing full well there's a better chance of Rogue Trader Nick Leeson walking into the Job Centre in the next 5 minutes. We'll continue the back and forth as long as I can claim, even though it's playing havoc on my diary - any gigs booked have to be rearranged so I can be home for when I sign on. The sooner I find a job that suits me the better.

Our string of gigs arranged to plug the album are with North Hampshire, U.S. band, The Queers. Known for their constantly changing line-up and Ramones-style songs, they should be a good fit for us. Similar to the Sloppy Seconds arrangement they borrow all our gear. Being at the receiving or the giving end of shared drum kits has its challenges, especially if you're touring with a band from another country who have brought nothing to cut costs. Being a drummer, the worst thing to ask (and to be asked) is to share a kit. Because smaller venues don't have the stage space or if bands have limited room in their cars, the first thing that needs to be shared is usually the drum kit. It then opens up a world of doubt for the kind drummer who is about to loan his precious kit - is the other drummer a complete animal? Will they steal my hi-hat clutch?? Will they tune my drums??

Normally, the standard protocol goes that you can let them use it, but they have to bring their own cymbals and snare.

One gruesome aspect of sharing drums is the hygiene issues; The Queers' drummer has a habit of spitting as he plays, so each night, I have to watch as my drum kit gets sprayed with saliva. Luckily, they seem more laid-back and less grimy than Sloppy Seconds when offstage.

The tour starts well in Birmingham, and things go without a hitch until we reach Brighton, where Chris feels like death. I'm coming down with something nasty too. Unable to play, we pull out and waste the evening in the van, feeling exhausted with ourselves and each other. We aren't getting paid anyway, so our stagnation in the van becomes a silent protest. The next day, blighted by their own drug related issues, we learn The Queers want to cancel the rest of the tour and go home. Not wanting to waste a set of booked gigs, we quickly contact the promoters and offer to play instead as the headliners. Only a few get cancelled, so we end up playing the rest of the dates to a Queer's audience that doesn't seem to mind.

26th April - with The Queers, The Boatrace, Cambridge
27th April - with The Queers, The Foundry, Birmingham
29th April - Peterborough
30th April – Nottingham

By Peterborough and Nottingham, most of the band is fighting the flu, but we dig deep and get through the gigs. A friend of Mac's puts us up in Nottingham and medicinal drinking games ensue – thumper, buzz fizz, fuzzy duck. A drink is concocted with wine, beer, and Baileys in it which is the closest thing to chunder you could taste. Miraculously cured, we go for a stroll around Nottingham, and I spot some old Three and A Half Minutes E.P.s in the record stores. Then it's back home for three days to fully recover.

Back on our now-headline tour and feeling refreshed, we act like rock stars all day, basking in the glow of our egos and contented nature. Headlining gigs does a lot for the band's morale. We stop at The Little Chef for a bite to eat and get some sun.

Post-soundcheck in Hull, we spot Paul Heaton of The Housemartins/Beautiful South at a pub near the venue - Roadie Paul is a tad starstruck. I wonder if he is coming to our gig. It's a no-show from the former Housemartin, but we do a tight set in front of about thirty-five people. We end up getting stoned at another stranger's house and start collectively calling ourselves Glynis.

The next day we arrive in Wakefield and have a few beers, then a few more... Well, you know the score. It turns into an afternoon sesh, I am a tad annoyed by being soberer than everyone else, and the gig isn't too brilliant, either. I can't think why. The venue is hot, which doesn't help. We nick some bollards. No reason: it's not that Wakefield has limited-edition bollards or anything.

"Not To Blame" is to be our third single. This time we have Jodie Foster's character from Taxi Driver adorning the front cover. Halfway through the tour, we stop in

Sunderland to record the B-sides with local legend, Frankie Stubbs of Leatherface. Highly regarded as one of the most talented punk bands of the 90s, it's a badge of honour to get Frankie involved. I quickly lay down the drums for "In Vain", "Scars" and "Against the Flow".

The studio is next door to a working men's club that offers a pint for 50p. We consume the day yo-yo-ing between the studio and pub in between takes and mixing, then end up staying in the pub.

We kip in Frankie's chic flat, drunkenly arguing about Audrey Hepburn being in Philadelphia Story (I bet Frankie a fiver it's Katharine Hepburn). The next day, there is a glitch with Mac's bass part that could have brewed a rather dark cloud over our collective heads, but Mac and Frankie sort it.

We leave Sunderland feeling like a bunch of hobbits who sought refuge with a local soothsayer. Or something.

We drive to Sheffield to play with Bracket, another U.S. punk band from California, who, thankfully, are nice chaps.

It was another OK gig in an OK venue with fucking weird sound. Bracket are cool to hang with, so we politely ask if we can steal their beers. It dawns on me that all I've eaten today is a kebab and a Drifter.

1st May - Cumberland Arms, Newcastle
2nd May - Duchess of York, Leeds
3rd May - Nice n Sleazy, Glasgow
4th May - The Venue, Edinburgh
6th May - The Players, Wakefield
8th May - with Bracket, Leadmill, Sheffield

We play a few more gigs with Bracket, then finish with a headline slot that should have been for The Queers at the Garage in Highbury. Making desperate calls, we add bands Reverse and Shutdown to join us and get a few hundred people coming along - I make the mistake of taking some speed before the gig. Hence, my memory of this performance is fleeting.

17th May - St John's Tavern, Archway, London
18th May - The Stage, Worcester
19th May - with Reverse, Shutdown, The Garage, Highbury
24th June - The Laurel Tree, Camden
30th June - with Snuff, The Venue, New Cross
10th July - with J Church, The Laurel Tree, Camden

Not to Blame press release:

"After many deliberations, Travis Cut will release "Not to Blame" from the debut LP "Serial Incompetence" as a single. The A-side of this, their third single, was produced by Big Ant of Collapsed Lung fame and is backed with two new tracks recorded by that maestro of punk Frankie Stubbs.

The single, on 7" vinyl only, comes out on Damaged Goods on October 9th. The band sail straight out to Europe to promote it with a handful of Swiss, German and French does, before embarking on a full-length UK tour.

While everyone rambles on about the new "punk explosion" with Green Day, Rancid, Offspring, Bad Religion et al., Travis Cut are just one of a whole new breed of UK melodic hardcore bands. Without the pretensions of Britpop, without the commercial trappings of the "punk explosion", just honest, poppy, infectious, brash, punk rock - bitter fucked up love songs full of barbed hook lines and choruses as catchy as the pox!"

In the last eighteen months, we've toured with four US punk bands, collaborated with Ant Chapman and Frankie Stubbs, recorded three singles and an album, and have appeared on TV. So only natural for us to get ideas above our station.

The first hare-brained scheme involves asking Damaged Goods to include us in a promo campaign, whereby copies of our single get sent to promoters who play the tracks in the venue and then send us back their feedback forms. We offer to cover the cost but end up paying for some constructive criticism of our work and not getting much more. This causes friction between Damaged Goods and us.

Secondly, we ditch Ian, our booking agent, without telling him - I was up for this, still feeling wound up with the Sloppy Seconds disaster. The problem is Ian soon finds this out via gig promoters who have had phone calls from our new agent. With our egos bruised, morale low and an album that was only doing OK, it wasn't long before I was tempted to try the boy-band thing again.

CHAPTER 34
SKREAM FOR ME, ROMFORD

Two former friends I have kept in touch with also happen to be up to musical things. Peter is a hell of a singer and a student at the "tits and teeth" Performing Arts school, Italia Conti. We'll come back to Peter in a bit. My other friend is Carl, an acid jazz-loving, Deee-lite-listening, Madonna super-fan. We were in the same class at secondary school, did stints in the Junior operatic club and spent many a school holiday visiting his beloved waterparks. I even indulged his Madonna obsession to the point of us bunking off school and getting a train into London to watch 'In Bed with Madonna' on the most giant screen we could find. Carl and I have a similar look too, with our olive skin, brown eyes, and dark hair. Gregarious, quirky, and outgoing, he was always destined to do something musical; it was in his DNA.

We go to Dukes Nightclub in Chelmsford every Thursday and dance all night to the latest house tunes and classic party songs. Dukes is your typical cheesy nightclub. The doors opened in 1983, there have been parties five nights a week ever since. Each week there is a standoff on who should be the designated driver, with my mate Alastair regularly drawing the short straw. We drive to the club in his Vauxhall Nova, smothered with Escape by Calvin Klein, breaking in our new clobber purchased from Mister Byrite. Queues snake around the block. To get past the burly fashion-conscious doormen, you have to wear shirt, shoes, and trousers. A friend who wasn't wearing socks was denied entry, so he ran over to the local pub and bought a pair off someone for a fiver. Once inside, we strut the sticky gaudy carpet, give the finger to the overpriced cigarette machines, and keep a cautious eye out for any Chelmsford or Harlow chavs fixing for a ruck. The DJ refuses requests, and there is always a slow dance section. The perfect opportunity to grab a wet snog to the dulcet tones of Richard Marx.

It's easy to get lost in Dukes, with two floors and about six bars, all providing shots of Aftershock, bottles of Hooch or pints of Hoffmeister. There is a ludicrous light show that happens halfway through the night, with smoke machines and a cheesy 80's fanfare, a sampled jingle proclaiming 'D-D-D-D-DUKES EXPERIENCE' at full blast. Carl is making a living in catering, but Raf, a friend of his, is working on a pop act, and Carl wonders if I would go along to see if this is worth pursuing together. He asked me because of my industry experience and maybe there is a role going for a percussionist. We drive to an industrial estate unit where Raf works and uses as a place to rehearse after hours. There are no instruments, just extra band member James, whom I've never met, and Raf - a short and spritely Belgian dude with steely blue eyes and cheekbones to die for. He's brandishing a tape player containing a pop song he's written and recorded. The rehearsal will be to choreograph a dance routine to the song, something I'm not entirely prepared for. A gig is promised at a different cheesy nightclub called Hollywood's in Romford, and the slot will be available once the act is ready.

Since the Upside Down audition debacle, I have worked on my dancing, and regular nights at Duke's have helped me expand my repertoire of moves. We practise over the next few hours, mirroring Raf's choreography and coming up with a routine for his song "Day in Day Out" - a funky number using a sample from Cross the Tracks by Maceo and the Macks. I manage to keep up and adapt to the idea of not sitting at the back anymore, but part of a multi-limbed, gyrating sausage fest.

After being screened successfully and with Carl on board, they ask me to join. I weigh up the odds. Swap a fresh-faced boy band with one song for a punk band with a record deal, a growing fan base and some burgeoning mental health issues? I have a good hard think and finally say no. They recruit another school friend, call themselves Skream! and give it a go. Their gimmick is wearing tartan trousers. This second boy band experience leads to my decision to leave Travis Cut.

CHAPTER 35
GET ON THE BUS

Sam is back on the scene, and we deploy countless evenings down the pub trying to right wrongs and solve each other's relationship issues. His younger sister has matched me with a friend of hers, a quiet, cute girl called Emily. She lives in a big creaky old house in a hamlet called Stocking Pelham, with undulating floorboards and dark, musty corners smelling of fireplaces. The similarity to Alice's abode is comforting and surreal at the same time, as I struggle to navigate a new relationship with someone who must share me with the demanding lifestyle of being in a band.

With finances at an all-time low, I've managed to get a job through a family friend. He has left his position as a runner in London, working at a TV post-production editing facility and studio. The location is a labyrinthine building in St John's Wood called CTV Facilities, with a grand, white-pillared frontage that wouldn't look out of place in Ancient Rome. It's a classy old building that used to be a church; the back of it was replaced after being bombed in World War II. My role involves making tea for the staff as they work long hours to edit TV programmes, driving tapes into Soho, parking the boss's car and manning reception. The reception task includes a night shift, looking after the whole building once everyone has gone home. It's a chance for me to scribble more in the diary, and to reflect. Other runners have had run-ins with the ghost that lurks around Edit Suite 5, but luckily, I've been spared. There were stories of the reception switchboard lighting up like a Christmas tree, as if everyone was suddenly calling from every room at 2 in the morning, followed by groans and knocking against doors. Built on top of the crypt, there is a TV studio, rented out to a children's channel called TCC. Despite the horror stories, the pay is good, and it's exciting to stand in the edit suites, see a programme come to life, and get to know the crew and presenters at TCC. With the news of a massive European tour in the offing, Chris and Mac plead with me to cut the job short for the band's sake. Once again, I weigh things up. What would I rather be doing? I tell CTV I'll be gone by October. With the job now short-term, I try to make ends meet by offering private drum lessons. Most of my students are youngsters who have received a kit for their Birthday/Christmas. Their parents want to hear something better than "We Will Rock You" all day. I cobble together my notes from the lessons with Alan and armed with my trusty practice pad and spare sticks,

I start visiting homes to train the next Dave Grohl. Back down to a trio, the news circulates during the summer that Raf, James and Carl's band Skream! have been signed to Telstar, recorded "Day in Day Out", and flown to New York to record the music video.

Back in the world of The Cut, we've been drafted on to a sleeper-bus tour, a sort of hop-on hop-off routine where you start the tour in your local town, join the bus for a string of dates, then switch places with another band.

Sleeper bus Tour dates:

17th September - The Square, Harlow
18th September - Princess Charlotte, Leicester
19th September -Fibbers, York

The bus is fantastic; a proper tour bus, the kind used by major artists. The beds are the size of coffins, and it feels like slotting yourself into a letter box when you get in it to sleep. There's a nice lounge section at the back with a CD player and TV. I feel like I'm in Aerosmith on a bus like this.

Our first tour gig is at The Square, where we play an OK set. The next day we're playing Princess Charlotte in Leicester, a venue I've been to countless times. I'm back on a diet of crisps, beer, and fags, so the free chips and salsa we get on the rider are a bonus. As the tour continues, my back starts to hurt from the beds, and the gigs are not well attended. The concept for this sleeper bus rotation is excellent, but the delivery is poor. Refreshingly, all the bands are diverse, ranging from The Gyres to Audioweb (who we love). They go on to have a few hit singles and support U2. Audioweb are a great live band and do not take prisoners when dealing with hecklers. During the tour, I learn Carl was on TV with Skream! on a light entertainment show called After 5.

Our last stop in York is a good day. Chris and I go to the Jorvik Museum and York Minster, eat a lovely lasagne, and the gig has an audience. Audioweb bond with us and play the funniest gag I've ever seen with a fake turd. The bus has a no number 2 rule to prevent blockages - and with a 100% male passenger count, the tour manager is keen to avoid this. Spotting an opportunity, one of Audioweb buys a fake turd and leaves it in the toilet. As we all sit around the table, they inform the poor tour manager that someone has defied the rules and dropped a floater. Visibly annoyed and flustered, he asks who has done the offending dump as we all snigger behind our beer cans. Eventually, he decides to go into the cubicle to fish out the poo with a plastic bag. Walking past us with the turd, warning everyone to hold their noses, one of Audioweb suddenly grabs the bag and bangs it on the table. We all fall about in hysterics.

Despite all the fun, things are not helped by the half-empty gigs and killing time wandering around different towns. I still have a burning desire to do something less punk. But first, it's time to embark on an extended European tour.

CHAPTER 36

AUF WIEDERSEHEN

Just my luck. What started as a France, Switzerland and Germany tour ends up with one gig in Germany and then a 5-day stint in Switzerland. The new agents we've dropped in favour of Ian are less than helpful. To think I left CTV for this. Having cast aside the boy band opportunity and a well-paid job, I'm starting to wonder if Travis Cut will ever become bigger than we currently are. We're a popular band, but the money needs to come from somewhere and I think maybe this has an expiry date. I've tried to restore my faith with Travis Cut but it's not being helped by the opportunities I've turned my back on. It's becoming an albatross around my neck and my dilemma of what to do grows with every gig we play. To add insult to injury, I hoped I would avoid hearing Fairground by Simply Red once I'd left the UK, but no such luck.

We are booked alongside another UK act called 95:Nil, who sound like Depeche Mode minus the talent. They change their name each year to match things up, so if you see "insert year here": Nil playing any time soon, you'll know what to expect. Paul is along for the ride as our Tour Manager/roadie. We've taught him what he thinks are chat-up lines in French, which are "Je suis ivre et anglais, s'il te plaît, frappe-moi" (I'm drunk and English, please kick me) and "Il y a des traces de sperme dans la barbe de ta mère" (There are traces of sperm in your mother's beard).

The long drives are made more pleasant by Switzerland's incredible scenery, and it feels more like a holiday than a tour. We frequently stop the bus at every corner and run out to take pictures of the stunning vista. We experience gruff in human form with a promoter who says everything is dead - the scene, the venue, the crowds. I'm tempted to ask him what his philosophy on life is but can already guess the answer.

Playing to no one each night, the trip starts rubbing us up the wrong way, and we take our frustrations out on each other. If we weren't in such a picturesque country, we would be plotting escape methods.

Things get hairy at a border security checkpoint. Mac has to conceal a thumb-sized piece of pot in some brie, which luckily goes undetected. Our last gig has the best attendance in a venue more suited for Octoberfest. This may well be my last tour.

12th October - Aarau, Switzerland
13th October - Thun
15th October - Bulle, Switzerland

I've done a lot of soul-searching. I sit down with my parents, who must be exasperated at this constant quest for success, as I jump from bandwagon to bandwagon. They can see I'm torn between my love of drumming and the need to earn money and start a stable career. I'm still living at home, and with Charlie studying at drama college, I feel like I've missed out on further education. Again, the advice is do what makes me happy, but the underlying message is find something that makes you happy but also earns money.

It's late October and just after my 21st birthday.

I pluck up the courage to tell Chris and Mac I'm going to leave. I don't need to give an exact reason; they know I want to go. Similar to Three and A Half Minutes, the music difference puts us at loggerheads. And they can read between the lines that the constant touring, moody ups and downs and my predilection for all things pop are rising to the fore.

Adding further awkwardness to my timing, they've had a birthday whip round and bought me a proper hardware box for my drum stands, having grown tired of lugging my homemade wooden box around for the last two years.

They are graceful about my decision, but I can tell they are gutted I'm going. Without blowing my own trumpet too much, I'm a good drummer, and we are sometimes hard to find.

I promise to stick around for the booked gigs in Ireland and Scotland, with my final gig being—where else—The Square.

For the Ireland tour, we drive to Holyhead and take a snail-paced ferry to Dublin. The venue is tiny, but goes well, and we all order pints of Guinness to celebrate the newest destination on the Travis Cut world map. We are cautioned not to go out in case we get mugged by junkies. I'm keeping an eye out for Ronan Keating. I have kept the boyband plan a secret; it's like cheating on the band or something. If I mention it, I will be the butt of all jokes, or they will try to talk me out of it; I'm a pushover when people try to talk me out of stuff. But trying to remain positive amongst the band is hard, and I feel like an imposter.

As I wallow in my hangover from the night before, we take some mad prick to Cork with us as he tries to force whiskey down us all. For Cork, we play a smaller venue than the night before. It's a crazy gig with a band called Monkhouse. The lead singer has an extra-long cable that lets him run into the crowd to scream in everyone's faces. He climbs the speaker and chomps down on the cables. Chris and Mac take turns asking if I'm OK. I feel guilty being so distant, but I can't help it.

Back in Dublin, we rush through our set at a pub called the Old Chinaman. If we're quick, we can catch an overnight ferry to avoid staying an extra night. We make the ferry in the nick of time. I stay up for the journey back, listening to Van Morrison as we drive home through the Welsh mountains.

3rd November - Dublin
4th November - with Monkhouse, Cork
5th November - The Old Chinaman, Dublin

Even though Ireland was another experience and a privilege to travel somewhere new, I am still committed to ending it, and the Scotland tour is the penultimate hurdle. Chris and I must drive the van for the Scottish gigs, so there is to be no wistful gazing out of the window for me. Chris and I alternate driving so we can drink. I forget driving with a hangover is just as bad.

The tour starts badly, with the long journey north, followed by a gig where I can't hear shit on stage. With every hour that passes, I do not want to be here. I can't be here. The next gig is better, but this isn't me anymore. One more to go. We spend the day in Arbroath and kill time watching a match on the coldest football ground I've ever been in. With the gig done, we decide to drive home overnight. To add insult to injury, Mac is so drunk he throws up in the van. This was not a good start to the nocturnal journey, but I'm determined to get us home. The hum of the engine and the rhythmic patter of raindrops against the windshield were not helping my eyelids. I try to battle the weariness that threatens to envelop me. The winding roads and desolate stretches demand unwavering focus, and I turn up the music to stay awake. The melodic strains of upbeat songs and energetic beats echo through the vehicle, infusing me with a renewed sense of alertness. As the hours wear on, fatigue becomes an unwelcome passenger. I resort to singing along to my favourite tracks at the top of my lungs, the sheer act of vocalization a jolt to the system. Windows down, the brisk Scottish breeze sweeps through the van, invigorating me with its chill. The occasional pit stop at deserted service stations become a respite, a chance to stretch my legs and gulp down caffeinated drinks, each sip a lifeline against the pull of sleep. Driving more, I swerve a few times, succumbing to the sleep and break into a cold sweat as I jump back to life, grabbing the steering wheel and bringing us back into the driving lane. I need to stop and ask Chris to take over.

16th November - Subway, Edinburgh
17th November - Kirkcaldy
18th November - Arbroath

With the final days of Travis Cut now in sight, I get invited by Carl's family to watch him perform at the Royal Albert Hall. Skream! are first on stage, followed by a young US group called The Backstreet Boys and then PJ & Duncan. PJ & Duncan (real names Ant McPartlin and Declan Donnelly) are two actors from a TV drama called Byker Grove, where a bunch of kids from Newcastle shout at each other for thirty minutes.

I've never had a real urge to be seen. It comes with the territory when you're at the back, playing the drums, with two or three bodies bouncing around in front of you. But the need to be more visible becomes a thing. Don't get me wrong; I know I'm a talented drummer. But right now, watching Skream! - an opportunity that I turned down; standing in the Royal Albert Hall as they perform, with a record deal, single, and music video under their belt, I can't help but feel jealous and useless simultaneously. Was it because I deserved to stay in the background, that I should know my place, a reminiscence from Three And A Half Minutes, that being upfront is not something a softly-spoken wallflower should entertain? Have I got what it takes to step out from behind the drum kit and express my musicality in another way? If it means ending up on the stage at the Royal Albert Hall, I'm well up for trying.

The last track Travis Cut record with me as their full-time drummer, is a cover of "Stranglehold" by UK Subs. We set up a recording space in The Square during the night, with all our friends and girlfriends watching. The mood is akin to the final days of The Beatles, without the impending roof gig. I play as fast as I can to give my time with Travis Cut the rightful send-off it deserves. I may have shown off in front of the gang too.

A 21st birthday present from my parents is an 8mm camcorder, which will document the next few years of antics in excruciating detail. I have a friend film the final set I play with Travis Cut at the Square, an all-dayer with UK Subs headlining. We storm through our set in time-honoured fashion, with the odd disruption from the STE collective as they jump on stage and berate the audience for their lack of dancing.

As I play the final strokes of "Open Letter," one half of me doesn't want to leave the stage, whilst the other half is donning the CKOne and ready to hit the dance floor. Chris announces my departure on stage; one of STE finds me after the gig with a look on his face as if someone has told him The Ramones have broken up. From first entering the building four short years ago and creating so many memories, it feels surreal and treacherous I will be trying something different next. But I've made up my mind. Time to leave them all behind.

22nd November – The Drum & Monkey, Ipswich
16th December - The Joiners Arms, Southampton
18th December - The Square, Harlow

1995 - Mixtape

Just - Radiohead
Wonderwall - Oasis
Hey Man, Nice Shot - Filter
On Your Own - The Verve
Lenny - Supergrass
Just When You're Thinking Things Over - The Charlatans
This is a Call - Foo Fighters
Brown Sugar - D'Angelo
Hyperballad - Bjork
Broken Stones - Paul Weller
Back for Good - Take That
Inbetweener - Sleep

CHAPTER 37

THE LONG GOODBYE

1996

Dunblane Massacre, Dolly the sheep, Tamagotchi, Wannabe by Spice Girls, K by Kula Shaker, Return of the Mack by Mark Morrison, Trainspotting, Jerry Maguire.

On the 21st of January, a single called "Spaceman" by Babylon Zoo enters the charts at number one. It is another one-hit wonder courtesy of a Levi's Jeans ad, where the intro is excellent, but the rest of the song is meh. I found out the frontman Jas Mann was the vocalist for popular indie band The Sandkings. I later discovered that because of Spaceman's massive success, there was a redistribution of PR teams at the record company, leaving label-mates In Aura with zero support for their album and tour. Not helped by the sudden departure of their A&R rep to another label, it seems this was the final straw for Matt, Laurence, and Steve. That is it. No more music. I feel sad for them, as the Inaura album is a fine piece of work, and they had so much potential to go further. Having spent Christmas reflecting on the Travis Cut days and still wondering if I've made the right decision, a phone call from Chris pulls me back in for one last job. They have found my replacement, an American chap called Bud, but he hasn't had enough time to learn all my drum parts. Chris asks if I could come up to Purple Rain and record my tracks in super quick-Alex style. I have nothing else to do, so it's back to Great Yarmouth.

Purple Rain is rapidly turning into my second home. We arrive in the evening, set up my kit, and then move on to The Gunner for a nightcap. Except it's been closed down. As a back-up, I've brought some homebrew with me that has mixed reactions, and I'm already regressing to fags and beer. My visit will be swift, but it's nice to be away. By 3pm on day one, I've recorded eight tracks. Because of this speedy work, I'm tempted to go home sooner, as all I'm doing now is filming stuff with the camcorder. The rest of my day is munchies and more munchies, fags, beer, fags, wine, fags, beer. I'm going to regret it.

I visit the beach and nearly get frostbite, the salty air stinging my cheeks. Even with some filming, I feel like I've been sitting around eating all day. Richard's studio assistant Helen invites us for a curry, and we head to her place for a great dinner. Bud is still timid; it must be weird to be with the original line-up as he learns the songs I wrote. They already have a new number called Save Me Now. Having spent a lovely evening, it's time to leave. It's fun up here, but I'm killing time. I'll miss this place.

I've recorded tracks for a new E.P. called "Complicated" and B-sides "Scars", "Look I'm Wrong" and "Interrupted". "Complicated" is a typical energetic Travis Cut song, with some intricate tom-tom work from me and an excellent Sugar style edge to the track. Ironically, these songs feature my best work. But the Travis Cut era is over for me and with Mac and Chris supportive, the split amicable, we part on good terms. They have their new drummer, so I've not left them in the lurch. I will miss the light-hearted moments and sessions with our loyal entourage at The Square.

travis cut

travis cut

7 - PRESTON with Down By Law

20/7 - LEEDS with Down By Law

22/7 - HARLOW with Down By Law

7 - CHELMSFORD Army & Navy

29/7 - LONDON New Cross Venue (tbc)

- LONDON Camden Falcon

UT SINGLE

AKING HOURS

INCOMING!

dist. by S.R.D.

ppy Seconds Tour

- LEEDS Duchess Of York   16/8 - GLASGOW Cathouse

- EDINGURGH Venue   18/8 - DARLINGTON Venue tbc

/8 - LIVERPOOL Venue tbc

21/8 - BRISTOL Fleece & Firkin

22/8 - STOKE Wheatsheaf

23/8 - BIRMINGHAM City Tavern

8 - DERBY Wherehouse

25/8 - LEICESTER Princess Charlotte

waking hours

THIS PAGE:
TRAVIS CUT BAND PHOTO (CREDIT: RUSSELL KENNEDY)
TOUR FLYER
WAKING HOURS SINGLE COVER

GIGGING AT THE SQUARE (CREDIT: UNKNOWN)

HAD A GUN SINGLE PICTURES (CREDIT KELLIE)

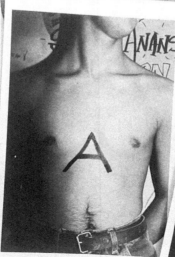

TRAVIS CUT ON TOUR (CREDIT: UNKNOWN)
INSET: ALBUM PHOTO (CREDIT: UNKNOWN)

travis

cut

AND PASS

19 FEB '95

OLD... WINDSOR

ARTIST / CREW

PASS

VALID FOR NIGHT

17 / 8 / 95

TO BE USED FOR VENUE ACCESS
MAIN DOORS AFTER 8.30 p.m.
BY PASS HOLDER ONLY.

THE ONLY ALTERNATIVE!
Fourth Ave, Harlow, Essex, CM20 HDW (0279) 437025
Harlow Town BR - 30 miles from Liverpool St BR

ALL DAY BASH!!!!!
Doors open 3pm - 1st band 4pm

SNUFF + WAT TYLER +
CHINA DRUM + TRAVIS CUT
+ REVERSE + SHUTDOWN +
GOOBER PATROL + THIRST
+ DJs + VIDEOS + DRINKING!

ORDER TO BE ANNOUNCED
SO BE EARLY!!!
BANDS SUBJECT TO FINAL
CONFIRMATION

CHEAPER THAN
LONDON SHOWS
PUB PRICES

Tickets £3.50(adv) £4(on the door)
Saturday 7th January

travis cut

APRIL '95
Mon 24th - London Camden Dublin Castle
        with Collapsed Lung
Weds 26th - Cambridge The Boat Race ($)
Thurs 27th - Birmingham The Foundry ($)
Fri 28th - Brighton Beachcomber ($)
        + RKL
Sat 29th - Peterborough Purple Haze ($)
Sun 30th - Nottingham Narrowboat ($)
MAY '95
Mon 1st - Newcastle Cumberland Arms($)
Tues 2nd - Leeds Duchess Of York ($)
Weds 3rd - Glasgow Nice'n'Sleazy ($)
Thurs 4th - Edinburgh The Venue ($)
Fri 5th - Hull New Adelphi ($) (tbc)
Sat 6th - Wakefield Players #
        with Chopper
Sun 7th - Manchester Star & Garter ($)
Mon 8th - Reading After Dark ($)
Tues 9th - Bristol (venue tbc) ($)
Weds 10th - Rayleigh Pink Toothbrush
        with Bracket
Fri 12th - Canterbury Penny Theatre #
Weds 17th - London Archway St Johns
        Tavern #
        with Gan + The Strookas
Thurs 18th - Worcester The Stage #
Fri 19th - London The Garage ($)
Weds 24th - London Camden Laurel Tree
        with Dr Bison

'SERIAL   (S) = supporting THE QUEERS
           # = headline shows
INCOMPETENCE'

THE WHERE HOUSE
Promotions
ARTIST TRAVIS CUT
VENUE THE WHEREHOUSE
DATE 24/8/94

THE garage

BAND PASS

22 MAR '95

VENUE
LONDON

BAND
Snuff

DATE
20/6/98

MAIN: BACKSTAGE PASSES / INSETS: SQUARE ALL-DAYER FLYER / WHERHOUSE PASS

TRAVIS CUT IN SCOTLAND (CREDIT: UNKNOWN)

TRAVIS CUT AT CLUB KIFF (CREDIT: UNKNOWN)

SNUFF GIG PASS

COMPLICATED 7" COVER

VENUE
LONDON

BAND

Snuff

DATE

30/6/95

ACCESS ALL AREAS

TRAVIS CUT

COMPLICATED

PART THREE

CHAPTER 38

BOY NEXT DOOR

With my new change in direction, the dream of making it could be tantalizingly close. I'm not ready to drop everything and become an accountant. It feels weird not focusing on drumming, but after being at the back for the last four years, its liberating to try something different. Emily has accepted a seasonal job working in chalets in France for the ski season. Rather than prolonging things with delayed letters and fuzzy phone calls between shifts, we agree to end our relationship. She's been a steadfast presence over the last few months, kept me grounded and a beguiling distraction from the Travis Cut rollercoaster.

I've bought the performing arts paper The Stage, hoping the perfect opportunity will appear and answer all my problems. One boldly captioned advert catches my eye. Boy Next Door is a management/record company, advertising positions for all kinds of acts and groups to be launched in early 1996. My mate Peter is still studying at Italia Conti and has already auditioned. Italia Conti has spawned many household names, including Russel Brand, Patsy Kensit, Louise Redknapp, David Van Day, and Tracey Ullman. I'm not entirely sure if I can meet the same calibre Peter has, but I take the plunge anyway and sign up to audition.

With the date, time and venue provided, I had imagined entering a vibrant office building fronted by a receptionist who is also a model. The lobby would be adorned with gold discs and framed, signed pictures of the CEO hugging NKOTB and Bruno Brookes. I'd imagined being ushered into a plush conference room with glass bottles of water everywhere, a faint smell of vetiver, the arrival of said MD, chewing gum, chatting on his mobile and wearing an Omega. Nope. Turns out the company is one rotund guy called Glenn, in his one-bed flat in Tulse Hill. At least the Upside Down auditions had numbered tickets and important people wearing headsets.

Here, I can smell bacon sandwiches mingled with a cat tray that needs sorting. Noticing my apprehension, Glenn talks about my travel to London and why I called the number. When I mention Peter, the vibe gets friendlier, and it looks like Glenn is nobly trying to build something exciting. The audition involves singing karaoke to a Take That music video. Singing is not my strong point, but I battle through "Back for Good" while Glenn makes me a cup of tea.

Upon his return, Glenn requests to take some photos and so I stand in front of his kitchen door, trying to look hot and sexy, distracted by onlookers from the double-decker bus passing by the window. Glenn clumsily readjusts his glasses and tries different angles with his disposable camera. He suggests a few more, but maybe this time with my top off. Now, at this stage, the red flags should have been waving furiously and the words "ABORT ABORT" ringing loud and clear, but no. I think, well, everybody's got to start somewhere, right? And boy bands do tend to be half-dressed most of the time. I'd inherited a fabulous sheepskin coat, so I put that back on to salvage the slowly evaporating dignity. I pose half naked, trying to breathe in, channelling Patrick Swayze from Roadhouse. Thankfully this is all that is asked of me.

Still flinching from the dodgy visit to Glenn's, I am comforted by the fact Peter is still involved, and I hope we can both smell a rat if things get seedier. Days later, Glenn calls me and asks if I would join his flagship act, Duo. I am flattered, and forgetting the budget audition, I accept. My co-member is a lovely chap called Mark, who looks like he could be Brett Anderson's younger, skinnier brother. Right before Telstar drop them, Carl decides to call it a day with Skream!. Still wanting to stay in the game, he introduces himself to Boy Next Door. He joins us with his pop socialite friend Jolene, where all things come to a head at a "label launch party" in a gay bar called Brief Encounter in London's West End. Glenn has three acts to showcase: Our band Duo, a trio Peter is in and a six-piece boy band Carl has his eye on. It's a motley crew of people, a selection of young men of different heights and hairstyles and Glenn's family who look remarkably like a Royle Family tribute band. Throughout the afternoon, group photos of each act are taken, champagne is distributed, and contracts are handed around.

The contracts have stipulations that include a 5-year management deal. Debts if you leave. A requirement to pay personally for booking agents. The whole thing feels worrisome, and we are concerned that we are expected to sign our careers away after merrily swigging glasses of champagne. Realising this could be a big mistake and a flawed enterprise, Carl, Jolene, myself, and another savvy guy we've befriended called Matt, make a swift exit. Matt is a suave handsome chap with a winning smile, not dissimilar to Brad Pitt. He had refused to take his top off for Glenn, which won me instant respect. I mean, why didn't I say no? It turns out Matt's family are showbiz royalty, with his mum being Clodagh Rodgers and his father John Morris, who is also his mum's manager. Clodagh is an Irish singer and former Eurovision entrant, still performing in musicals and shows.

We grab a drink in Leicester Square and stuff our faces at an all-you-can-eat Chinese buffet, chatting about the surreal afternoon we've just had. Jolene invites us to stay at a flat she is renting in West London with her mum. Numerous cups of tea are consumed, with each of us talking about our lives. Then an idea dawns. We don't need Glenn. Let's go it alone. With our collective industry contacts, Matt's famous mum, this could be exciting. We stay up all night scheming until a new boy band is finally born. The next day I leave a message on Glenn's answerphone to say it isn't for me and then to Mark saying the Duo would have to be Solo.

CHAPTER 39
DELUSIONS OF GRANDEUR

The three of us decided on a band name: NV (basically how you would say Envy, but cooler and shorter). We dive into an intensive two-week bonding period – going out, blagging free entry into clubs, and being with each other 24/7 to ensure we get along. On most days, we're either in London or wandering around Bishop's Stortford filming the band's antics with my trusty camcorder. We have high ambitions. Three hopefuls sitting in my shitty Nissan Cherry on Carl's driveway, listening to Take That's farewell single on the radio. Who will replace them, we mused as knowing smiles spread across our goateed faces. There's no way they could reform so why not us?

We feel some networking is needed, to get our name out there. This involves attending all the party hot spots in London. The Met Bar. Mezzo. The Emporium. The Atlantic Bar and Grill. Hanover Grand. Brown's. All are on our hit list. Additionally, we have no qualms about phoning local nightclubs, pretending to be the band's manager. We tell them we are booked to perform soon and would like to visit the club in advance (for free, of course). This fraudulent claim mostly proves successful, so we manage to blag-free entry to regular haunt Dukes and Harpers in Guildford, Matt's old stomping ground.

We stay over at Matt's for a bit too, getting to know his mum. It was surreal to chat with Clodagh in her kitchen, wearing a baggy jumper and leggings as she cooks spaghetti bolognese for Matt and his younger brother, Sam. She'd worked with light entertainment legends Bruce Forsyth, Jimmy Tarbuck, Mike Yarwood and Des 'O Connor, but is still a regular mum putting food on the table at home. Carl was quite taken with Clodagh, he also saw her as another opportunity, especially when it came to blagging free tickets to see her in the musical Blood Brothers. Carl has a rare talent for blagging his way into almost anywhere.

Our first big piece of exposure comes from an "Exclusive" feature in the Herts & Essex Observer, lamenting the split of Skream!

"In an exclusive interview with the Young Observer, Carl (20) of Bishops Stortford revealed the reasons behind the decisions to split and his bid to make it big with his new band, NV. He said each of them had been unhappy with the band's progress. "James basically didn't want to do it anymore and was dubious about the whole music industry. Things went very quiet after Christmas, and we decided to split because we weren't happy, and everybody wanted to go their separate ways. The announcement was met with mixed reactions - some had thought the band would hit the big time, while others were more sceptical. Carl has remained on good terms with Telstar and talks were underway about striking up a deal with his new band. Again, there are three members of NV. They include Carl, 21-year-old Alex Boucher and Matthew Morris (20). Now we'll just have to wait and see whether the latest band can make it big in the pop world."

One venue we frequent is The Chilled Eskimo in Ladbroke Grove, linked to actors John and Nick Pickard. Nick is starting a role in the new Channel 4 soap opera Hollyoaks. The Chilled Eskimo becomes our local, with many lock-ins courtesy of Nick's younger brother and plenty of celeb-spotting whilst we hang out attempting to look famous. I love the vibe there, with its wooden flooring, shabby chic decor and acid jazz background music. The Hanover Grand or Brown's in Holborn are the places to be seen. Branded as "exclusive" I always feel a shiver of imposter syndrome as the rope is pulled across and I'm waved in by the attractive door staff. Brown's is a world away from Dukes; no fag machines in sight, or a two-for-one deal on shots of Aftershock. When the bartender does eventually notice you, the choices are champagne or champagne. The dancefloor is smoke and mirrors; they line the walls, encircling tall and slender women in slinky dresses throwing elegant shapes amidst the dry ice, hoping to get spotted by a talent scout or just waiting to be picked up by a coked-up millionaire. I wonder if I'll get found out, wearing my shirt from C&A and a pair of jeans that were on offer in Burton. The shiny and dimly lit toilets are not used for such bodily functions, the cubicles are permanently engaged and used for business meetings where execs talk rubbish at each other as they hoover up a white line or two. Bottles of aftershave are littered around the wash basins, looking more like the men's fragrance counter at Debenhams. I fritter long nights in Brown's catching up with Carl's Telstar mates and wondering if Kylie Minogue will ever show up (she doesn't). My favourite haunt is the Atlantic Bar & Grill, a stylish venue that feels like the inside of the upper-class deck of The Titanic. I get a sore neck constantly looking around, spotting artists like Tracy Emin and Damien Hirst, or members of Pulp and Elastica wandering in.

We pick up a manager on the way - a big guy named Phil who had managed Ultimate Kaos. Phil is softly spoken but doesn't suffer fools. He looks like he could be our bodyguard too. Seeing our potential, he drops a boy band called Tracer to work with us. Phil plays us some song demos we might want to use for record companies and gigs. This is a different set-up to what I'm used to; rather than investing a week writing a song in a chilly rehearsal room on an industrial estate, the work has already been done. There are two songs we like. One is a moody, soulful pop track called "Keep on Loving", and the other is a dance track written by Tim Hegarty (Irish co-writer for D:Ream) called "Free to Love". The problem is, that these songs are currently "optioned", so recording them might be a waste of time if another band with their eyes on it secures the rights.

Desperate to get in the studio, we end up recording a different track altogether, called "Last Kiss", written by flamboyant singer-songwriter Drew, in a draughty studio near Dartford. There is a picture of Tony Hadley from Spandau Ballet on the wall, not exactly Lemmy, but I'll go with it. With Pot Noodles packed, we record the demo overnight (at cheaper rates) with Drew, some engineers, and producers. The song is a saccharine sweet ballad about catching that first kiss before the last dance finishes. If you dip a strawberry in treacle and melted chocolate, then feed it to a unicorn on a bed of roses, you're halfway there. Even Boyz II Men would tap out on this one.

Here's the chorus:

"I've been saving my first kiss for the last dance of the night
You're trying hard to resist, the chance of a kiss goodnight
And if it's the last dance, it's the last chance
For our lips to be falling in love
So, I'm saving my first kiss for the last dance of the night"

This is a far cry from sweary punk-pop songs about unrequited love and hate mail. Drew stoops over the extensive recording desk, keeping his blonde dreadlocks at bay, a packet of soft duty-free cigarettes never far from his pinstriped elbow.

It's my big moment in the vocal booth. I walk up to the microphone and slide on the chunky headphones that are lying on a stool. It's dimly lit, freezing and quiet. There's a hint of mildew. Drew's voice interrupts the damp silence.

"Hello Alex, can you hear me?"

"Yep."

"Great. This is how we'll communicate from now on - we'll play the backing track through the cans, and you just sing your lines into the mic okay?"

I stop myself from mounting the high horse to tell him this isn't my first rodeo.

I say understood and wait for the track to start. The piano strikes up. The Upside Down audition comes flooding back and I shake my arms ready to sing.

"So, as we come to the end of the night"

The track stops.

"Hi Alex, can you hear me?"

"Yes"

"A bit flat there, needs some more tuning and give it a breathy kind of vibe, yeah?"

I evoke a whispering tone and try to hit the notes.

"So, as we come to the end of the night".

"Hi Alex, can you hear me?"

"Yes."

"So that breathy thing you do is nice. Still not getting the notes and the phrasing is off. I want you to pause after *come*, so it goes like: So, as we come.. to the end of the night"

Drew sings it perfectly and I squirm in the darkness knowing full well I'm under-rehearsed and nowhere near the standard of Backstreet Boys.

We go again.

"So,"

"Hi Alex, can you hear me?"

I'm tempted to stay silent.

"Yep"

"That first word, "So" needs to have some real impact - give it some welly in a sexy way yeah? Like this - "So""

Drew sounds like a gravelly Mick Hucknall when he sings. I'm more like a builder with delusions of grandeur.

"Alright, I'll give it a try".

"Nice one. Here comes the track, we are now recording".

"So, as we come".

"Hi Alex, can you hear me?"

We stumble on for what feels like an age trying to get my one line right. It becomes clear Carl has the strongest singing voice, so Matt and I attempt to bluff our way through our given sections of the ballad. It's taken me forever to sing one line of a lyric that isn't tone-deaf. It's another "learning" experience for the band, but I burn all the demo evidence. It is truly awful.

With the recording over, Jolene arranges a press trip near her home turf of Nottingham, setting up a local newspaper interview and photo session. It is a chance to hit the road as a band, and see some old friends based in the area too. With nothing tangible to promote, this might be deemed a waste of time, but it's great being in a new band and going on road trips again.

Using Jolene's home as a base, we look in on our friends, visit quaint pubs and go to a nightclub called The Black Orchid. The Black Orchid is rough. Like a Northern version of Dukes. The air is thick with the aroma of spilt beer and the unmistakable scent of cigarette smoke lingering from the designated smoking area. The men sport a uniform of football tops, checked shirts with rolled-up sleeves, tight tops and tight denim, while women showcase an array of high heels, miniskirts, and fur-trimmed jackets.

We do a photoshoot the next day, but Matt doesn't get into it for some reason. It's hard to work Matt out sometimes; he's quiet and more of an observer than a doer. We get an invite from Telstar to see PJ & Duncan for free in London, so we head back south. On the way, Phil makes a pitstop in Cambridge. We wait patiently inside the sleek black van as Phil runs an errand for a promoter. There's a pop roadshow concert taking place and Phil has parked up alongside the venue. As the minutes tick by, we peer through tinted windows, our eyes scanning the surroundings for any sign of his return. Suddenly, a burst of giggles and whispers erupts from the pavement. A group of girls, their faces adorned with expressions of curiosity, have spotted us through the van's windows. The realization dawns that we must be performing tonight, or at least someone notable, and a wave of excitement ripples through the group like wildfire. Within moments, what started as hushed whispers turns into a crescendo of ecstatic screams. The girls, unable to contain their enthusiasm, rush towards the van. We exchange wide-eyed glances, hearts pounding with a mix of exhilaration and apprehension. The van's windows are soon adorned with the imprints of eager palms and smeared lipstick. The girls fire rapid questions at us, their voices muffled by the glass, "What band are you" "What are your names" "You're fit", their faces pressed against the windows like eager spectators at a sold-out concert. Inside the van, I'm navigating a whirlwind of emotions. Laughter mingled with nervous chuckles as we swap bemused glances, realizing the surreal nature of this sudden popularity. I find myself grappling with the novelty of being the object of such intense adoration. Just as the excitement reaches its peak, Phil emerges, calmly dividing the crowd with both arms, mobile phone in hand. The door creaks open, and Phil, sensing the overwhelming situation, turns the ignition and very slowly pulls away. He turns back to us, once we're in the clear. "I think you've got something special, lads!"

PJ & Duncan are playing at the Royal Albert Hall again. In the bar, I meet Anita, who works at Creation Records, the label that signed Oasis. Turns out she was the girl on the Wonderwall single cover. I also find out Andy Saunders from Scared Hitless works there too. Backstage, I'm bought a drink by a lovely woman who works for Telstar. She's about eight years older than me and has a cheeky but forthright way about her; I can tell she's the kind of lady who always gets what she wants. She likes my sheepskin coat and is impressed to hear I've been in this crazy game for 5 years. A beer fight ensues with a mad bloke called Phil Seidl, who also works for Telstar. Anita puts us up for the night, where the rest of the evening is spent talking about Oasis, boy bands and my photographic memory of James Bond films.

The NV entourage is growing, and with each day comes a new invite to attend a party and meet someone from Carl's network. It usually takes about 2 hours to get ready as we try on new togs, recheck ourselves in the mirror and swap clothes. We're a close-knit trio, and I love that we share everything, even cigarettes. Matt's family has a stake in a bar called Volley's in Wimbledon, so this becomes a regular rendezvous spot before we jump in a taxi and head to somewhere like the Ministry of Sound or the Met Bar to meet with Anita, Jolene, and Phil from Telstar.

At a Top of the Pops after-party at the Ministry of Sound, I bump into the feisty woman from Telstar again and we use the evening trying to flirt and chat over the deafening dance music. After downing another drink, she stands up, takes my hand, and says, "Let's go."

We jump in a cab back to her place and stay up all the night listening to all our favourite songs and getting to know each other. This never happened after visiting The Ship Inn in Oundle, so I'm buzzing, getting used to this new shiny trainee pop star life. She suggests some ideas about how to give NV the best chances to make it, and reckons we've got what it takes. It seems we are rapidly becoming the flavour of the month. But where are the songs? We need to get back in the studio and record a hit single.

CHAPTER 40

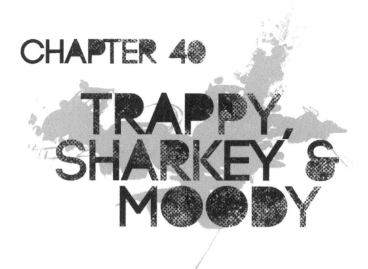

TRAPPY, SHARKEY & MOODY

The partying continues with a group trip to Bagley's in Kings Cross, a massive club based at the former site of a coal yard and warehouse. The colossal building houses about three dance floors, all playing different types of techno, rave and hardcore choons. Bagley's is a mecca for Carl, who has the infinite energy to dance through the night, with or without drugs. I am still an indie fan but throw on Disco's Revenge by Gusto, and I'm in. At one point, I end up on a staging area, dancing in front of a massive crowd. A raver next to me passes me his joint, which has an odd green glow, rather than the usual orange embers. I take a drag as he says, "get some zero zero down you mate".

I have no idea what he meant, but thirty minutes later, I am having the hottest flush I have ever experienced. I start to feel disorientated, constantly wiping my arm across my sweaty forehead, looking around for someone sympathetic who might notice what I'm going through. Desperately needing air, I stumble and stagger as if I'm on a rocky ship, through three packed club rooms to get to the fire exit, murmuring, "Sorry mate", "Excuse me", and "Passing through" to the beats of Bizarre Inc. It feels like I've walked for miles, trying to keep it together and not lose myself in a downward spiral of paranoia, a voice in my head repeatedly asking, "What have you taken?"

Outside, I take a seat and attempt to calm down, my stomach now feeling it's been put on spin mode. After a few deep breaths of the night air, I soon spot Carl, Matt and a few others who have come to look for me outside. I find out zero zero is another word for crack. I've spent four years in indie and punk bands, but no, it's during the boy-band era I end up smoking crack. The drugs don't work. Unable to make it home in one piece, I find a telephone box and call my guardian angel using my BT phone card. She lets me crash at hers again, and even with my monologues about James Bond, she still doesn't throw me out and says I can stay as often as I like.

Her flat in Clapham occupies the ground floor of an old, terraced house just off the Common. The front room has undulating floorboards and a fireplace, a sofa draped in leopard print, Persian rugs and piles of takeaway menus. When the sun hits, it feels like Janis Joplin might wander in and ask for a whiskey. I love the decor and the vibe. Her bedroom in the back is a storage room for CDs with just enough space for a bed. She shares the flat with another young professional who is hardly ever home so during the day, I get to have the place to myself. It's a nice place to be, listening to Aphex Twin, compiling mix tapes and journaling until dusk, waiting to hear her keys jangle in the door. I get conscious that I might be staying over too much, so I remain a maximum of two nights before the food or water usage becomes an issue; I am still a fan of taking long baths and listening to music, but now fully aware that someone else is paying the bills. Her lifestyle seems idyllic, a beautiful flat, cushy job at a record company, Swinging London, the epicentre of Cool Britannia and all its diversions on her doorstep. Free parking outside and Clapham Common to stroll around in the summer. Maybe I should start thinking about leaving the family nest.

The Dartford experiment was proof to appoint Carl as main vocalist, and we end up back in a studio in Camden with Tim Hegarty. The track "Free to Love" sounds like D:Ream, but at least we can dance to this one. Tim is a lively hyperactive chap, and it takes a full day to record. Carl sings the lead, with Matt and I bringing up the backing vocals with an "It's Alright, It's Alright" refrain and joining Carl on the chorus for "I will be free, free to love when I'm here with you". If you sing "Things Can Only Get Better" in your head, it's kind of the same vibe.

From visiting Matt's home in Surrey and seeing a photo of Clodagh sitting with Ringo Starr on the same sofa I was on, a few favours may be called in if the band start to make some waves. One such request is made by Clodagh to her friend and photographer, Patti Boyd. Yes, Patti Boyd. Sixties icon and the ex-Mrs George Harrison, ex-Mrs Eric Clapton. We book an afternoon at her West London studio. The weather is good, so we end up on the roof, attempting to look sexy in all those stock boy band poses you can think of. We have a few sessions with an opera singer who trains us in breathing and projection. We even get a free clothing endorsement from Mossimo. Remember them? The band dynamic is well balanced, with Carl being the chatty, excitable puppy who can't keep his mouth shut, Matt ready to pounce on the ladies given the chance and myself being the silent, frustrated artist and deep lukewarm water in the middle. Somebody labels us Trappy, Sharky and Moody. This nails it, to be fair. With the track in the can and a nice line of clothes on our backs, all that is left is to perform.

CHAPTER 41
THE BEACON RADIO MIMING DISASTER

Finally, a gig opportunity has turned up. All that mingling and networking is about to pay off. Right?

A day-long outdoor radio roadshow by Beacon FM is happening in Dudley, Birmingham, featuring mid-tier pop acts, such as Blair, Gemini, and Crush - another Telstar-signed Byker Grove duo featuring the actress Donna Air. We work for an afternoon in Brixton with a choreographer, Derek, who teaches us our "Free to Love" dance routine. He provides us with some cheesy moves including the "elbow pump", the "falling to the knees and slipping a coat off one shoulder" move, and the ever popular "pointing to the left and slowly panning it to the right". We still have reservations about this song; it's off the shelf D:Ream, and there are other tracks we would have preferred. Nevertheless, the big day comes around quickly, and we all journey up to Dudley in Phil's car. We listen to the Trainspotting soundtrack on the way, it's good to hear "Sing" by Blur again.

It is a cold and wet day, with our slot somewhere in the afternoon. The vibes are similar to a festival, with a slow procession of cars snaking into the grounds of Himley Hall. The grey weather has not improved as we transfer from Phil's car into a golf cart that takes us to the backstage area. The mood is quiet and tense, a feeling that could be translated as massively unprepared or about to make a huge impact on the pop world. I am veering between both and wondering what Travis Cut are up to. Filming with my camcorder, we are visibly nervous, wandering around the backstage tents in our oddly fitting beige Mossimo clothes.

Time for our turn. We take to the stage to rapturous applause and screams from our friends. There are hundreds of people, all soaking wet and cheering us on. It is a great reception, and we feel welcome. This is it. I'm finally at the front, waving at the audience and lapping up the attention. I've done it; the plan has worked! My transition is now paying off, and I don't even care it's raining. Why didn't I do this sooner? Who cares about this new flash-in-the-pan scene called "Britpop" everyone is into? Get some Europop tunes down you, courtesy of NV!

We are to perform the song miming from the backing track, with Carl improvising vocals using a live microphone. We take positions, our backs to the audience, hands crossed and feet apart. I'm channelling Robbie Williams, ready to win over hundreds of new fans. Come on, Alex. The track starts. We spin around and stomp toward the front, using the moves Derek had shown us. Then within seconds, the music jumps like a broken record. Fuck.

We look at each other confused, as Carl tries to remedy the situation with a quick gag and reassurance to the crowd. What the hell? This isn't good. We glance backstage and see a thumbs-up from Phil as he cues the track to start again. We go again from the top. Positions. Hands. Feet apart. I'm Robbie Fucking Williams. Tape jumps again. Fucking Fuck. By now, my worst fears are being played out on stage; nerves are more frayed with each second. Laughter is coming from the crowd, and Carl is stuttering into the mic, saying, "What's going on? They've completely mucked it up!".

Time stands still. I can feel the Jedi ghosts of Three and A Half Minutes and Travis Cut shaking their heads at me in sorrow. The compere comes on, jokes about batteries running out, promising the crowd we will be back once the technical glitch is fixed. We go backstage to see Phil sweating and flustered over the DAT player, in denial about it being broken.

I stand there, holding my useless switched-off microphone, wondering what the hell I've gotten myself into. If we can't perform then this was a monumental waste of a day, and all that practice has been for nothing. Then, Carl runs to the car and grabs a cassette of the song that we can use on our return to the stage. We must wait for another act to finish and pace the backstage area, silent and tense. Matt and Carl's faces are dark and stormy, flustered by the embarrassing mess.

Back on stage, my heart is pounding, and I am praying this will work out. Positions. Hands. Feet apart. Not now, Robbie. At this point, I'm going to give it my all. The adrenaline has kicked in, and I feel exposed without a drum kit in front of me. I put this to one side and go for it and savour it. The performance runs fine without any further issues - our dance moves are a tad dodgy, and Matt prowls the stage, shaking his stick mic like Liam Gallagher. Due to the technical fault, we even get a mini on-stage interview from the DJ compere. We've done it. NV has debuted their first performance. It's a hollow victory because of the false start and shit weather, but I hope it's upward from here.

Stopping at a service station, we sit down in various heaps, drawing a collective sigh. `Don't worry boys, we'll get you a record deal.'

Phil talks with such a laidback tone I'm not sure if I'm hearing quiet confidence or a polite lie. He walks off, patting each pocket before finding his mobile phone, extending the plastic antenna and making a call, strolling away from earshot. He never takes calls in our presence, so I'm starting to wonder if these are crucial industry conversations or the number three set menu from the local Chinese.

We're feeling despondent from today's sordid events, a veritable clusterfuck that we managed to crawl our way out of, salvaged by our collective charm and the sympathy of a kind audience. I've been dealt a double whammy after phoning home and finding out my grandfather has died. Matt has gone mute again, surveying the services station surroundings, like Clint Eastwood from a western. Carl grows uneasy at the silence, before creasing his face into a smile, standing up with a flourish and announcing he is off to buy cigarettes. I know I'll be asking for one later, so I am thinking about requesting a certain brand, not the Rothmans he buys, just because they come in packs of 25 and not 20. But I can't be arsed. I look down at my damp designer shoes and shuffle my shoulders in my baggy Mossimo jacket; this garb has been wearing me all afternoon, not the other way around. Jolene, in her homely Nottinghamshire drawl, asks if anyone would like a cup of tea. Matt requests sparkling water in a voice that's more Claridge's than M1 Services, and I give a meek nod, not used to being waited on like I'm George Michael. I find a couple of plastic stirrers and start a rhythm around the cups and ashtray to keep my mind off things. Sensing irritation from the gang, I stop with a solo worthy of Keith Moon and break them in the process which is appropriate. I look around the desolate cafeteria, taking in the atmosphere of temporary pitstops, a halfway house for full bladders, hungry kids and weary truck drivers. The WHSmith store is bulging with stacks of Angela's Ashes and Bridget Jones' Diary, a tiny casino with 4 fruit machines blinks and tinkles in the corner. The corridor leading to the toilets has a revolving procession of visitors, the hand dryers roaring in the background like a mythical sea beast ready to drown another victim. I've been here before. It could have been two years ago with Travis Cut, or four years ago when I was in Three and A Half Minutes. Now I'm in a boyband. Even though Britpop is ruling the charts, the youngsters still crave handsome boys singing perfect pop. Four months in, it's been an interesting experiment, one that I'm not sure is proving successful based on today's fiasco. We have to put faith in Phil. He does another lap of the cafe. I need to pull this band together, convince Matt that he can follow in his mother's star-studded footsteps and work with Carl on bettering his previous experience with record companies. Jolene places the tea, with a friendly `There you go luv´ - I stare at the shiny brown surface, moving it closer to avoid Carl's flamboyant use of the ashtray. Life on the road. Life in a band. I ask him for a spare cigarette, attempt to reset the jacket on my shoulders and sit up. I want to make this work. This time around, the band will get there. Phil canters over, whirring his forefinger in a military style, our signal to get back to the people-carrier and return to London. We slowly gather our things, I look back at the makeshift drumsticks, lying in pieces on the table and try not to smirk at the irony. I can't help but ask myself, 'What the fuck am I doing?´

On the drive home, the car breaks down. Hours later, I finally make it back to Stansted, a nervous wreck.

CHAPTER 42

KEEP ON LOVING

With the debacle of Dudley still ringing in our ears, we have some leverage to convince Phil our song should have been "Keep on Loving" from the get-go. With Clodagh joining us, we book an afternoon recording the track in a studio near Bognor Regis. This is another favour called in by Phil, and it feels like his free credits are drying up. Carl takes lead vocals, with Matt and me on "sexy talk" duties, plus backing vocals for the chorus. Clodagh adds an excellent "Keep on" refrain to the last section of the song, giving it a haunting edge. The song has heart, with funky Soul II Soul vibes. If this song ever gets released, Jazzie B will probably lawyer up. Regardless, we now have a demo we are happy with, so it is time to try and pitch NV to the record industry. We still have an in with Telstar, so we build a presentation pack featuring a biography of the band, plus the shots from the Patti Boyd shoot.

With some inside help, Phil meets with the label to discuss our potential. Then, right as this could be the crucial turning point, Carl goes on an impromptu holiday. Closely followed by Matt to the US. Like Vincent Vega in Pulp Fiction, I'm left gazing around for company. The set-up in the band always pinned me as the more grown-up member, having the battle scars from former groups. A role I haven't asked for. I want to have fun for a change!

On his return, I discover Matt has re-recorded the song, singing the lead vocals instead. I choose not to share this obvious power-play with Carl. With no progress from Telstar and unable to get past the Dudley gig, we decide to end our relationship with Phil. Having made the exit speech before with other bands, I must give Phil the bad news. We sit in his black van as I explain why it's best to part ways. Most of what I say is waffle; we all know it's the Dudley gig, and the lack of favours left as the main reason. Judging by the lack of energy from Matt and Carl, I feel like our last chance saloon is a man called Tim Smith, former manager of Skream! He's looked after other Telstar signings and PWL groups. Without a good manager, we'll be left high and dry. I ask Carl if an urgent meeting with Tim could be arranged. Tim's open to having a chat, so we meet in his office in Holborn. As with many boy-band managers he's a big, heavy-set dude with a cap and a no-nonsense energy. We play him the "Keep on Loving" and "Free to Love" demos, watching Tim nervously as he quietly nods his head, avoiding eye contact. After a dramatic silence he asks us what we think of our image. We glance at each other, checking to see who will do their best to describe our look first. Before one of us can attempt it, Tim suggests we change our identity to something edgier and current, closer to an act like The Prodigy. Their number one single, "Firestarter", has turned them into a mainstream act, and the heavy guitar on the single gained them a new rock audience on top of the ravers. This is something I am well up for. A boy band with a punkier edge and rocking songs. Fuck yes. But this idea doesn't sit well with Carl, and things slowly falter for the three of us as we try to cling to something that is fading fast.

CHAPTER 43
TOO CLOSE

In a last-ditch attempt to revive things and get our creative juices flowing, the three of us are invited to a song-writer's house to come up with original material. The plan is to write and rehearse, have dinner, and stay over. Matt, Carl, and I arrive at his lovely house outside London, and we chat around the table as he prepares the food for later. We crack some jokes about our band name and the embarrassing events at Dudley. The mood is buoyant, and this is what the band needs; a proper creative afternoon working on music and building morale.

We head up to his studio, a long thin room with a keyboard, speakers, and an 8-track recording desk. We all squeeze in around the keyboard.

Cigarette smoke fills the room within seconds, all of us idly wafting the smoke away from our faces. I start to suggest the type of song we want to compose, instruments we should use, that kind of thing. I hope we can come up with something that resonates with each of us. Carl is into funky bands like the Brand New Heavies. Matt has a fondness for Take That and MOR music. I can't bring punk or alternative vibes to the table, but I want that raw emotion to be captured. I am the most vocal with suggestions, having spent the last few years in and out of studios and rehearsal rooms.

I know the back and forth needed to be creative, the sounds we should utilise, and the dynamic and structure of a song. The seed of an idea you grow through collaboration. Unfortunately, Carl and Matt get bored quickly. If smartphones had been invented back then, they would have been glued to their screens. Sensing bored reluctance, the session is cut short, and we all head downstairs for drinks and dinner. We talk about the band, plans, the songwriter's career, etc. People start to yawn. Time to retire.

As we head up the stairs, our host announces there is a bedroom for 2 of us to share; the other person would have to share with him. Quick as a flash, Matt and Carl dart for the bedroom and close the door. I've slept on many floors, squats, and backs of vans to be prepared for a rough night and whilst I feel annoyed to be separated, I go along with whatever makeshift bed is available. It is a double mattress laid on the floor. It's in the smoky thin room we'd been rehearsing in.

I take the side closest to the wall, and he strips down to T-shirt and boxer shorts, turns off the light, gets into bed and mutters a "G'night". I've had a few glasses of wine, so it doesn't take me long to drift off.

I wake up suddenly. Sensing it too early to be morning, I realise something has stirred me. Something feels odd. Then I realise a hand is in between my legs. It's right up near to my buttocks. I want to quickly check if it is my hand, stupidly hoping, praying even, that this is the case. Nope. Not mine. I break into a cold sweat. He can tell I've woken up, so I move my body as close to the wall as I can, pressing myself against it, making as much space as possible between him and me. I don't know what to do. He's a well-built man and could easily overpower me, given a chance.

My imagination creates so many scenarios, each one worse than the next; rape scenes from movies, the desperation in a victim's face, unable to move, having the worst of violations inflicted on them. I can't move; it is as if my whole body has frozen in stasis. The hand withdraws and he turns over. I've gone over this scenario many times, and the same "should haves" always arise. I should have decked him. I should have found a sofa downstairs. I should have knocked on Matt and Carl's door. But as everyone does in these situations, I froze. And the weirdest thing? The next day, we all act like nothing happened. We have breakfast and then leave. I try to tell Matt and Carl what happened, but it gets misheard and shrugged off. Just a grope from some horny songwriter trying his luck after too much wine. I lock it away, counting myself lucky. Lucky. What a coward I am to be "thankful" nothing else happened.

It happened; no escaping that. I tell that guy to go fuck himself whenever this memory surfaces. Like many abused people, there's a mixture of guilt, anger, and embarrassment. Coming up in a cold sweat as the memory reappears, trying desperately to push it back in its box in my head, brushing it away and getting on with things. "It's nothing" and "I'm fine" are the mantras used. I even begin to feel guilty. Did I say something that gave him the wrong impression? Touch his arm without thinking? Maybe because I'm in a boy band there's some expectation that I'm gay, or bi-sexual or probably up for it either way? The whole thing starts to feel tainted. There's no camaraderie in this pop industry, just vanity, shallowness, and an expectation to succeed if you rub yourself against the right person.

"The Old Adage"

In times of strife and prosperous nerves
Humming the tune, forgetting the words
Having another one, checking the time
Acting the lemon, feeling sublime
Eyelids drooping, tasting the dark
Remembering dreams, vivid and stark
Fuck me I'm bored, what shall we do
A pointless existence, left there to stew
Refusing to smile, wanting to cry
Talking of riches, letting time fly
No motivation, a childish big wish
Mad drunken ramblings, shooting no fish
A gift long forgotten, contacts let slip
Moan fucking moan, a sarcastic quip
He stands before you, small and bereft
A faded wannabe, the only one left.

The last official appearance of NV as a band is at a glamorous fancy dress party for a friend of Carl's called Miranda. She was one of Gina G's backing dancers for the Eurovision entry, "Ooh, Ah, Just a Little Bit" and has performed with PJ & Duncan numerous times.

We head down on a double-decker party bus to deepest Sussex, decked out in Heroes or Villains attire. Carl is dressed as a mobster; I am James Bond, and Matt is Brad Pitt from Se7en. We're sat near two members of pop band Deuce clad in black catsuits, Gina G's other backing dancers, Michelle, and Chloe, dressed as army recruits and a dance coach called Kevin Adams, decked out as Marcellus Wallace, holding court at the back of the bus.

The party is more like a wedding in a big tent, with a three-course meal and various music industry guests milling about. No Gina G, or PJ & Duncan, though. We hardly talk about band-related plans that night, so I take it as a signal nobody cares anymore. We get roaringly drunk, though, so every cloud. After the fancy dress party, I head to Clapham to check in before my drive back home. It feels as if I've walked in on the wrong flat. She's cold and mono-syllabic; recoils when I go in for a kiss. It feels transactional, as if I am there to mend the boiler. She moves back. I move forward, frustrated and confused at this tense standoff we're suddenly having in the front room. As the trade-offs increase, I can tell she's becoming upset, and then I remember our conversation the last time I was here. The penny drops. She broke up with me. The age difference becomes a yawning chasm, with my only experience of break-ups thus far consisting of being a cad. From her 28yr old point of view, she was likely being diplomatic, but it didn't register. Or maybe I was in denial and had subconsciously moved this to the recycle bin, like I'd missed an episode of Eastenders. It was my turn to be upset, taking in her face and surroundings for the last time, acting like I was about to leave for the Undying Lands. With NV finished and my future uncertain, it was safe to assume our paths would not cross again. Losing the only good thing to come out of this whole chapter.

Reluctantly I say my goodbyes and drive back home to my bedroom in Stansted.

With the party physically and figuratively over, there's no more band correspondence. No final band meeting or mutual agreement to give up. Carl and Matt aren't even on speaking terms. They never clicked as mates, and I was stuck in the middle. The band fizzles like some bargain sparkler from a pound store. It's like NV never happened, an embarrassing but laughable diversion for six months. Once again, I am without a band or a muse. With NV officially beyond saving, it is time to find a full-time job. Again.

Discus Music has closed and I've no other job to return to. There is nothing else to take up my time, so I coast for a bit. Back to the Job Centre I guess, and it's dry, soulless conveyor belt of menial jobs. It looks like a dry season is about to occur on the music front, but then I get an invitation that leads to one of my darkest days.

CHAPTER 44

THE WRONG BUSINESS

It's June and Travis Cut are without a drummer as Bud needs to return to the US. Chris has a favour to ask. They don't want to cancel their gig supporting punk band The Business, so can they pull me in for one last job? With NV now a "fucked around and found out" scenario, it's nice to hear from Chris and feel wanted. I check the diary in case Dukes, Brown's or drum lessons are scheduled in, but the day is free. I accept. Chris tells me the gig is at the Water Rats, having been moved twice. "Why?" I ask. "The Business are against racism and far-right extremism, which is good, but...this means racist political extremists don't like them. So, they try to sabotage the gigs or threaten anyone who books them". I feel apprehensive but shrug it off and hope this gig won't be targeted. Besides, The Water Rats is a good venue to play in, always busy and a great location; there's been a pub in the same spot since 1517. It was the first London venue Oasis headlined.

It's a strange feeling to be back on a bus with Mac, Chris, and the team. Any giggling interrogations about the boy band foray are mercifully short. The atmosphere is convivial and a happy reunion, the air isn't too awkward being only six months since I left. It feels like things are going OK with Bud, but I can tell they aren't sharing everything about their drummer. No bother. The original line-up has a gig to do. We arrive in Kings Cross with our yellow Essex County Council-owned minibus (courtesy of The Square). The soundcheck goes well, the muscle memory brings the last two years flooding back, and I'm happy to be helping them out. Chris and Mac turn to me after a run-through of "Complicated", beaming and saying, "Welcome Back.".
Ah, shucks.

We return to the van and help Chris find a place to park. Driving off, I notice a lot of skinheads gathering at a street corner. Big boots, white polo shirts, some with braces. Unnervingly, some of them look like ordinary blokes with regular clothes and appearance. It looks like a mass '80's drug deal, but they're not distributing wraps, its tickets. They start approaching the Water Rats' entrance in small groups. It looks odd.

Soon the venue is full of these types, and the vibe doesn't exactly scream "music lovers". Even Mac, who has been to hell and back various times, looks concerned. There's an air of hostility, and Mac is scanning the crowded bar, shaking his head, making me nervous. We watch the first band. They don't fare well and are visibly rattled by the intimidating crowd lined up to watch them. Even though the mood is tense, we decide to play. I am out of practice but still play the fastest set Travis Cut have ever played. We rush through it, dropping a few songs as we go along too, Chris looking more scared by the minute and keeping banter between songs at a minimum. By now, the atmosphere is palpable, so our show is followed by the quickest de-rig of gear you've ever seen. With help from everyone who came to see us, all the guitars, drums, and amps are packed and carried to the fire exit. We need to get the fuck out of here, so having stationed the mini bus outside the venue, we are ready to open the door onto the street and get it packed.

Then it kicks off.

We're in a corridor that runs alongside the venue, and from the other side of the wall, we hear glass being smashed, tables getting broken and shouts of "Seig Heil". It's like a football crowd from the depths of hell. We hit the street the same time as the neo-Nazis do, finding ourselves standing like lemons as they trash the minibus windows, with one skinhead caving in our windscreen with a tabletop. A guy takes my cymbal bag off me, asking, "What are these, mate? What have you got here?" and starts throwing them at people like frisbees. He didn't look like the rest, just a normal-looking man but with a fucked up far-right head.

We run back towards the building next door and up a flight of stairs to some poor bloke's flat. With the shouts of "Come on then" and "D'you want some?" ringing from below, we bang on the door, and thankfully a man in his dressing gown opens, and we burst in with no time to explain. We sit tight for ten mins until the police sirens are audible, then creep down when it's over. It was Far Right mob Combat 18, an organisation formed by the BNP. They trashed the venue and our bus and successfully stopped the headline act from going on. A punter with half an ashtray in his head is talking to the police. We get towed home, as the inside of the minibus is covered in shattered glass.

My parents take advantage of my rare appearance at the table the following day at breakfast.

"How was the gig?"

"It was OK. Just a typical Travis Cut gig."

"Oh, that's nice. Do you think you'll re-join them?"

"When Satan ice-skates to work, Mum."

CHAPTER 45

TAKE IT EASY CHICKEN

With the Nazi event now logged in my brain for the grandkids and boyband NV one I can't ever erase, I reflect on my CV. I'm a 21 year old former drummer/boy band member with two old recording deals, four singles and two E.P.s, a soundtrack song, one full-length album, two compilation albums, a live album, AND a singles compilation under my belt.

As summer approaches, my thirst for being in a band remains strong, so I turn to NME and Melody Maker to scan the "Drummer Wanted" ads. I come across one that looks good. The ad asks to send details and a demo tape by post. I choose songs from Three and A Half Minutes and Travis Cut that showcase my drumming, find a suitable picture from an old photo shoot, and send it off.

A few weeks later, I receive a telephone call requesting to head up to Liverpool to audition for a band called Mansun. They suggest I listen to the previous singles, "Stripper Vicar" and "Take It Easy Chicken". I head to Woolworths and manage to get hold of the songs so I can learn them. Mansun's previous drummer Chad was unreliable, so they are searching for someone else. The drummer from Kinky Machine has even filled in for them. I like their songs and Paul Draper's vocals. They are an up-and-coming band signed to Parlophone. There are influences in their music of Bowie and new wave, but with a rockier edge.

My folks are on holiday in Italy. As my Nissan Cherry is on its last legs, I ask to borrow dad's company car for the four-hour journey. For the 220-mile drive, I compile a blinding mix tape and the Mansun tracks to play on rotation. These were the days before affordable sat navs and GPS, so I have to rely on directions from a massive AA road map.

As I get closer to Crash Rehearsal Studios, the butterflies begin to take hold. This is the first professional audition I have been to, and I'm not sure I've done enough preparation mentally. I also need to figure out what to expect from the audition. I guess it will be a live jam and rehearsal with the band, playing through the songs and getting to know each other, similar to that garage meeting many moons ago.

Except for Travis Cut, I've had to audition a lot in the past few years. But even though I am becoming a veteran, the nerves rarely disappear.

Once there, I use a nearby pay & display car park and pray I've left the BMW somewhere safe. A typical Boucher trait is we are always early, so I wander around the streets for a bit, making my nerves worse. I find a sandwich bar and pick at a cheese and ham panini, mulling over the last few years and how this opportunity could be a real game-changer. I look onto the street, watching Liverpool's residents go about their daily lives. It's a sunny day with a chilly breeze. One key fact I never considered is I will probably need to move to Liverpool if I get the job.

Finally, it is time to ring the bell and head upstairs to the rehearsal rooms. The band's manager is there to greet me. Behind him stands frontman Paul Draper, in a boiler suit, quiet and poker-faced. The whole room is dark. There is a solitary drum kit on stage, with a spotlight. No guitars, amps, or microphones. I stride over and take my seat. Paul and the manager sit on a sofa at the other end of the room.

I play a drum solo, add in some rhythms, doodle around a bit, and then stop when I think it's enough.

"Can you play some funk?" shouts a request from the darkness.

"I'm sorry, what?" I spoke.

"Funk. Can we hear some funk?"

Their single "Stripper Vicar" has a funky drum pattern, so no surprise they want to hear what I can do. I duly play some funky drums, involving James Brown and whatever else I can think of, then stop abruptly when I realise it has morphed into a disco rhythm.

"OK, cheers - thanks for coming."

In a surreal blur of goodbyes and thanks, I stumble back onto the street, where I was less than ten minutes ago. Dazed, I wander back to the car, grateful to see it still in one piece and drive home.

A few weeks of silence ensue; I won't be the next drummer for Mansun. It has been a strange exercise in humility, but it will also prepare me for future auditions. Putting on your "game face" is accurate, and meeting strangers in a job interview-style setting is always a daunting prospect, no matter who you are.

These days, we have the luxury of vetting people on social media before we even meet them, but back then, it was raw. I'll always ask myself what if or why I didn't cut it, but in the end, it doesn't matter. I'm fucking lucky to have been there.

CHAPTER 46
NEW BROOMS

With Matt's chiselled good looks, charming demeanour, and celebrity mum, it means a lot of things come easy for him. This is proved true when he's sent free passes for the Oasis Knebworth gig by Anita from Creation.

As predicted, Oasis are the biggest band in the country and could have sold Knebworth out for a whole week of August if they'd wanted to. Even though Blur are from my turf Essex, I've bought into the natural rock n roll swagger the Gallagher brothers bring to the scene, and What's the Story (Morning Glory) is a classic album. Matt asks me to join him, and I'm thrilled to be going to a festival-type gig. It sends me fully back into the indie sphere, and it's great to be in a field again, watching bands playing with instruments. We even manage to get backstage to the hospitality area, where I bump into Ben Wardle, get introduced to Tim Burgess and spot my Telstar ex wandering around too. Other celebs ligging about are Julia Carling, Anna Friel, Darren Day, Kathy Lloyd, Boo Radleys, Super Furry Animals, Jo Wylie, Kula Shaker, Kate Moss, and Jason Orange. It's like a who's who if you watch shows like The Big Breakfast and TFI Friday, read FHM, Loaded magazine or listen to XFM.

Matt and I head back to watch the Oasis concert and stand in silence with the massive crowd. Since that night at the Town & Country Club with Suede and Blur, it is weird to think I have observed the Britpop phenomenon from start to finish. The Oasis gig at Knebworth heralds a closing chapter on the genre, and it goes even more mainstream over the next year, taken over by laddish culture, more Oasis band-a-likes you could shake a stick at and Chris Evans trying to get people to swear on his TFI Friday show. I preferred the early days when Suede, Pulp and Blur were trying to start a new wave that celebrated all the quirkiness of being British and demonstrating a pushback to all things grunge. It is a great time to be into British music despite the whole Blur Vs Oasis shite and the lurid schoolboy humour directed at female musicians by the media. Looking back, it was odd I chose to be in a punk band, then a boy band, rather than following the trend. Annoyed? Definitely Maybe.

I was used to joining bands in my local area but what if I was missing a trick by not living somewhere more vibrant? Feeling ready to fly the coup, I decided I wanted to move to London. With CTV not needing runners, I found work as a Night Porter at the Hilton Hotel near Regent's Park. I quickly renamed it the Hellton.

My first shift involves lugging the South African cricket team's equipment to the lobby. Most of my time is spent patrolling the hotel corridors, sliding newspapers under doors at four in the morning and arranging mini cabs for drunk people. On one shift we had to let ourselves into a jet-lagged air stewardesses room; she'd started a bath, then fallen asleep, causing a leak in the room below.

My daily commute takes me through Camden, reminding me of where I've spent most of my time in recent years, The Dublin Castle, The Monarch, The Laurel Tree, Underworld and The Falcon. Wandering around Camden Lock and buying dodgy bootlegs of Suede on cassette. Shopping with Carl, seeing who could buy the biggest New Rock boots. Tired of working nights and the drive to London for every shift, I request to be transferred to the Hilton at Stansted Airport instead. It's a temporary setback from the quest to move to London. The new role is bartender, working evenings and late nights wearing a tasteless waistcoat and plastic name badge. I was hoping for a Tom Cruise in Cocktail lifestyle, but this is wishful thinking. Empty pint glasses are impatiently waved at me, orders are shouted for a Cosmopolitan, and it takes all my restraint to come back at them with a "Do you know who I am" but I need this job and anybody who hasn't read NME/Melody between 92 and 94 won't have a clue anyway. I hide behind the optics as I ask myself, "How has it come to this?"

I need to rectify the situation fast and find a more appealing job. I would have liked something closer to my skill set, but as I left school early to become a rock star, my GCSEs were not great, and my relevant skills specialised.

Carl is keen to relocate to London too, so we hit the West End armed with a stack of CVs. I spotted a job notice for Showscan's Emaginator, a simulator ride based in the Trocadero Centre, a multi-floor tourist hot spot in Piccadilly Circus. The ride has six pods that can fit four people, jumping around on hydraulic legs to the frenetic action on a cinema screen. It's next to Alien War, a live-action immersive experience putting you in the movie Aliens. You join a bunch of soldiers (actors) and Xenomorphs (actors in suits) running around a dark facility, scaring the bejesus out of tourists.

The Emaginator interview process is an all-day workshop. The job is suited to out-of-work actors/performers who can choose flexible shifts between auditions. It is the perfect chance for me to work somewhere full-time and relocate to London. I get the job and use the rest of the year couch-surfing, as I figure out where to live. Carl and Peter have found a shared flat in Walthamstow, so I crash there, or end up staying with Charlie at her rat-infested student house in South East London. Sometimes an Emaginator staffer puts me up, or I head back home to Stansted for a brief spell and a change of clothes.

I love my job at The Emaginator. Surrounded by talented actors and creative types who are constantly joking, laughing, and working double shifts so we can afford our next big night out. They do the splits in the staff room and help each other with lines for auditions, hoping to get their dream gig. There is always a copy of The Stage lying around, and one day I see an ad for open auditions for Stomp. Stomp is a percussion-led West End show using dustbins, brooms, newspapers and much more. It's an opportunity to try something different, and with no band in the picture, the timing is good. It's an open audition. The venue is bustling with dancers limbering up and drummers and performers waiting to be called. We are led onto a vast stage in groups of ten, taught a few exercises and rhythmic steps by the Stomp cast that we must replicate, followed by an improvised solo using our hands and feet.

The main aim is to show them we can learn quickly and keep time. They thank us for coming and ask the following to come back tomorrow. I am gobsmacked to hear my name called out. Being pessimistic that this would be another audition ending with a no, I hadn't planned to be in London the next day. I blag a space on Carl's cousin's floor for the night.

Day two is a more extended session but with twelve of us left. They bring out some more props for us to learn about, including the brooms, iconic bin lids and other fun elements that make up the show. We workshop some of the parts, perform them individually and as a group, and before I know it, the day is done. I'm having so much fun. Such a great day of learning percussion with some awesome creative people. It reminds me of the drum lessons with Alan when I'd learn a new rhythm, and he would join me with a tambourine or cowbell, and we would have a massive drum battle for the rest of the lesson.

To my uncontainable excitement, they ask me to come back for day three, the final audition. Making a last-minute phone call, I stop for the night at Sam's place in Guildford where he is a student at the University. We have remained pals, and I frequently visit for boozy nights out. As I'm sure every twenty-something male will testify, once a girlfriend joins the scene, there can be periods where you don't see your mates as much, but we've managed to spin the plates and stay in touch.

On the final day, eight of us remain. Only two performers are required to join the European tour. I am fired up to nail the final day, a full-on workshop of everything in the show, more improv, and the same routines as before with all the props. I give it my all, sweeping the brooms across the floor with gusto and incorporating some flourishes here and there, adding extravagant stage moves I'd learned from Am-Dram and NV. With dustbin lids in both hands, I stalk the stage and perform an energetic duel with another cast member from Stomp. I make one last push, leaping high, before slamming my dustbin lids onto the floor in a sweaty heap.

At the end of a fantastic day, they thank us for our time and tell us we will receive a phone call on Christmas Eve. I have a shift working at the Emaginator that day and ask to work from the ticket desk so I can take the call. The day drags on, and I wonder if the call will ever come. The daydreaming begins, picturing myself on a tour bus, performing Stomp in cities from Berlin to Barcelona. This will be the best Christmas gift or a good reason to get started on the eggnog ASAP.

Making me jump, the phone underneath the box office counter rings. It's the office transferring a call for me. I answer the phone and hear the softly spoken voice of Stomp founder Steve McNicholas. Sadly, I didn't get it. Gutted. But it was a hell of a ride, and I am chuffed to have gotten far. I went on to audition for Stomp twice in the next six years but never got the gig.

CHAPTER 47

CAUGHT BY THE FUZZ

Following the epic Knebworth Oasis gig, I see Matt for a night out on New Year's Eve. I should have realised by now going out on New Year's Eve never bodes well for me, but I can't resist his invitation to do a pub crawl along King's Road in Chelsea. Matt brings a friend along who seems to be good company as we go from pub to pub, talking to very rich and very attractive young ladies who are already set for life. Things are fun until we end up at a house party on early New Year's Day somewhere in Pimlico. I can't recall our third person's name so let's call this wonderful human being Tarquin. It's about 2 in the morning, the party is winding down. After opening other people's mail in the hallway to see if there is any money in the Christmas cards, Tarquin decides we should get a black cab back to Wimbledon, where he and Matt are staying. Unbeknownst to me, it turns out we don't have enough money for the fare once we are in the cab and heading south. I sit in stunned silence as Tarquin plots to throw what change we have left into the driver's cabin once he's unlocked the doors, and we will make a run for it.

My heart is pounding. Stealing some random disused item from a box backstage at a gig is one thing but threatening a cabbie's livelihood and not paying is on another level. I try to think of alternatives, but they are limited. Walking home from anywhere in London with only the shirt on my back is not an option and I'm thirty miles away from the reliable service that is Mum and Dad cabs. The driver will stop and turf us out if we say we have no money. Back then, you needed cash for a cab; contactless and Uber were not a thing for another twenty five years. Once again, I'm wondering how I got here, facing another drama on New Year's thinking this must be some kind of curse. Did I throw away some random ancient artefact, was I rude to a little old lady with mystical powers? Maybe I'm not a good judge of character, but I think the main culprit here is alcohol. We do strange things and turn into stranger people under the influence. I'm sure Tarquin is a nice enough chap any other day of the year, but right now in this cab he's a prize knob-jockey.

The cabbie pulls up in the centre of Wimbledon, and we wait for the doors to unlock. I think if I hang back and explain, maybe the driver will go easy on us, understand our plight. Then I remember it's London, and he's a Black Cab driver. He's seen everything. They probably have a bingo card on passengers who will likely throw up, do a bunk, or try other ways to avoid the fare. As soon as the doors unlock, a fistful of coppers is flung into the front, with a "cheers mate" and a frantic exodus from the vehicle. Having not planned what to do once exiting the car, we scatter, with Matt and me going in one direction and Tarquin going in the other. Choosing our next move as we crouch behind a bush, we dart into the car park of a building directly opposite. We listen for the cab, as he drives around to find us.

I cannot believe this is happening. Fucking New Year's Eve. As Matt and I pin ourselves against a wall to catch our breaths, we look into what we think is a car park and notice a row of police cars. Then it dawns on me. We're hiding in a police station car park. Our heads slowly look up and stop at the camera pointing at us on the wall. Before we decide to move on, a police officer appears with a casual "You all right, lads?"

With proper bad timing, Tarquin runs past, notices us, stops, starts to speak, and then realizes we have company. With the policeman's Spidey sense tingling, he suggests we go into the station for a chat. Before we know it, the three of us are sitting around a table in a small interrogation room as he asks what is going on. Tarquin confesses we've bunked from a cab, even though he had enough money. I'm speechless. He actually had the money to pay the fare. The officer says he can't do much unless the cab driver stops to press charges, so after stern advice, he sends us on our way. It's only here I find out there is no room for me to stay with Matt in Wimbledon, so I withdraw some cash from an ATM and get another cab to a friend's flat in South East London.

I don't see Matt again for two years. I bump into him at Soho House, a trendy private members club in London. He is making a living as Brad Pitt's body double and making new friends, milling about with Robert Redford and Guy Ritchie. He plays me a voicemail the actor Kevin Spacey has left on his mobile. I wish him luck with his attempt to crack Hollywood.

1996 - Mixtape

Everything Must Go - Manic Street Preachers
Stagger Lee - Nick Cave
Hey Dude - Kula Shaker
Fast Love - George Michael
Say You'll Be There - Spice Girls
Novocaine for the Soul - Eels
Virtual Insanity - Jamiroquai
The Day We Caught The Train - Ocean Colour Scene
Scooby Snacks - Fun Lovin Criminals
Nancy Boy - Placebo
Ready To Go - Republica

The dream ends as Skream! split

EXCLUSIVE BY
HOLLIE DARKEN

FIRST came the devastating news that pop sensations Take That, were to break up, but now Bishop's Stortford's very own boy band has announced its decision to split.

Just months after Skream! released their debut single, the dream of making it big in the pop world is faded and died.

Despite a successful British tour with PJ and Duncan, partying alongside groups such as EYC, Damon Deon, all EYC, a trip to New York, to film their first pop video, all disharmonic fans, a difference of opinions behind the band has lead.

Now, the three lads — Carl McAleer, James Gordon and Matthew Burnite — are seeking to go their separate ways to the music industry.

In an exclusive interview with the *Frenzy Observer* the break, Carl (23) of Record Gardens, Bishop's Stortford, revealed the reasons behind the decision to split and his bid to make it big with his new band, NV.

"I've seen each of those had been unhappy with the progress of the band," James basically didn't want to do the hard work and it all became about the whole music industry. Things went very quiet after Christmas and we were really happy and everyone started to go their separate ways.

"There was a bit of a clash between us because we'd hit the limited creatively found out what was going on and it wasn't happy either because things weren't happening as fast as they wanted it to," he says.

"The record company also found out we'd finished with our manager so we decided to finish with Manager B so we'd have fought for the deal, but the others didn't want to carry on.

"The new-improved man with mixed emotions is Bishop's Stortford — even his though the band weight of the big idea, while others were more sceptical," said Carl. "We had quite a big fan-base on the scene and a big of touring in Manchester last and we've had terrific success in getting a lot of people were just great.

"They had contacted on 'good music' with former Knoutlle PL and who were under way those picking up a deal with his new band.

Agents have put three members of NV. They include Carl, Thornbhull Alex Beneker of Quarter Close in Stortford, and Matthew Montez (16) of Stortford. Between us it just been to earn and see whether the latest and can really make a big in the pop world.

● OUT: Skream! (left)
Matthew Burnite (top)
James Gordon (middle) and Carl McAleer
have gone their own ways.

● IN: New boy band, NV, with (left to right)
Carl McAleer, Alex
Beneker and Matthew
Burnite.

FRENZY SHOOT IN LONDON (CREDIT: UNKNOWN) / INSET: FRENZY PROMO PHOTO (CREDIT: UNKNOWN)

CHAPTER 48

BACK FROM MARS

1997

Channel 5 launches, Tony Blair elected, Princess Diana dies, Urban Hymns by The Verve, Polythene by Feeder, Titanic, The Full Monty.

My hair is long. Again. I also have a girlfriend. Gina is an Emaginator colleague. We've grown close over the months, working long shifts together, sitting in the darkened auditoriums and flirting in the staff room. She has a dirty Sid James-style laugh and could easily replace Scary Spice if the job arises. She is vivacious and dominant; I love how much she empowers me, making me feel anything is possible.

I've found a room to rent with co-worker Eddie in a spacious flat that backs onto Crystal Palace Park. Eddie is the synth/keyboardist for an industrial band called Inertia and used to manage the local venue in Wakefield, so we have loads in common. We regularly get stoned until the early hours, drinking cans of obscure German beer, and listening to ambient tunes. The lounge has a poster of Iggy Pop, a flea-infested Persian rug, a cat called Billy and a Christmas tree we can't be bothered to take down. I couldn't be happier. Leaving the family home was ok, seeing as I've spent most of my life out and about since 1992 - but I miss the Sunday roasts, homemade Banoffee pie and honest counsel.

I go on a shopping spree to get new togs, as I'm trying my luck with an open audition for another boy band that I'd seen advertised in The Stage. The ad says they are looking for boys with "attitude and edge" so, maybe an ex-drummer for a punk band is just what they'll need. The location is Pineapple Studios, Covent Garden. There were no drunken revelries the night before, and my song of choice this time is "(Sittin' On) The Dock of the Bay" by Otis Redding. Strong, safe. Maybe too safe, as, once again, it's a polite "thanks for coming". I later learned this was the audition for what resulted in the edgy and attitude-filled boy band 5ive.

It takes a few slaps of my face in front of the mirror and some good northern advice from Eddie to convince me my place on stage is not preening out front with a switched-off microphone. It was behind a drum kit and giving it a bloody good seeing-to.

So, the search begins once more for a band. Being based in London, this isn't too hard. I place a Drummer Available ad. Eddie soon gets bored of the numerous phone calls, answerphone messages and post-it notes he must leave for me. Off the back of a few missteps and hard passes, I hear from a French chap called John, who has a band called Jaff. With scrappy black hair, John has the look and demeanour of an inquisitive mouse, with a tendency to close one eye as he speaks. Luckily, he lives right around the corner in Sydenham, and the proposition for me is to join temporarily, play some urgent gigs in France and get paid for my time.

We utilise two intense days rehearsing as I desperately try to memorize their songs in time for the gigs. It's mainly pop-punk with straight-froward song structures and time signatures, with catchy songs and irrelevant titles, like "Back from Mars". The night before I leave, I still don't feel ready and break down in tears in front of Gina. It's an anxiety attack I've never experienced before, leaving me shaken. I usually can tour, play, and blag things with my eyes closed. Since when did I become so emotional? I realise it's been a tough year or so, experiencing assault, neo-Nazis up close and rejections from Mansun, Stomp and 5ive all contributing to my sudden lack of confidence. I head to France with John and bassist Jimmy, a tall Brit with spiky blond hair, to play the gigs in Metz.

I'm in at the deep end, doing a gig in a massive tent, with only two days of rehearsal. To keep my mind off things, we bond with a Spanish band called Casa Home, and I enjoy visiting Metz for the first time. I feel homesick and miss Gina a lot. Not living at the family home has made me dependent on her, and at twenty-two I feel more like a sixteen-year-old on tour again, vulnerable, and nervous. She's an absolute force of nature and able to weather any storm.

It's the day of the gig, and I walk onto a big stage with John and Jimmy, the first large-scale gig I've done in a long time. We crash into the songs, and mercifully, the set is short. I survive, using all my listening, improv, and drumming skills to get through it. I now understand what Bud felt like, playing another drummer's rhythm, trying to give it a personal touch and making it their own.

The next gig is to fewer people, which helps me grow in confidence after the night before. We pass through Lille, meet some fans of Jaff and drink Limoncello in the sun. We head home on a 1.45am ferry, and I'm back in Crystal Palace by four in the morning, with another shift at the Emaginator starting in a few short hours. It feels good to have helped John, and I hope we can stay in touch. But for now, there might be one more Pop trump card to play.

CHAPTER 49

FRENZY

The brief stint with Jaff is over, and I am back in touch with friend and all-around pop uber networker Jolene. It turns out she is working with Glenn from Boy Next Door. Hopefully, he's become more legit since the last time we met. He now has an office which is a good step up from the bacon and cat shit, but I'm still unsure about working with him.

From years of hobnobbing with pop stars, Jolene is keen to have a taste of the lifestyle herself. I feel compelled to support her, considering how well we get along. And seeing as Jolene knows everyone in the pop world, this project could have potential. Gina is drafted in too, as she has a strong singing voice due to her gospel choir roots.

Even Matt is interested in the band but never commits. I sense an air of FOMO from him, but I think he remembers what a shit-show NV was and withdraws. To round up the gang, Jolene's mum Irene oversees things, and big Phil returns to help us out but chooses not to be our manager full time, more of a consultant and driver where needed.

Before long, the three of us are having photo shoots in Central London, walking calmly through Oxford St, having "caught unaware" photos taken on a sunny day in Hyde Park by a photographer friend.

Just like the NV/Mossimo agreement, we are loaned a fashion line provided by Junky Styling; two female entrepreneurs who have a stall at the trendy Kensington Market (demolished in 2001). Even The Chilled Eskimo is back on the radar, where we attend an EastEnders birthday party for Phil Mitchell, AKA Steve McFadden and dance all night to funky tunes provided by Carl's brother Elton. Seeing how it worked so well for the Spice Girls, there are idle talks of us sharing a flat, but after a few viewings, the stark prospect of living together is quietly forgotten.

The next plan is to find a song, and after listening to various demos, we agree to record "Taking Care of Business", or TCOB for short.

Again, with zero vocal training or experience, I'm shouting the song from start to finish - a live gig would have been intimidating, with young kids watching us yell, "TCOB: I'm taking care of business, TCOB: I'M TAKING CARE OF BUSINESSSS" We allocate a night recording it with the patronizing dude who wrote it, only for the song to never see the light of day.

On top of our regular appearances at the Chilled Eskimo, random invites would always be coming in due to my NV connections or from social butterflies Carl and Jolene. One such invite is for a new girl band launch event, who are inventively called "Girl Band". Since their huge arrival in June last year, The Spice Girls have taken the pop world by storm and now the music industry is on the frantic search for another girl band. The act we are going to see features Gina G's former backing dancers, minus Miranda who is now concentrating on song writing and producing. The three of us head down, and twin sis Charlie tags along too. The venue is Stringfellows, a glamorous nightclub owned by the King of the Mullets, Peter Stringfellow. Things get off to a weird start when I bump into a young TV actor who is a regular at the Chilled Eskimo.

"Hi mate, how's it going? This is my sister, Charlie."

"Ah, cheers, mate; I'm well up for a line!"

"I'm sorry?"

"I thought you said you had some Charlie?"

We shake heads politely as I point at Charlie to explain over the loud music and then make an excuse about needing to find someone at the bar.

My experience of the white powder thus far is only through movies, and I've not been brave enough to take ecstasy or anything with life-changing results like heroin, MDMA, or ketamine. I've kept everything at arm's length, choosing only to indulge in the odd spliff and some speed. Beer is my vice, followed by tequila slammers (licking tabasco off the wrist, not salt) or quaffing the gloopiest, richest red wine I can find. "Alcopops" seem to be latest trend, with bright coloured bottles of lemon-flavoured Hooch, Metz (martini and lemonade) or the odd-tasting Smirnoff Ice and Bacardi Breezers.

We wander about and wait for the girl band's unveiling, which never happens. Instead, we explore a bit more of Stringfellows, then make a swift exit and head to the nearest Pizza Hut. I feel I'm getting too old for these 'be seen at' parties and would much prefer sitting in a pub with my friends, talking rubbish all night.

Frenzy gets a gig presenting (but not performing) at a pop roadshow event near Shirebrook. The place has no natural pull except Jason Statham was born here. Phil drives us up to the gig in his Previa, with a young magician called Steven Mulhern tagging along for the ride. Seeing how new and shy we are, he opens the sunroof, stands up and starts shouting, "Everybody! I've got Frenzy here!"

The three of us have fun on stage, dressed up to the nines in the latest London streetwear and shouting "Give it up for The Boyz" or whatever generic bands are performing that day. We return to our hotel bar and chill with abbed-up antipodean, Peter Andre. Sitting at his booth, I'm boxed in by his stocky entourage and see a legion of girls peering in from outside, misting up the glass as they clutch their autograph books for dear life.

In the end, Frenzy fizzles out quickly due to the realization that this is doomed to fail. My relationship with Gina survives unscathed; it's nice to be back as boyfriend and girlfriend without the added band-mate drama. Still, we got some lovely photos out of it.

CHAPTER 50
ZUT ALORS

John calls - he has a new bass player and asks if I would be up for joining Jaff permanently. I jump at the chance, and we meet regularly in a rehearsal space in Brixton. Bassist Sean is a super easy-going guy alongside John, a constant ball of energy. Our style is Stone Roses meets early Radiohead, with John's high-pitched vocals and talented ear for an infectious riff. Similar to Travis Cut, our productivity is quick, and we write some great songs in a short space of time. Must be a trio thing. We have something for everyone - anthems ("Back from Mars", "I Want Ya"), slow-burner epic tracks ("Hello" and "Misunderstanding"), something baggier ("Call it a Day"), and a proper wig-out set-closer called "She Don't Care", with lyrics written by me. Because of John's contacts in France, we often drive to Paris and its surrounding areas for well-paid mini tours.

I love playing in Paris; my favourite venue is Le Pop Inn. It's a speakeasy-type venue with a bar at the front and the venue via a secret door in the back. The French way of gigs is a game-changer, too, with later stage times, proper food, and guaranteed payment. John often finds us a floor in a friend's flat or a commune to sleep in for the night.

Things are starting to settle into a routine. I do a few shifts at the Emaginator, appreciate quality time with Gina, rehearse and record songs with Jaff, play the odd gig and then repeat.

The Brixton rehearsal rooms are great, and John is always happy to ferry Sean and me around. My happiest times are after a successful writing session, nailing a few new tracks, followed by a satisfying Pot Noodle in the kitchen. I'm hearing about mobile phones, with Motorola and Nokia providing affordable handsets to take on the road. I can't wait to get hold of one, so I can call Gina from anywhere and "text" her - whatever that means.

Pretty soon, we have enough songs to make a demo and have a great little tape of songs called "Please". It's a banging mixture of songs and feels like the good old days of Three And a Half Minutes, sending tapes to all and sundry and holding something in my hands I'm proud of.

Before long, we're off to France again. This time I know the songs, fully prepared, and I'm raring to go.

To the tunes of Summercamp and Our Lady Peace, John keeps the band morale up in the car. This comes in handy when ferries or the new Channel Tunnel have delays. We play a mix of intimate gigs, all with varying results.

Sometimes we drink from the rider too much, and John's guitar tends to go out of tune. The late performance times mean we're not sleeping somewhere until 3 am. Sean snores, so it's a race against time to fall asleep before he does. I'm more relaxed now, as I know what to expect and the calls home to Gina help me focus. We have some time off during the tour and record some new tracks in a rehearsal space. "Call it a Day" and "Misunderstanding" are long six-minute tracks that keep me engaged due to the complex drum parts I've written for them. My experience with the other bands pays dividends, and I can delve into my headspace, filled with drum parts from Led Zeppelin to RIDE and Nirvana.

Sometimes the language barrier shuts Sean and me out as we politely wait for John as he speaks to someone in French for what seems like an hour. This proves to be a challenge when he says, "Au Revoir", remembers one more thing, and we don't leave for another thirty minutes. This may seem petulant, but it can be frustrating if you've had only four hours of sleep. Still, it's an excellent way to learn more French. Once again, as I approach the end of an eventful year, I hope the next one brings a big break. But first, I need to survive another New Year's Eve.

20th November - Paris
21st November - Paris
22nd November - Paris

1997 - Mixtape

Bittersweet Symphony - The Verve

Paranoid Android - Radiohead

Song 2 - Blur

Place Your Hands - Reef

High - Feeder

Tonight - Supergrass

Your Woman - White Town

Block Rockin' Beats - Chemical Brothers

Firestarter - The Prodigy

Da Funk - Daft Punk

To The Moon and Back - Savage Garden

CHAPTER 51
PLAYING IT SAFE

1998

Good Friday Agreement, Clinton impeached, France wins World Cup, Mezzanine by Massive Attack, Celebrity Skin by Hole, Shakespeare in Love, The Big Lebowski.

You'll be glad to know my New Years' Eve seeing in 1998 was spent safely indoors with Eddie, Gina, and Jools Holland on the TV. Throughout the last year, my life with Gina has endured, despite the occasional fallout. Prone to outbursts, our relationship becomes elemental, with equal doses of fire, ice, and earthquakes.

More Jaff gigs are lined up in London and France, but there seems to be little interest in finding gigs elsewhere in the UK. The money is too good in France and gigging in London is easy for the three of us.

I think about our stage presence and have an idea to add some colour. John and Sean have orange amps, so I buy purple fur from Brick Lane and end up using a productive day covering my kit. It's an easy process, loosening all the lugs, taking the drum skin off, wrapping the fur around the shell and then putting everything back- it seems to help deaden the drums too, which is an added extra.

My job at the Emaginator is becoming fraught. The place is under new management, normally the death knell for any workplace. With morale at a low, all my workmates are starting to leave. It's the end of a golden age, and the commute becomes more harder with each shift I have. To stay in the band, I will have to find a less stressful job that pays well but has flexible shifts. It's a big ask, but I hope London will deliver. It is good to get away with Jaff and escape the country to relieve work stress. We play another string of dates - our first night in Evry is long, with a receptive audience clamouring for an encore after encore. We get in at 3:45 am. We stay in a squat, sleeping in a crawl space similar to the quarters at Purple Rain. It's full of artists and cold as hell. I try to have a shower the next morning, standing under a clogged-up shower head that may have been used for painting, as freezing water trickles over my face.

Our next gig is a massive college event in front of dwindling crowds. I'm getting used to the running order of each day, a lie-in, a long drive to the next venue, a late gig and waiting for John as he chats to everyone in French, with Sean and I standing by feeling awkward.

We stay in a Novotel for the final night, and I contemplate what to do on my return home. I need to find a new job and escape the Emaginator. A few weeks later, the final straw comes when a disagreement between Gina and management forces her to quit. With the new bosses being dicks, and in an act of solidarity, it's time for me to leave. I find something, but depressingly, my new day job is a far cry from the zing and brightness of the West End.

In the heart of the East End of London, where the city seems to fade to grey, stands my new place of work, a run-down call centre. Day after day, I trudge through the dreary routine of scripted conversations and disinterested responses. It's a banal world of scripted greetings and robotic queries, a relentless tide of irritated homeowners and complaints and lonely old-age pensioners that simply want to stay on the phone for the company. Each keystroke, each call, is a reminder of my aspirations left unfulfilled. During breaks, we huddle in a dimly lit breakroom, conversations a mix of resignation and yearning for something more. We are cogs in a machine; our individuality swallowed by the relentless grind.

Jaff needs a lift up the ladder and fast.

17th January - The King's Head, Fulham
29th January - Calais
31st January - Evry

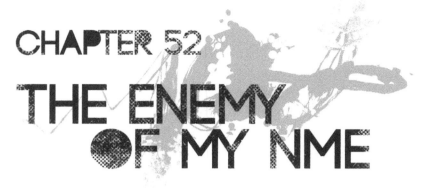

CHAPTER 52

THE ENEMY OF MY NME

For the first time in over five years, I am in a band that I'm a real fan of. I love our songs, our setlists, and the easy-going nature of Sean and John's quirkiness. This is a real opportunity to make it, so I call in a favour from an old acquaintance. Tim Paton is still managing bands but focuses more on photography these days. I call him, we catch up, and I ask if he could come and check us out at our next gig at the Hope & Anchor in Islington. In hindsight, I should have stressed the importance to John and Sean of playing this gig with all we've got. We aren't in good form at all. It doesn't help that the gig is half-empty. Or that John has drunk too much cider. He needs to be more in tune and give it his all, but neither option is on the cards.

I spot Tim and another chap watching us from the bar. My heart sinks, but I'm glad the venue is half-empty, reducing any risk of heckling or bad press. When I call Tim the next day, he tells me the other chap was Mark Sutherland, Editor of NME. We had a golden chance right before us, and we fucked it. Tim explained this to me more politely, but I could tell what he was really saying. This is a huge downer, and after telling John, he tries his best to put on a brave face. Every gig should be played like it's your last. We all have off days, but the timing for this one couldn't have been worse.

We decide to ramp things up on the London front and by March, Jaff is enjoying residency-style gigs at the Bull and Gate in Kentish Town and the King's Head in Fulham. It feels like we are playing these two venues every other week. For one gig at The King's Head, we have the pleasure of supporting Chesney Hawkes' band "Ebb" with his brother on drums. "The One and Only" is not played.

On a good day, our setlist is a finely honed dynamic thing of beauty, and I suggest we wear suits to enhance the stage image. We are willing to try anything to get noticed, and it feels superb playing in a shirt and tie like being in The Jam.

We have another gig to do at The Bull and Gate. I love playing at this venue. Even if the promoter has a habit of leaving without paying. Sometimes we would have to call him at his house and ask about the money. His reply would generally be, "well, you didn't bring enough people in, so there isn't any."

Here, John 'Fat' Beast made a name for himself and Carter, whose fans would shout 'You Fat Bastard' when he came on stage to introduce them, wearing just his pants. Like most pub venues in London, this had started as the Boulogne Gate in 1871. Everyone has played here, including Elastica, Coldplay, PJ Harvey, Keane, and Manic Street Preachers. The venue closed in 2013 and was turned into a gastropub. An open kitchen stands where the stage used to be.

Playing regular gigs means friends that we constantly invite to see us would have to say no at some point. Instead, it's up to us to win over another band's audience to make it all worthwhile. This is one such evening where the room is filled with unfamiliar faces, so it's clear we need to blow them away and become their new favourite band.

During the evening, a dark feeling creeps in. It dawns on me that time might be expiring for this 'being in a band' lark. With the sobering realization hitting me moments before taking the stage, my head is suddenly in an odd place. I sit at the kit and finish my cigarette, scanning the audience and seeing who's out there. The room seems ambivalent, and I take a swig of beer, and pick up my sticks. I check the cymbals, move the hi-hat closer in and fire off a quick rat-a-tat on the snare drum to alert the crowd. I count John and Sean in, and we plough through our first song, a new number called Lipstick.

As with every gig, I am playing my heart out but can't help but notice how distracted the audience is. They are talking during and in between our songs, even John addressing the crowd is making no impact. I grow angrier and angrier. The heat is rising inside me, reaching the tips of my ears, and causing me to hit the drums harder and harder. There's no denying it. I am in a rage. Angry with the audience. The lack of success. The bad luck. My mistakes. I have nobody to be mad at except myself. Seven fucking years of this. Now I'm 23, in the fucking Bull and Gate, next door to the place where I've supported Blur, and no one is fucking listening. Seriously just fuck it all. Time to look back in anger.

At the end of our set, after a blistering version of 'She Don't Care' I've decided I don't care either. I flip out and trash my drum kit. Through gritted teeth, I push the bass drum over, fling the cymbals aside and storm off in a huff.

I have nobody to be angry at except myself. It was a petulant rage, and all I want is oblivion. I feel worthless. I'm a joke, a pathetic opportunist with shit timing and terrible foresight. What's the point of this? How long do I have to continue this before I get lucky? I slide down the dressing room wall and sink my head in my hands. Seriously. This is all I want to do. But I can't. John bounds over to check on me. "Hey, Alex, are you OK? Is your drum kit ok? What happened?"

"The sound was terrible onstage ", I lied, "I couldn't hear anything, so I lost my temper".

John can tell something is being held back, but he nods and heads to the bar. As most bands will know, when playing in a tiny venue, you have to return to the stage to remove your gear to make space for the next band. So, I sheepishly step back on to see the sound engineer untangling cables and mics from my pile of drums with a weary and disappointed look on his face.

7th Feb - The Bull & Gate, Kentish Town
7th March - with Ebb, The Kings Head, Fulham
1st April - The Dublin Castle, Camden
3rd April - The King's Head, Fulham

CHAPTER 53
STOP THIS TRAIN

Drained of motivation and from years of touring, recording and letdowns galore, the reality of life has caught up with me. I need a break, so I head home to see the parents for some proper meals and helpful conversation. I ride home to Stansted in an empty train carriage in the middle of the day. It always feels good to go home, catch up with the folks and see if Charlie is around.

I look out the window as London gives way to green fields and churches. I start planning my schedule, wondering who else might be about. Maybe I'll meet up with Sam if he's home and have a pint at The Boar's Head or The Three Horseshoes.

A newspaper has been left on the seat, so I idly flick through the pages to catch up on what's happening in the world. Clinton and Blair are still doing their thing. George Michael has been caught doing rude things in a public toilet in LA. I flick to the classified jobs. And there, right on the first page, is an ad for CTV. They are looking for runners. Having left on good terms with them, I know all it takes is a phone call, and I will get my old job back. Then I can afford to stay in London and have a career. With below-average GCSEs to my name, it feels like a lifeline to work my way up from the bottom. Besides, the TV studio is now rented by Disney Channel, so being close to a former employer might be nice.

With this playing on my mind, I set off on our next France tour, trying to stay positive for the gigs we are about to play. The tour starts with two nights at the Cirq Cafe, Metz, where we play unplugged. This doesn't help my downbeat attitude toward things, and the whole day is spent getting there, carrying a headache I gave myself with a morning pint on the ferry. I want us to step up, but John has autonomy with our France schedule, and sometimes money plays a more crucial part than where or who we're playing with. We play a set three times in one night in a pizza restaurant. By this point, I'm ready to play a gig in a kid's soft-play room and be unsurprised. For the next night, I have to play an electric drum kit in a pub called the Horse's Mouth, which wasn't on the Jaff weird gig bingo card. My relationship with electric drums is standoffish at best, but I know we need to get paid, so I relent. But, this has an air of finality to it, and I resolve that this could be it for the band.

My last gig for Jaff is at The Kings Head in Fulham, and I invite everyone along, work friends, Sam, Charlie, Gina, and my parents. They'd snuck into the Pogues gig in Harlow, but since then, they haven't seen me play. I like Jaff and our songs, so the situation is more distressing this time around - leaving out of necessity, not for personal reasons.

To prevent a low-key performance, I haven't told them I'm leaving. We play a blinding set. I keep it together, stay in the zone and do not let the air of finality cloud my performance. As I glance out from behind the kit, I think about how a reunion would look if everyone was here. I'd spot Alice weaving through the crowd, avoiding my gaze with a cheeky smile. I'd see Ollie in the audience, nodding his head and telling the sound engineer I need more bass in my monitor. Steve is smoking a fag and flashing a grin as I end another song with a flourish. Matt is twirling his hair in the corner, thoughtful, a wry smile starting to form. Laurence beams widely as he tucks his hair behind his ears. Chris is swaying and swigging from a can of Stella, Mac has bought the sound engineer a pint and tapping his foot as he takes another drag from his rollie. Matt and Carl are dancing in sync, enjoying the moment, and being slick as always. They're all here, in spirit, joining me as I signal the end of an era. Come on, Alex. I smile as I play, looking up to Alan as he adjusts his glasses, beaming proudly at his student. The quiet kid who likes to play loud. I even managed to leave the drum kit in one piece this time. Well, I didn't want to embarrass the parents.

CHAPTER 54

CALL IT A DAY

Break-ups can be shit. You rehearse the speech with its gentle intro, go through all the reasons, and try to round things off with a generic "just going to have to call it a day" line. Beforehand, there's been forty-eight hours or so of back and forth, asking friends for advice, dramatic wringing of hands and pervading clouds of dilemma after dilemma. Also, you don't want to hurt any feelings, right? Want to remain friends? (You know, just in case).

It is a sunny morning in our flat. Eddie and I have recently moved across the road to a smaller place after our landlord evicted us. It takes a while to adjust, and the smaller rooms and rising damp in the bathroom are not a good start. I still work odd shifts, so time is spent shuffling about, making coffee, playing music, and waiting for John to arrive. Eddie had spent the previous evening getting stoned and listening to Ozric Tentacles until 3 am. The new age prog music and sweet herby tang are still fresh in the air.

John still lives on the next street, which means a short wait between the phone call and his showing up. I've been pacing my bedroom all week, going over scenarios to save things somehow, but it's no use—time to end it. John mooches into the kitchen and helps himself to a cuppa. I'm perched on the sofa, and after some small talk, I launch into 'the speech.'

"So, I've been thinking about my future in the band. It's been tough for me to pay the rent and commit enough time these days. My old employers have offered me a job in St John's Wood. I've looked at this in every way I can, but short of sleeping on someone's sofa until we get signed, I think I'm just going to have to call it a day. Sorry."

John takes a minute to let things sink in. It's a cast-iron excuse, and I know he doesn't have a sofa to spare. Or record label interest. In his typical gallic way of smacking lips, John quietly takes it on the chin, we finish our drinks, and we agree to keep in touch, you know - just in case. Then off he goes.

I sit in silence for a bit, band-less once again. I reach for the latest diary and sit, pen in hand, to reflect. I recall how everything started in December 1990. Crazy to think answering an ad in a local paper would be followed by eight years of trying to make it big.

I write about the highs, supporting bands like Blur and Ned's Atomic Dustbin, flying to Los Angeles. The camaraderie in Travis Cut and the back catalogue of songs we created, sealing our name as one of the most popular punk pop bands on the UK circuit. Messing about with friends and loved ones in pop bands and the bittersweet ending with Jaff - a band whose songs I will always listen to.

The lows are fleeting, dealing with toxic personalities, Far-Right thugs, sex pests and a tape that kept jumping. It is a lot to unpack. I've broken a few hearts here and there, but in the end, I was breaking my own. Not because I didn't get to be famous, but because I always left. Looking back, I was always the one heading for the exit. And it makes me sad I didn't stick around with Three and A Half Minutes, Travis Cut and Jaff. Why am I so impatient to move on? I feel like Sam from Quantum Leap, or an idiot nomad, giving everyone eighteen months max and then fucking off. It dawns on me that I create temporary friendships, a temporary lifestyle and then, for some reason, I throw it all away.

Sitting alone in my flat, listening to "Speck" by Mega City Four, I break down and weep uncontrollably. Seriously? A big turning point in my life and the music I'm playing makes this feel like the end credits to a rom-com or something. But it was true. I could blame my life on many variables, but in the end, it's down to me.

I look at the drum cases stacked in the corner. I think of all the times I've carried those cases out of the garage, into a car or van, onto a stage. For me, I was at work. I would sit down at the kit and pick up the sticks. It was my desk, my operating table, my easel. The place to create something powerful, and have a room witness it. I have learnt a craft, and nobody can take that away from me. I've been lucky to get as far as I have and get the opportunity to try again and again. And again. I may have been impulsive and childish to move on so many times, but everything happens for a reason doesn't it?

1998 - Mixtape

Iris - Goo Goo Dolls
One Week - Barenaked Ladies
No Regrets - Robbie Williams
Kelly Watch The Stars - Air
Angel - Massive Attack
Here Comes The Breeze - Gomez
Lonely Soul - Unkle
Much Against Everyone's Advice - Soulwax
Praise You - Fatboy Slim
Celebrity Skin - Hole

JAFF AT THE POP INN, PARIS (CREDIT UNKNOWN)

JAFF BAND PHOTO (CREDIT: JOHN DAVEY)

JAFF (CREDIT: JOHN DAVEY)

WAITING AT THE BULL & GATE (CREDIT UNKNOWN)

TRASHING THE KIT (CREDIT UNKNOWN)

EPILOGUE

Paddington Train Crash

After graduating, Sam and I got back in touch after my relocation to London and his new job. Sam always landed on his feet. Savvy, intelligent, and interested in tech and good music, he was destined to be another Richard Branson. He rented a flat in Bloomsbury, and I would often stop by, quickly chatting about Van Morrison's new album, before sinking a few pints at The Hope pub near Goodge Street tube.

We spent two weeks doing work experience around the corner at Palace Pictures in 1990, and now here we were, both living and thriving. We always had a great time reminiscing and talking about our future. Sam had a new role set up with a telecoms company in Slough, and I was learning the ropes in live television at Disney Channel; we were all set up for the next stage in our lives: career, adult life, and good times.

It was an odd experience working at Disney, with a constant conveyor belt of guests, mainly pop bands. Meeting the likes of A1, 5ive, Steps, Atomic Kitten and S Club 7 made me wonder if any of these people would be friends if NV had actually made it.

I was working at the studio, enjoying the quiet period after rehearsals, with about 45 minutes until we were live on air when a call was transferred to me. It was my dad. His voice was breaking, and I could tell he was not sure what to say and how to say it.

"It's Sam, "he said.

"What about Sam? He left me a voicemail yesterday, is he trying to get hold of me?"

"No, Al. He was on the train. The train that crashed near Paddington. They can't find him".

"No. No, he can't be. There's a voicemail. We're meeting up soon. No, no."

I kept saying no, denying it as the weight of it hit, and I started welling up, trying to keep my composure in front of my colleagues. I stumbled over my words and told him I was coming home, placing the phone back in a mess of tears as people gathered, telling me to go and be with my family. I darted into the sound booth to gather my things, glancing at the phone where I'd listened to Sam's voice yesterday. My stomach clenched and I wailed, gripping the desk to hold myself steady.

I rushed back to my flat and picked up what I could, phoning Megan to tell her what'd happened. All the way home, I played Astral Weeks whilst going through a series of emotions that would prey on me for the next year or so. Life was never the same again without Sam.

I'm sure I speak for many people, but it knocks you for six when they go as unexpected as Sam did. I think we are prepared for grandparents or family friends with ailments to depart in a gradual and sad but expected manner – but when someone the same age is suddenly taken away from you, it's a classic mixture of denial, anger, sadness, and grief. It was hard to deal with the fact I wouldn't see Sam again. I sought comfort in spending time with his family as we shared raw feelings of loss and anger. Why him? Why now? It wasn't fair.

I had the heart-breaking job of suggesting songs for his funeral, songs I still can't listen to without breaking down. Seeing his coffin lowered into the ground as his family wept, will never leave me.

Sam would appreciate or smile at whatever I do now and who I chose to be. I know his death is responsible for my apprehension about making new friends. I only go so far with new friends now, to the point that if it gets any closer, I will take a step back at the risk of losing them too. I miss him and always will, but he motivates me and reminds me of family, a time of opportunity, and the thing that brings us all together, music.

POSTSCRIPT

It's been twenty four years since that moment when I had to stop the whole band mission and try something else. And if I had chosen to stick with Jaff, sleep on sofas, and tour France again, I wouldn't have met my wife, Megan.

I wouldn't have had a fruitful career in television (I might write a book about that) or travelled to Southeast Asia and Australia (I might write a book about that too). And I wouldn't have the amazing kids I've got, either. So, it's not all bad.

I joined Travis Cut for a couple of gigs at the end of the century. Then we reformed to play at The Square one more time before the council demolished it. I joined another band called Psychic Kids, and we played in London several times.

The drum kit is set up in my home office, I've got a growing vinyl collection of 90's indie. I still love gigs. Everything about them I live for. The announcement by the band, checking the poster for the nearest venue, and finding out when the tickets go on sale. Swooping in to get a ticket before they all sell out. Waiting impatiently for the ticket to arrive through the post and putting it somewhere safe until the big day. Then when the day comes, to make the pilgrimage to the venue, constantly checking my pocket to make sure the ticket is still there. Queueing up patiently outside the venue, scanning everyone's T-shirts, looking at creative tattoos, wondering if we'd shared a mosh pit at another gig in our lifetime. The last-minute panic of making sure it's the correct date on the ticket and that it's not too dog-eared to be accepted by the door staff. Walking in and heading straight to the merch stand, hoping for a nice-priced long-sleeved T-shirt that comes in a medium— then to the stage and joining the fray, waiting with arms folded for the band to come on. The hit of adrenaline as the lights go down, everyone cheering as the silhouettes of each band member walk on stage and pick up their instruments. I love the communal nature of the gig; we're all there for one reason, to sing along and shout and cheer when our favourite song's first chords are played. I close my eyes and drink it in, feeling grateful I am alive simultaneously with the band I'm hearing. Ticking off the songs in my head as I pray they're saving my all-time favourite for the encore.

Then it's all over. The crowd asks for more until the house lights show everyone in their raw form, acting as a signal to slowly wade through the plastic cups and into the cold night air.

I admit I wallow in the past. It helps me get through the days sometimes, with all the doom and gloom we face as a species; modern life can be rubbish.

Yes, I hark back to simpler times, even though I know it didn't feel like it at the time. How did I have so much energy? Some diary entries show I didn't stay home and chill for nearly three weeks. A conveyor belt of pubs, clubs, gigs, parties, house parties, and restaurants.

Oh, to be young again, irresponsible, and adventurous. I've made peace with my mistakes. Some people in this book will be surprised when they read about my personal experience. This book started as something I wanted to write for posterity, to share with my kids when they wanted to know what the '90s were like. It was the last decade before social media recorded everything, and it has a special mystique. So many creative earthquakes took place in that short time it's hard to list them all. Shoegaze, Grunge, Britpop, Trip-Hop, Big Beat, Nu Metal. I like that there are only rare photos or recordings. But for those of us that still remember, it was magical. That's the thing about the '90s. You had to be there.

.

WHERE ARE THEY NOW?

I'd be lying if I said I've kept in touch with everyone, but here's that bit you get at the end of films based on true-life on what happened to everyone. Thankfully, nobody from this book is serving life for murder in a US Penitentiary.

Three And A Half Minutes/In Aura

Matt moved to Sweden.

Laurence works for a music therapy trust.

Steve is Chief Experience Officer at a creative branding agency.

Ollie lives in Canada.

Simon is still searching for ganja

Mike Smith is taking a hiatus from running music conglomerates and working on several personal projects and ongoing charitable work, which includes board positions with Teenage Cancer Trust, EarthPercent, In Place of War, and the Creative Society.

Laura Ziffren worked on many soundtracks as a music supervisor, including Shark Tale, Spiderman 2, 28 Days Later and Moulin Rouge! Now Laura Z. Wasserman, she is a philanthropist.

Steve Lamacq is Steve Lamacq

Graham the Toilet - missing

Travis Cut

The band went on to record two more albums and even toured Japan (I'm not jealous).

Chris is a Headmaster, avid supporter of Walthamstow FC and plays guitar for Amesbury Banks.

Mac moved to Leicester, runs a mail-order merch company and is still fighting the fight.

Ant Chapman still writing music and gigs with Collapsed Lung, a music producer.

Paul the roadie moved to New Zealand.

NV

The memory of our debut and final gig lives on, via YouTube.

Carl works in catering and dresses like he's about to go onstage at a rave in Ibiza.

Matt moved to New York, no longer doubles for Brad Pitt, and has a family.

Clodagh still cooks a mean spag bol.

Jolene after working in TV and devising a little-known show called Celebrity Juice, now runs an interior design company with her partner.

Jaff

Just after I left, the band were "signed" to a record label, but it turned out to be a dodgy outfit where everything was promised, and nothing was delivered.

John continues to play gigs all over London as part of a covers band. He still takes ages with everything and commutes from France.

Sean plays with John occasionally and lives in South London

ACKNOWLEDGEMENTS

I first had the idea (like a lot of people with time to kill during the pandemic), to put together the bones of a book. I'd already written short blogs about the boy band, and some of the key beats, such as the Nazi gig and my trip to L.A. I didn't hit my stride until I worked with Sara Nadine Cox, whose honest, open, and unwavering support pushed me to make this a story worth sharing. I always knew I'd be up against the household names who have made it big, but her suggestion to spill my guts and come clean about everything lifted the book to a higher level.

I also met with Mike Smith, the first time we'd seen each other in nearly thirty years. He suggested the title of this book. Additional thanks go to fellow author James Batchelor, who gave me some great ideas and was truly out of his comfort zone reading a book like this.

My brilliant wife Megan for her patience, as I made her read numerous drafts; I think she may be sick of the '90s now, along with the endless playlists I would put on to feel inspired. I'd like to thank my parents for letting me stick with the music during those formative years and my sister for enduring ten years of drumming in the room next door, while she tried her best to listen to her Jenny Morris tapes. A massive thanks to all the bands I was in, you shaped my decade, my future, and my personality.

THE VENUES

I can't remember them all, but here is the list of nearly every venue & location I've played.

KIFF, Aarau, Switzerland
Thun, Switzerland
Bulle, Switzerland
Cafe Drummond, Aberdeen
Sports Centre, Arbroath
Esquires Club, Bedford
Bishops Stortford Football Club
City Tavern, Birmingham
The Foundry, Birmingham (now an office block)
Bracknell
The Fleece & Firkin, Bristol
The Louisiana, Bristol
Moles, Bath (closed in 2023)
Queens Hall, Bradford (Derelict)
Brentwood
Madeira Hotel, Brighton
Sussex University, Brighton
Brunel University
The Tivoli, Buckley
The Junction, Cambridge
The Corn Exchange, Cambridge
The Boatrace, Cambridge (now called Six Six Bar)
The Y Club, Chelmsford
The Army & Navy, Chelmsford (demolished to make way for a Travelodge)

The Penny Theatre, Canterbury

Cork

Polytechnic, Coventry

Darlington

The Wherehouse, Derby (now called Mosh)

The Old Chinaman, Dublin

JB's, Dudley (closed)

Dundee University

The Clay Pigeon, Eastcote (now an Indian Restaurant)

The Subway, Edinburgh

The Cathouse, Glasgow

Nice n Sleazy, Glasgow

Gillingham

Godalming

Rico's, Greenock

The Forum, Hatfield

The Adelphi, Hull

The Square, Harlow (a car park)

The Town Park, Harlow

Drum and Monkey, Ipswich (a car park)

Kent University

Kingston University

Kirkcaldy

Loughborough University

Lancaster University

The Princess Charlotte, Leicester (now a supermarket)

The Duchess of York, Leeds (now a Hugo Boss store)

The Krazy House, Liverpool

LONDON

The Amersham Arms, New Cross

The Archway Tavern, Islington

The Falcon, Camden (Apartments)

The Camden Palace (now Koko)

The Grand, Clapham

The Town & Country Club (now The Forum), Kentish Town

The Bull & Gate, Kentish Town (now a gastropub)

The Borderline, Soho (closed)

The Dublin Castle, Camden

The George IV, Brixton (now a Tesco)

Imperial College

The Monarch, Camden

The Laurel Tree, Camden (now a BrewDog bar)

The Powerhaus, Islington (Halifax bank)

The Orange, Kensington (Sainsbury's Local)

The Kings Head, Fulham (permanently closed)

The Marquee Club, Soho (now a Wetherspoons)

The Garage, Highbury

St John's Tavern, Archway (Gastropub)

University of Westminster

The Mean Fiddler, Harlesden (demolished to make way for Crossrail)

The Venue, New Cross

The Water Rats, Kings Cross

The Half Moon, Putney

PCL, London

The Roxbury Cafe, Los Angeles (now a Taco Eatery)

Metz

Middlesex University

The Boardwalk, Manchester (now offices)

City Hall, Manchester

Manchester University

Cumberland Arms, Newcastle

The Riverside, Newcastle

The Arts Centre, Norwich

Nottingham University

The Narrowboat, Nottingham (demolished)

The Ship Inn, Oundle

Jericho Tavern, Oxford

Pop In, Paris (permanently closed)

Marquee Rooms, Peterborough

Twa Tams, Perth

Preston

The Pavilion Rooms, Portsmouth

The After Dark, Reading (Temporarily Closed)

Hallamshire Arms, Sheffield

The Leadmill, Sheffield

The Horn, St Albans

The Joiners Arms, Southampton

Southampton University

The Wheatsheaf, Stoke (now a Wetherspoons)
The Bowes Lyon, Stevenage (now Bowes Lyon Young People Centre)
The Monkey Club, Swindon
The Rat Hole, Tamworth
Snow Dome, Tamworth
Four Alls, Taunton (now an Indian Restaurant)
The Forum, Tunbridge Wells
Psychic Pig, Trowbridge (closed)
Players, Wakefield
The Old Trout, Windsor (closed)
The Cumberland, Workington (hotel)
Monroe's, Workington
Worcester
Fibbers, York (permanently closed)

THE BANDS

All the notable bands I've shared a stage with

Adorable
The Adventure Babies
The Auteurs
Audioweb
Back To The Planet
Bang Bang Machine
The Bardots
Bark Psychosis
The Barlows
Big Fish Little Fish
Big Boy Tomato
Blur
Blind Mice
Bivouac
Bracket
Boo-Yaa T.R.I.B.E
The Business
Captain America (later Eugenious)
China Drum
Chopper
D.O.A
Dr Phibes & The House of Wax Equations
Down By Law
Ebb

Echobelly

Electric Sex Circus

F.F.F

The Family Cat

The Fluid

The Fuzztones

Gallon Drunk

Genius Freak

Goober Patrol

Great Northern Electrics

The Gyres

Huggy Bear

Hyperhead

Jamiroquai

Jawbone

Jawbreaker

Joeyfat

J Church

Kinky Machine (changed name to Rialto)

Kingmaker

Lagwagon

Luna

Love Battery (changed the name to The Presidents of The United States of America)

Love's Young Nightmare

The Meat Puppets

Mega City Four

Mint 400

Midway Still

Mondo Popless

Monkhouse

Murray Torkildsen

Neds Atomic Dustbin

The Nubiles

Orange Deluxe

Peach

Pele

Pop Am Good

The Pogues

The Queers

Radiohead

RatCat

Resque

Reverse

Rugrat

The Sandkings

Scorpio Rising

Sensitize

The Sect/Skimmer

Shonen Knife

Shutdown

Skyscraper

Sleeper

Sloppy Seconds

Snuff

Sofa Head

Sugarblast!

Sp!n (changed name to Gene)

Spitfire

Strangelove

Sultans of Ping FC

The Senseless Things

This Year's Blonde

Tribute to Nothing

Suede

Sunshot

UK Subs

US:UK

Wat Tyler

Zu Zu's Petals

95:Nil

ABOUT THE AUTHOR

Alex Boucher is a writer and musician based near Colchester, Essex. Keeping a journal during the 90s, he has a detailed archive of his experience as a drummer and performer in acts including Three And A Half Minutes, Travis Cut, NV and Jaff. Since then he has worked for Disney Channel, ITV, BBC and Channel 4 as a sound engineer. He now runs his own company offering services in the video games industry. During the lockdowns, he decided to write down his memories of trying to become famous during the 90s and has produced a memoir that showcases the unseen story of what happens when you don't make it big. Creds: BAFTA member, Music Venue Trust shareholder, PRS Member, Trustee for Safe in our World.

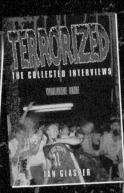

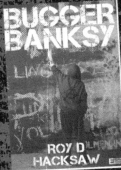

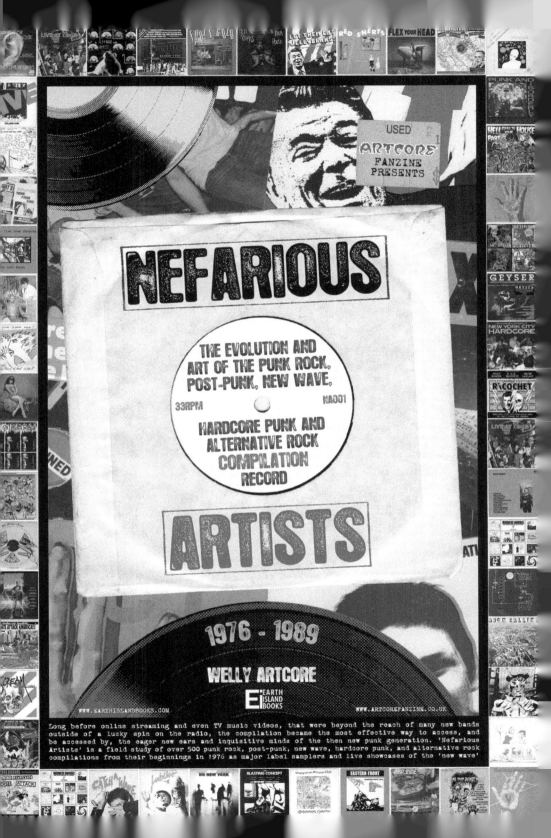

USED
ARTCORE
FANZINE
PRESENTS

NEFARIOUS

THE EVOLUTION AND
ART OF THE PUNK ROCK,
POST-PUNK, NEW WAVE,

33RPM   NA001

HARDCORE PUNK AND
ALTERNATIVE ROCK
COMPILATION
RECORD

ARTISTS

1976 - 1989

WELLY ARTCORE

E EARTH
ISLAND
BOOKS

WWW.EARTHISLANDBOOKS.COM   WWW.ARTCOREFANZINE.CO.UK

Long before online streaming and even TV music videos, that were beyond the reach of many new bands
outside of a lucky spin on the radio, the compilation became the most effective way to access, and
be accessed by, the eager new ears and inquisitive minds of the then new punk generation. 'Nefarious
Artists' is a field study of over 500 punk rock, post-punk, new wave, hardcore punk, and alternative rock
compilations from their beginnings in 1976 as major label samplers and live showcases of the 'new wave'

SILENCE IS NO REACTION FORTY YEARS OF SUBHUMANS
IAN GLASPER

ISBN: 9781629635507
£24.99 • 640 pages

Formed in Wiltshire, England, in 1980, the Subhumans are rightly held in high regard as one of the best punk rock bands to ever hail from the UK.

Over the course of five timeless studio albums and just as many classic EPs, not to mention well over 1,000 gigs around the world, they have blended serious anarcho punk with a demented sense of humour and genuinely memorable tunes to create something quite unique and utterly compelling. For the first time ever, their whole story is told, straight from the recollections of every band member past and present, as well as a dizzying array of their closest friends and peers, with not a single stone left unturned. Bolstered with hundreds of flyers and exclusive photos, it's the definitive account of the much-loved band.

THE REVOLUTION WILL BE TELEVISED

RAY STUART

Ray wrote 'The Revolution Will Be Televised' because he finall[y] realised that if our presen[t] government wasn't going t[o] trigger open rebellion, the[n] nothing would.

Instead, he has embraced hi[s] middle-class roots; where h[e] used to be full of passion an[d] rage, he is now full of artisa[n] bread and locally source[d] cheese. Meat may be murder bu[t] so are his knees. He's leaving th[e] street fighting and statu[e] tipping to the young. Instea[d] 'The Revolution Will B[e] Televised' is an appeal t[o] people from all backgrounds, to imagine and work for a better, fairer society withou[t] the reliance on the straightjackets of traditional left-right politics or inherited privilege[.]

An important book in changing times, available now, direct from Earth Island Books, or any good book or record shop, or online retailer.

Remember, in this age of media, 'The Revolution Will Be Televised'.

EARTH ISLAND BOOKS

WWW.EARTHISLANDBOOKS.COM

MY PUNK ROCK LIFE: THE PHOTOGRAPHY OF MARLA WATSON

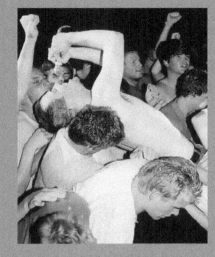

MYPUNKROCKLIFE.COM
EARTHISLANDBOOKS.COM

EARTH ISLAND BOOKS

PUNK ROCK LIFE PRESS

This book supports the Music Venue Trust and Grassroots Music Venues.

Music Venue Trust is a UK registered charity which acts to protect, secure and improve the UK's grassroots music venue circuit.

Created in January 2014, Music Venue Trust aims to secure the long-term future of iconic GMVs such as Hull Adelphi, Exeter Cavern, Southampton Joiners, The 100 Club, Band on the Wall, King Tut's, Clwb Ifor Bach, Tunbridge Wells Forum etc. These venues play a crucial role in the development of British music, nurturing local talent, providing a platform for artists to build their careers and develop their music and their performance skills. We work to gain recognition of the essential role these venues fulfil, not only for artist development but also for the cultural and music industries, the economy and local communities. We provide advice to the government, the cultural sector and the music industry on issues impacting GMVs and are the nominated representative that speaks on behalf of the Music Venues Alliance, an association of nearly 1000 venues from across the UK.

These grassroots music venues aren't just home to great nights out. From them emerge local scenes of music, styles and fashion that grow to become regionally important, then national trends. Sometimes they even become global movements. But it's when they are first starting in and around their local venue that they create an identity that is unique; special to that place, special to the people who create it. A Hardcore Heart is the history of just one such scene, but it tells the story of literally hundreds if not thousands more.

www.musicvenuetrust.com

Music Venue Trust